The **AP*** Comparative Government and Politics Examination

What You Need to Know

A Test Preparation Guide by Ken Wedding, Regional Consultant to the College Board

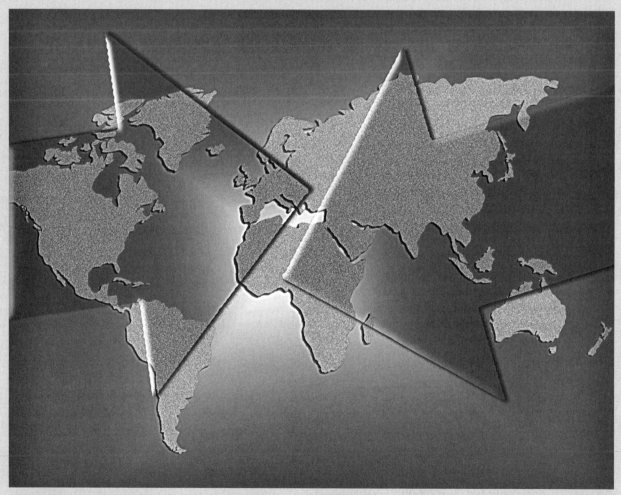

Published by College City Publications, Northfield, Minnesota 55057

All inquiries should be addressed to:
   College City Publications
   925 Ivanhoe Drive
   Northfield, Minnesota 55057

E-mail: *information@apcomparativegov.com*
Web site: *http://apcomparativegov.com*

*AP and Advanced Placement Program are registered trademarks of the
College Entrance Examination Board™, which was not involved with the
production of and does not endorse this book.

International Standard Book No. 978-0-9746379-7-6

PRINTED IN THE UNITED STATES OF AMERICA

**Check for corrections and updates
at this book's supporting web site:**

http://apcomparativegov.com/tools

At this site you will also find links to

- **Internet Links Cited in the Book**
- **Online Sources for Review**
- **Web Sites for Major Textbooks**
- ***What You Need to Know* Facebook Group
  (for discussions and questions)**
- ***Studying Comparative*, the Blog Quiz**
- ***Teaching Comparative*, a Blog for Teachers**

What You Need to Know ...

ACKNOWLEDGMENTS

The suggestions I make in this book are meant to help you prepare for the Advanced Placement Examination in Comparative Government and Politics. Neither the College Entrance Examination Board, the Advanced Placement program, nor the Educational Testing Service was involved in the writing nor do any of those organizations endorse this product.

However, my suggestions are based on more than 15 years of my work teaching courses at Hopkins High School in Minnetonka, Minnesota, to help students prepare for the comparative government test. My suggestions are also based on my experiences, since 1992, reading and grading student responses to the Advanced Placement Government and Politics Examination.

While working on these suggestions, I referred to the AP Program's publication *AP Comparative Government and Politics, Preliminary Course Outline.* I also consulted the following textbooks:

Almond, Gabriel A. and G. Bingham Powell, et al., *Comparative Politics Today, A World View,* Longman
Hauss, Charles, *Comparative Politics, Domestic Responses to Global Challenges,* Wadsworth
Kesselman, Mark, et al., *Introduction to Comparative Politics,* Houghton Mifflin
Kopstein, Jeffrey and Mark Lichbach, *Comparative Politics, Interests, Identities, and Institutions in a Changing Global Order*, Cambridge
Lim, Timothy C., *Doing Comparative Politics,* Reinner
McCormick, John, *Comparative Politics in Transition,* Wadsworth
O'Neil, Patrick, *Essentials of Comparative Politics,* Norton
Sodaro, Michael J., *Comparative Politics, A Global Introduction,* McGraw Hill
Theen, Rolf H. W. and Frank L. Wilson, *Comparative Politics, An Introduction to Seven Countries,* Prentice Hall

While I am responsible for the contents of this book, including any errors or omissions,* no one can claim sole credit for a project like this. My wife, Nancy Ashmore, who is the editor and designer of the book, has been an invaluable help. I also owe thanks to Kris Wedding Crowell, Jim Wedding, and David Ashmore for aiding and abetting my growth. Chip Hauss has been a friend and a role model. He showed me new and fruitful ways to stay engaged in teaching. Students in classes I taught helped me learn better ways to explain the nuances of complex topics.

Several people and their students have contributed to this project with valuable feedback about early drafts of chapters, among them: Bill Babcock and students at the Bolles School in Jacksonville, Florida; John Unruh-Friesen and his students at Hopkins High School; Sarah Fisher and her students at Central Kitsap High School in Silverdale, Washington; Serene Williams and her students at the Convent of the Sacred Heart High School in San Francisco; and Michael Schaffer of the Central Academy of the Des Moines Public Schools.

Ken Wedding

---

* **Check for corrections, updates, and other valuable links at this book's supporting web site:**

http://apcomparativegov.com/tools

1: Know ... YOURSELF

The AP test is coming in May.

Maybe this is going to be your first AP test. Maybe you've done this all before. Maybe you've done this before and been marvelously successful. Maybe the last time you took an AP test was not fun. Maybe you've been thinking about getting ready for months. Maybe the test is next week. No matter what the situation, I can help you prepare.

I can't teach you all the things you need to know. I **can** help you put the pieces together in ways that will be helpful.

The place to begin is with yourself. Yes, you need to know some specifics about the test. In my mind, that comes later. If it comes right now for you, skip ahead to Chapter 3. That's the wonder of books. You're in charge. Use this test prep guide as you will. I've tried to label things clearly so you can find what you want.

PREPARING YOURSELF, PART ONE

I once had a student with eidetic memory. She could scan a chapter of a book and retain an image of that chapter in her mind. In a sense, she could look things up even though she didn't have the book with her. Most of us don't have that ability.

Then again, each of us has academic and intellectual strengths, and we need to use them. Do you know your strengths? Dr. Barry Zimmerman of the Graduate Center of the City University of New York argues that, "explicitly coaching students to think about their study processes and to monitor their learning can pay large dividends."[1] I'm coaching here.

Dr. Zimmerman identifies two common follies: students' overconfidence about their knowledge, making the assumption that they understand material just because they have sat through a few lectures or have read a few chapters, and students' tendency to attribute their failures to outside forces ("the teacher didn't like me," "the textbook wasn't clear enough") rather than taking a hard look at their own study habits.

His research shows that self-examination is important to academic success. In his own words, successful students are those who "personally initiate and direct their own efforts to acquire knowledge and skill rather than relying on teachers, parents, or other agents of instruction."[2]

Ask yourself: Do you memorize things easily or quickly? Can you take those things you memorize and link them to other things you've memorized? Can you memorize complex ideas as well as lists of terms? If so, do it. Memorization won't replace analysis, but it's a great start. And for multiple choice tests it can be a great advantage — **if** you memorize the right stuff. One of your analysis tasks is figuring out if you have done that.

Do vocabulary lists seem like isolated bits of trivia? Do you make sense of things by understanding whole systems? Do generalizations offer you insight into how things are related or why people act they way they do? Is it easier for you to identify which country a city is in than to make a list of cities in a country? If so, you'll still have to know some specifics about things like British local authorities, but you'll have a good conceptual idea of how they fit into the unitary system dominated by the parliament.

It's not like there are two camps: the specific-to-general experts and the general-to-specific experts. It's more like a spectrum. Some of us are better at generalizations and others of us are better at facts. Line us all up on the spectrum from extreme generalizers to extreme specifiers and you'll probably get a normal curve. **Knowing your strengths is a key to figuring out how to prepare yourself.**

If facts are your forte, learn those lists! If getting the big picture first is a key, then concentrate on the explanations.

In addition, you should be aware by now of what processes make learning easier for you. Traditional schooling focuses on reading and listening. If it helps you to talk things through, organize a study group. If you need to see things as well as hear them, search out video. If writing helps you make sense of what you read, hear about, and study, then write. An online study group may be just the ticket.

PREPARING YOURSELF, PART TWO

Dr. Charles Hauss, the author of a popular comparative government textbook, once visited my AP class. He asked the students about his book, which they were using, and then invited questions. Someone asked what he saw as the most difficult step in moving from high school to college. He said, "Learning to tolerate and appreciate ambiguity."

Up through high school, most answers seem to be right or wrong. But in the academic environment of a college or university there's less certainty about absolutes. This

> ... to say that it [existence] is ambiguous is to assert that its meaning is never fixed, that it must be constantly won.
>
> — Simone de Beauvoir, *The Ethics of Ambiguity*, translated by Bernard Frechtman

often causes consternation among new college students who have gotten good at seeking out and finding the "right" answers. But, especially in the social sciences, we have to learn to live with the fact that there may be many good answers and perhaps no right ones.

This difficulty is apparently not just caused by the structure of schooling. (Yes, we do want to avoid single causation.) W. G. Perry in his 1970 study, *Forms of Intellectual and Ethical Development in the College Years: A Scheme*, described four stages of intellectual development.

- The first one he called **"dualism."** It's the one most of us take to college. In this stage, we see knowledge as absolute. We expect teachers and other authority figures to know the truth and tell us.

- Perry calls the second stage **"multiplicity."** In this stage we realize that some answers are not yet known and believe that in those cases any rational-sounding theory is as good as any other. It's at this stage when we're likely to argue that our ideas are as good as a teacher's or an author's. This is the stage that many of us find ourselves beginning to enter sometime during the last year of high school or the first year in college. If we are lucky, we also discover that academicians are better at supporting their answers than we are. So we work at learning how to play the games of academia.

- The third stage Perry described as **"relativism."** In this stage, we learn to perceive knowledge as relative to its context and see that some "answers" are better than others. If we get beyond playing academic games, we begin to make choices from among multiple answers based on analysis and recognizing other perspectives. Many of us write research papers at this stage and feel we're finally able to refute some ideas and prop up some others.

- **"Commitment in relativism"** is the label Perry gave to the final stage of intellectual development. It's at this stage that we can commit ourselves to answers because we've made choices based on careful study and we can rationally defend those choices — even when they're different from the choices of our families, friends, and teachers.

Ambiguity: Is it a duck? Or is it a rabbit?

Dr. Hauss told my students that learning to tolerate and appreciate ambiguity was going to be their toughest and most important job as first-year college students. He was talking about making the transition from one institution to another and, at the same time, making the transition from one stage of intellectual development to another.

What does that have to do with you, a high school student preparing for an Advanced Placement test? The test is based on assumptions about knowledge and academics that are beyond high school. Your high school AP class may not have seemed all that different from other classes except for the homework. Your teacher may have insisted on you knowing the "right" answers. (You're probably very good at that.) But, what is the AP test going to ask you?

Half of the test is a set of multiple-choice questions. Those kinds of tests are often called objective. But AP questions are aimed at more than just absolutes. If you've taken old AP tests for practice, you know something about this. The questions are aimed at finding out how well you can distinguish between good answers and choose the best one. The test instructions read, "Each of the questions…is followed by five suggested answers…**Select the one that is best in each case**…" [emphasis mine]

If you're stuck in Perry's first or second stage of intellectual development, you might find these questions very difficult. You have to get beyond seeing knowledge as either right, wrong, or an opinion that's as good as anyone else's.

What's true for the multiple-choice half of the test is even more true for the free-response half. There are usually many ways to respond to these questions, and some ways are better than others. I've read 150-word responses that have been obviously superior to 800-word responses. I've read 10-word definitions that are clearly better than 50-word definitions. It's not just that some responses more directly address the question. It's also that the better responses show evidence of analysis and support for the choices the writer made. (More about how to respond to — notice I didn't say "answer" — these questions later.)

How do you get beyond those first two stages?

1. **Stop being satisfied with simple answers.** It's okay to accept the fact that Mahmoud Ahmadinejad is the president of Iran. But to answer the question, "Is the UK's parliamentary system better than the USA's presidential system?" with a simple one-liner is silly and unhelpful. Instead, you should see that there are probably good lists of advantages and disadvantages to each system and that the response you make probably will depend on the context of the question or the context of the example that goes with the question.

2. **Don't accept as gospel the assertions in your textbook or the words of your**

teacher. Do you know the academic, political, and intellectual biases of the textbook's authors and editors? Do you know who the authors are? Do you know how they are evaluated by their peers? Do you know what their areas of expertise are? Ask the same questions about your AP teacher.

3. **Stop playing academic games.** I don't think it will help to try to "psych out" the AP test. There are too many variables. Similarly, I doubt it will help if you restrict yourself to a textbook. Instead, learn the basic facts that are relevant wherever you find them and figure out how to understand the workings of the various political systems in their contexts. And, learn to "play" with those facts and processes so you can identify the "best" answers and write good responses.

PREPARING YOURSELF, PART THREE

Rehearsal is vital. No matter what your learning strengths, no matter what methods help you best learn, practice is necessary. It's hard to imagine you can overprepare. I know it's theoretically possible, but you have a life. There are other people, other things to do, and even other academic subjects (and perhaps other AP tests to prepare for), so I can't imagine you practicing **too** much.

So, what is rehearsal? Talk about the governments you studied. Describe them to patient relatives and friends. Answer their questions.

Pay attention to the news about politics in these countries. If you don't see any news on American media, go looking on other media. There are English language newspapers and web sites about these countries. Read them. Figure out what events are important in those countries and why they're important. If you go to the C-SPAN web site and choose "International Links," you'll find web links to all the governments and most of the legislatures. Use the links and see what's going on. See if what's going on makes sense based on what you know about government and politics. Explain

Hot Off the Press(es)

C-SPAN
www.c-span.org/international/links.asp

The Times of London
www.timesonline.co.uk/

London's Guardian newspaper
www.guardian.co.uk/

International Herald Tribune
www.iht.com/

The St. Petersburg Times
www.times.spb.ru/

ITAR-TASS News Agency
itar-tass.com/eng/

China News Agency
www.chinanewsagency.com/

Iran Daily
www.iran-daily.com/

A list of Mexican newspapers
(if you read Spanish)
www.ipl.org/div/news/browse/MX/

The Guardian from Lagos
www.guardiannewsngr.com/

it to someone. If you're not sure, ask questions. (This is where study groups come in handy.)

While rehearsal and this book are parts of your preparation, the textbook (even with its limitations) is more vital.

PREPARING YOURSELF, PART FOUR: TEXTBOOKS

It's easy to get overwhelmed with assignments like "This week read Chapter 4 on parliamentary structure." You read the chapter — or at least you look at all the words. You sigh. You've done your homework. But what have you learned?

Textbooks seem to be big, anonymous tomes full of information. It's all correct. It's all objective. Your job seems to be to internalize it. That can be daunting.

One Explanation of Things

Rather than approaching a text as some kind of ultimate source of knowledge, think about it as **one** explanation of things. Someone wrote the words for you. Some real person sat and put words and sentences together to help you understand some things (like I'm doing for you right now). Admittedly, authors — like everyone else — have mixed motives (like making ourselves look smart), but the primary one is making things understandable to you.

Think of the author of your textbook as a real person, not some Olympian authority figure. Don't think about static words on a page; think about what the writer is trying to tell you. Think about how she is telling you. Think about her attitudes toward the things she's writing. (Notice the recurrence of the verb "**think**" in this paragraph? Notice the implied subject, "**you**"?)

If, after "doing your homework," you can mentally sum up the chapter's main idea(s) about its topics, you have made a good start. If you can describe your impression of the author's attitudes about the topic as well, you've made a better start. If, in addition, you can recall how the author organized her presentation of the topic, you're in great shape.

If you have some notes about the big ideas, the structure of the chapter, and the author's conclusions, you're ready to move on.

If you can't recall the basics and you have no notes, you probably have **not** done your homework. Looking at the words is not reading. Reading the words without thinking is not really reading either. **There's no way around the fact that if you're going to succeed at this, you're going to**

have to work at it. Now's the time to figure out how to work intelligently as well as diligently.

Start at the Beginning

What are you to do with your few pounds of paper full of words called a textbook?

The best idea (especially if you're one of those general-to-specific people) is to compare the table of contents with the Advanced Placement outline. When it comes to what's important for the exam, remember it doesn't matter what you read in the text or what your teacher told you. The Advanced Placement outline is good and accurate about the test and it's **definitive**.

How does your textbook compare to the outline of the AP Comparative exam? Many textbooks are written with the AP course market in mind. (High schools may not buy textbooks every year, but

> **definitive**: "most nearly compete and accurate; authoritative"
>
> — *Webster's New World College Dictionary*

14,000 students each year is a big market.) Some of the books have tables of contents that look a lot like the course outline[3] published by The College Board. Other tables of contents look more like lists of country-specific chapters.

What you need to do is figure out how the textbook you're using covers things like the differences between states, nations, regimes, and governments which are concepts central to the first of the six major topics in the AP curriculum. Are the topics discussed theoretically with examples from specific countries? Or are they discussed each time a new country is examined?

If you're more of a specific-to-general person, your textbook's index and the College Board's course description are useful starting points. You just have to tease the details out of the descriptions. Go through the course description and underline the nouns (sometimes it will be useful to underline significant adjectives with nouns, as in "public authority"). Then go to the back of the book and look those words up in the index. Some of the terms may be listed under a country's name in the index. Make note of where the topics are discussed so you can clearly recognize the correspondence between the textbook and the AP outline. If the outline's specific terms are not in your textbook's index, you get your first practice at dealing with ambiguity. Can you find analogous terms in the index for the ideas in the outline? (Hint: you should be able to pretty easily.)

Whether you work with the table of contents or the index or both, you should get to the point of recognizing how comparable the outline and the textbook are. Then you're ready for some review of the topics you need to master for the Advanced Placement exam.

You can also use the annotated outline in Chapter 2. What I've tried to do is offer some explanations, elaborations, and exercises to help you master the simple facts, manipulate the concepts, and practice your tolerance and appreciation of ambiguity.

PREPARING YOURSELF, PART FIVE, THE PHYSICAL AND MENTAL ASPECTS

I obviously don't know about yours, but I do know my mother always said, "Be sure you get enough sleep." Still good advice.

In April 2002, the BBC reported[4] that " Research carried out at Northwestern University in Illinois has found that teenagers need extra sleep at the weekend to catch up on hours lost during the week."

However, Molly Webster, writing in Scientific American (May 2008) noted that other research showed that weekend "catch ups" were not adequate for long-term "sleep debt." She wrote, "Sleep debt is the difference between the amount of sleep you should be getting and the amount you actually get... Studies show that such short-term sleep deprivation leads to a foggy brain, worsened vision, impaired driving, and trouble remembering..."[5]

An Associated Press article published in the *New York Times* on October 9, 2003, reported on experiments done at the University of Chicago and Harvard Medical School. The results also back up "motherly advice to get a good night's sleep." The neurobiologists found that "sleep apparently restores memories lost during a hectic day."

The *New York Times* reported in January 2004 that, "Scientists at the University of Luebeck found that volunteers who had eight hours of sleep were three times more likely than sleep-deprived participants to figure out a hidden rule for converting the numbers into the right answer on a simple math test."

The article cited no sources, but asserted that "Some 70 million Americans are believed to be sleep-deprived, contributing to accidents, health problems and **lower test scores**" (emphasis mine).

The Nemours Foundation[6] suggests that research shows that people in their teens "need a whopping nine hours of sleep each night. But this number can be hard to reach." It's hard to reach not only because you have a busy schedule, but "Recent studies have shown that many teens have trouble going to sleep so early — not because they don't want to sleep, but because their brains naturally work on later schedules and aren't ready for bed."

Even the National Basketball Association is taking the need for sleep seriously. Teams are beginning to eliminate light morning practices called "shoot-arounds." The reason, Howard Beck wrote in the *New York Times*, is a growing realization that players need more sleep to be mentally ready for serious practice and games.[7]

Get Lots of Sleep

Why am I preaching about sleep? The son of a friend took the SAT on four hours of sleep. His results were disappointing. The second time he took the test, he slept much longer the night before the exam. His verbal score was 60 points higher than the first time he took the test.

So, "Be sure you get enough sleep." Not just the night before the test, but for several nights. You're probably taking the U. S. Government and Politics exam in the morning and the Comparative Government and Politics exam in the afternoon. Including time for listening to test instructions, that means about six hours of work. And the work is not easy. You need to be ready.

I know: You're young and you often feel you have boundless energy. You can do more than some of us older folk, but you have limits, too. Realistically recognizing them is important to your success.

As well as showing up with sharpened #2 pencils and a pen, you have to show up with your wits about you. Plan your academic work for the week of the exam. Adjust your work schedule. Abandon your favorite television (there are reruns and video on demand). Tell your band that rehearsals can continue the week **after** the AP exams.

And Relax

If you're rested, you'll be in good shape to take the exam. Being relaxed is important as well.

You're the expert on your relaxation. Go see a softball or baseball game the day before the exam. Go with some friends to an early movie.

Confidence? If you've worked at mastering the subject matter and rehearsed, you should feel confident. Don't give into the panic that promotes cramming. Unless you have specific goals in mind (like memorizing the dates of recent Russian regime changes), don't spend time trying to learn new things in the couple days before the exam.

Cramming and trying to puzzle out what to study at the last minute only create stress.

IN SUMMARY

Get to know your learning and thinking skills. Use them.

Learn to live with (if not appreciate) ambiguity. Look for what's better or best, not just what's right. Don't settle for other people's simple answers or your own simple answers.

Stop playing academic games. You're probably good at high school academic games, but as with ambiguity, the AP curriculum isn't high school.

Rehearse in ways that help you. Talk, argue, write, analyze cases, memorize lists, keep up with current events, look at pictures, or watch videos.

Rest and relax. Sharpen your pencils. Make sure you have a couple of pens with plenty of ink in them.

If you're taking both government and politics exams, eat a good breakfast the morning of the exams. Eat a light lunch between the exams. If you're only taking the comparative exam and you have to get up in the morning, same advice. If you can sleep in, the advice about lunch still holds.

And, as *The Hitchhiker's Guide to the Galaxy* advised its users, "Don't Panic."

FOOTNOTES

1   Glenn, David, How Students Can Improve by Studying Themselves. *The Chronicle of Higher Education*, 7 February 2010. chronicle.com/article/Struggling-Students-Can/64004/ (accessed 10 February 2010)

2   Zimmerman, Barry J., A Social Cognitive View of Self-Regulated Academic Learning. *Journal of Educational Psychology*, 1 September 1989, Vol. 81, Issue 3. *www.sfu.ca/~sbratt/SRL/A%20Social%20Cognitive%20View%20of%20Self-Regulated%20Academic%20Learning.pdf* (Accessed 10 February 2010)

3   Online at *www.collegeboard.com/student/testing/ap/sub_compgov.html* Here you will see a link to download the official course description for "Comparative Government and Politics." My annotated version of the outline is in the next chapter.

4   *news.bbc.co.uk/2/hi/health/1939284.stm*

5   Webster, Molly, "Can You Catch Up on Lost Sleep?" *Scientific American*, May 6, 2008.

6   *www.kidshealth.org/teen/your_body/take_care/how_much_sleep.html*

7   Beck, Howard, "Bowing to Body Clocks, NBA Teams Sleep In." *New York Times*, December 19, 2009.

REVIEW EXERCISE

This little exercise and the ones at the end of the other chapters are meant to get you thinking about some of the basic facts and point out areas you might have to review more thoroughly. My responses follow.

1. Understanding how you learn best
    (A) matters little in an AP course since the content is so structured
    (B) determines the things that will be most difficult
    (C) should help you decide how best to study
    (D) tells you what things you should memorize
    (E) means that generalizations are more important than specific facts

2. If Dr. Perry is correct, the level of intellectual development you have reached
    (A) will determine whether you are successful in this AP course
    (B) means that any logical answer you can think of is acceptable
    (C) allows you to challenge the authority of the AP question writers
    (D) suggests that being able to accept some "relativism" is important
    (E) requires commitment to those answers that are absolutely right

3. Multiple-choice questions on AP exams
    (A) ask you to choose the best answer
    (B) only offer right or wrong choices
    (C) make clear distinctions between right and wrong choices
    (D) are similar to questions from your textbook or those written by your teacher
    (E) require the memorization of huge lists of facts

4. The textbook you used for your AP Comparative class
    (A) included everything you need to know for the AP exam
    (B) is the final authority on topics for the AP exam
    (C) is an unbiased presentation of factual material
    (D) is a good beginning point for mastering the AP curriculum
    (E) was designed by the AP program

5. Which of the following is NOT a helpful suggestion for succeeding on the AP Comparative exam?
   (A) understand that there's a lot of ambiguity in our understanding of political systems
   (B) look for the simplest, clear-cut answers
   (C) don't assume that your class presented all the information you need to know
   (D) there are too many variables to make game playing useful
   (E) try to do analysis that goes beyond the basic facts

6. Helpful forms of rehearsal for this AP exam include
   (A) practice writing various forms of FRQs
   (B) explaining regimes and politics to family and patient friends
   (C) reading journalistic accounts of political events in the countries included in the AP6
   (D) participation in class discussions
   (E) all of the above

7. It's helpful to remember that your textbook
   (A) is the final authority on all issues related to this course
   (B) requires you to think about and manipulate the ideas it presents
   (C) is strictly a factual presentation
   (D) matches the AP curriculum very closely
   (E) is written in such a way as to require you to guess about which ideas are most important

8. Research shows that sleep
   (A) schedules have little to do with learning
   (B) is never a problem for adolescents
   (C) less important for younger people than it is for older people
   (D) is necessary for the formation of long-term memory
   (E) the night before the exam is all you really have to worry about

9. Understanding that ambiguity is part of the study of comparative government and politics is important because
   (A) there are no generally accepted facts in the field
   (B) prejudice and bias dominate the analysis of political scientists
   (C) normative analysis is more important than empirical analysis in comparative politics
   (D) cultural differences determine what is right in each political system
   (E) there are so many ways to understand facts in comparative studies

10. Being relaxed when going into the AP exam probably means
    (A) you haven't spent the weekend before the exam cramming
    (B) you're confident about your understanding of the main topics
    (C) you have been preparing for the exam for weeks
    (D) you relaxed and got away from your notes and textbook the night before the exam
    (E) all of the above

(For responses, see below)

2: Know ... THE AP CURRICULUM

If you gotten this far into the preparation for the AP exam, you probably don't need to be told much about the curriculum.

Below is the outline with a few of my elaborations. (The official version is available online at *www.collegeboard.com/student/testing/ap/ sub_compgov.html* .) The percentages listed here suggest the weight of each topic in the **multiple-choice** half of the test.

> **Remember: Everything in the outline is likely to be tested on the AP exam even if your teacher or your textbook did not deal with it.**

You need to "know important facts" about government and politics in the six countries in the AP curriculum (the AP6). The course description doesn't specify which facts are important. Presumably, the important facts are the ones that make understanding and comparisons possible. (Ambiguity raises its head already.)

The course uses comparisons between and among the AP6 to

- introduce major concepts, themes, and generalizations developed in the field of comparative government and politics
- examine patterns of political processes and behaviors and the consequences of them
- develop comparative generalizations about political institutions and processes in the AP6
- interpret and analyze demographic, economic, and political data in a comparative context

1. **Introduction to Comparative Politics (0 – 10% or 0 – 5 questions out of 55)**

- What are normative (value-related) questions and what are empirical (factual) questions?
- Can you describe the intellectual organization of political science?
- What are interdependence and globalization, and what are examples of them?
- What is meant by political and economic permeability of national borders and what effects does that have on political decision making?
- Distinguish between state, nation, regime, and government.
- What do power, legitimacy, authority and the bases of political power have to do with one another?
- Can you describe several types of political and economic systems and distinguish the ways these systems approach common situations?

2. **Sovereignty, Authority and Power (15 – 25% or 8 – 14 questions out of 55)**

- What is state power? What is sovereignty?
- What are the origins of the nation-state system? What effects do those origins have on nation states today?
- What contemporary pressures for supranational systems are recognized and how powerful are they?
- How are political structures created and maintained?

- How do these structures affect nation states?
- How do various political systems go about establishing legitimacy?
- What roles do governments play in economies? How are those roles integrated into the political system?
- Describe the political cultures and belief systems — religious or ideological — of the countries you studied. Explain the process and effectiveness of socialization and political integration in the political cultures.

3. **Political Institutions
    (30 – 40% or 16 – 22 questions out of 55)**

- Describe the basic formal and informal structures and operations of authority and policy making systems in the countries studied.
- Can you identify, describe and evaluate the relationships between parts of governments (degrees of separation or fusion of powers) and between governments and between governments and supranational organizations for the countries you studied?
- What are the roles and relationships of executive, legislative, judicial, bureaucratic, military, security (intelligence), and non-governmental institutions?
- Describe the systems for selection and recruitment of power elites.
- Describe how powerful interests within the state exercise their power.
- Understand the operation and effects of electoral and party systems.

4. **Citizens, Society, and the State
    (10 – 20% or 5 – 11 questions out of 55)**

- What are the politically relevant cleavages and what effects do they have on political systems theoretically and on the political systems you studied?
- What are the interrelationships between institutions, political practices, and cleavages?
- Theoretically and in practice what is the

relationship between civil society and power (especially domestic and international advocacy groups)?

- What are the forms and efficacy of political action (including transnational forms)?
- What are the political roles of media in the countries you studied?
- Describe the forms, efficacy, and representativeness of various forms of citizen participation in the countries you studied and political systems theoretically.

5. **Political and Economic Change
    (10 – 20% or 5 – 11 questions out of 55)**

- What types of political and economic change are common?
- What are the interactions between political and economic trends?
    - What promotes democratization? (preconditions, processes, and outcomes)
    - What are the political ramifications of economic changes?
    - What does corruption have to do with all this?
    - In what ways are economic inequalities relevant to politics?
- Describe the roles of supranational organizations and reactions to them.
- What cultural changes accompany political and economic changes?
- What economic policies have changed in the AP6 during the past two decades?
- What is the relationship between globalization and political and economic change?
- Why and how has the convergence of elites' attitudes been accompanied by the widening of ethnic, religious, and economic cleavages?

6. **Public Policy (in domestic and global contexts) (5 – 15% or 2 – 8 questions out of 55)**

- What are the influences on policy decisions?
    - Describe the formal and informal institutional influences.

Compromise Can Be Messy

AP courses are designed to resemble introductory university and college courses. The problem in designing a curriculum for comparative government and politics is the incredible variety in undergraduate courses. All it takes is a few minutes searching the web for syllabi (syllabuses) at political science departments across the country to recognize the diversity. At one extreme are courses that include the study of half a dozen countries. At the other extreme are the courses that examine only two or three countries. Some courses concentrate on industrial democracies; others deal only with developing countries. Some courses devote considerable time to complex theoretical processes; others seem to be primarily descriptive.

The AP curriculum then is a grand compromise of all these approaches reached by a course development committee. You study six countries: one industrial democracy, a former communist country now aspiring for industrial democracy status and prosperity, a communist country that more and more resembles an autocratic economic development machine, and three less developed countries exhibiting a wide variety of political and economic characteristics. Comparative theory ties these examples together.

* What are the requirements of new policies?
* What global pressures and institutions must be acknowledged?

- Identify the scope of policy agendas available to the governments you studied.

- What impacts the implementation of policy decisions?

- How does state capacity affect policy choices?

WHAT'S NOT IN THE OUTLINE

You need to master the basics about six countries: Iran, Mexico, Nigeria, the Peoples Republic of China, Russia, and the United Kingdom.

In addition, you'll have to learn how to do some basic comparative analysis.

If you keep the country information straight and do a careful study of the official course description, you may not need to read my commentary. On the other hand, perhaps my explanations here and in Chapter 4 on comparative theory will clarify some things. Once again, you get to decide what works best for **you**.

The Course

Because it's a grand compromise, many people had hands in writing the course description. That may make it difficult to make sense of. If you know what you're looking for, there are clues. Here are the clues I see in the course description (in the order in which I found them).

Methodology of political science
Normative questions
Empirical questions
Interdependence
Globalization
Permeability of borders
State
Nation
Regime
Government
Legitimacy
Authority
Bases for political power
Environmental politics
Social cleavages
Ethnic diversity
Economic performance
Power
Sovereignty
Supranational

Constitution
Limits
Obligations
Rights
Citizen
Economic system
Political economy
Belief system
Governance
Political culture
Core values
Political socialization
Ideology
Religious belief system
Formal state structure
Formal state operation
Informal state structure
Informal state operation
Unitary system
Federal system
Intragovernmental organization
Parliamentary system
Presidential system
Separation of powers
Fusion of powers
Legal system
Elite recruitment
Aggregation of political preferences
Electoral system
Political party system
Interest groups
Pluralism
Corporatism
Bureaucracy
Professionalism
Military politics
Intelligence community
Secret police
Civil society
Mediation of power
Advocacy groups
Social network
Media and politics
Global civil society
Transnational networks
NGOs
Participation (voluntary and coerced)

Change
Representation
Democratization
Elite pacts
Authoritarianism
State capacity
Economic reform
Income gap
Standard of living
Differential access
Corruption
Economic inequality
Public policy
Domestic policy
Global policy
Social welfare
Individual liberties
Inflation
Monetary policy
Fiscal policy
Population policy
Migration policy
Gender politics

Many of these should sound familiar, even out of context. Others are probably unfamiliar labels for concepts you do understand. Yet others may be total mysteries. You better look up those mysterious terms. The glossary in Chapter 4 will be helpful.

The course outline might be a more useful document right now. It can even provide an organizing plan (a paradigm, if you will) for putting your knowledge into serviceable order. There's an abbreviated version just below the next paragraph.

There are six major topics in the outline. If you think about creating six pages of notes for each country you've studied (a page for each topic), you will have organized a very practical document. The creation will be educational and the product will be a manageable, useful study guide.

The six topics are

1. **Introduction to Comparative Politics** — This topic is primarily about how to do comparative politics.

2. Sovereignty, Authority, and Power — This is about power arrangements and justifications.

3. Political Institutions — This is about regimes, how they function, political culture, and leadership.

4. Citizens, Society, and the State — This topic is concerned with how people relate to the political system.

5. Political and Economic Change — This topic is about change: what causes it, how it happens, and its ramifications.

6. Public Policy — This topic combines the four previous topics and emphasizes the results and limitations of the political process.

Does that seem more helpful?

If you're the organized type, you might want to go ahead and label 36 pages of a notebook with the topic titles (one for each country). If not, you might want to begin reviewing your textbook for information relevant to the topics. Or you might want to go ahead and look at my notes on each of the countries. I don't have all the answers, nor do I know where **you** will find the answers, but I have ideas to offer.

You will notice many of my source references are to web sites. While I have drawn upon my teaching experiences and consulted comparative government textbooks while putting these notes together, I wanted to provide you with access to up-to-date information if you want to seek it out. Looking for and reacting to information is a good method of rehearsal.

> **Live links to up-to-date information and to web sites mentioned in this book are also available at this book's web site, *apcomparativegov.com*.**

REVIEW EXERCISE

This exercise is meant to get you thinking about some of the basic facts and point out areas you might have to review more thoroughly. My responses follow.

1. The AP6 does NOT include
   (A) The United Kingdom
   (B) Nigeria
   (C) Mexico
   (D) Canada
   (E) Russia

2. The AP Comparative course outline includes all the following goals EXCEPT
   (A) determining which regime is best
   (B) interpreting economic data in a comparative context
   (C) examining patterns of political processes and their results
   (D) introducing major concepts of comparative politics
   (E) developing generalizations about political institutions

3. One of the learning goals of the first part of the AP Comparative course outline is to
   (A) integrate normative and empirical observations
   (B) eliminate false distinctions between various regimes
   (C) learn that legitimacy has little or nothing to do with political power
   (D) understand that factors outside the nation-state affect policy making within that nation-state's government
   (E) find evidence for the superiority of democratic regimes

4. Power refers to the
   (A) right of a government to make policy
   (B) ability of a government to make policy
   (C) legitimacy of a government
   (D) permission a nation-state obtains to use military force
   (E) independence of a nation-state

5. Supranational describes
   (A) huge nation-states
   (B) nation-states that are federations
   (C) a power over nation-states
   (D) nation-states that are much more powerful than most others
   (E) unitary regimes

6. Legitimacy
   (A) can only be achieved by representative governments
   (B) forces people to accept government decisions
   (C) is an acceptance of the right of a government or a regime to exercise public power
   (D) results from centuries of self-government
   (E) depends upon repression of human rights

7. Public institutions
   (A) are organizations to which anyone can belong
   (B) differ from private institutions in the way people are allowed to join them
   (C) are governed by democratic procedures
   (D) are most common in new nation-states
   (E) are government organizations

8. Separation of powers
   (A) is common among governments
   (B) requires some parts of government to have power over other parts
   (C) describes the division of power between political parties
   (D) is most functional in unitary regimes
   (E) ensures executive authority in a regime

9. Political cleavages refer to
   (A) the ways that geographic features separate people from one another
   (B) socio-economic classes
   (C) religious beliefs held by various groups within a nation-state
   (D) ethic identities of groups within a nation-state
   (E) all of the above

10. A nation-state is
    (A) a cultural or ethnic group
    (B) an economic elite and the wealth they control
    (C) always able to exercise sovereignty
    (D) is a territorial unit controlled by a single state and governed by a single government
    (E) none of the above

(For responses, see below)

3: Know ... THE AP EXAMINATION

The AP exam is well described in the course and test registration material provided by the College Board and the Educational Testing Service. You can get information directly from them on the web at:

www.collegeboard.com/student/testing/ap/compgov/exam.html

There you'll find the official description of the test, sample multiple-choice questions, and the actual free-response questions from the past few years.

Here's my summary of the description. There are two sections to the test. The first is a set of 55 multiple-choice questions. You'll be allowed 45 minutes to work on this section. The multiple-choice section accounts for half of your exam score. The second section consists of an eight-part free-response section. You are allowed 100 minutes to work on these questions.

That's a total of 145 minutes of test taking (2 hours and 25 minutes). If you've taken AP exams before, you know there's a certain amount of time required for filling out forms and listening to directions. Your time in the testing room for this test is going to be close to 3 hours.

TEST QUESTIONS

The questions on the test are different from questions on tests that come with your textbook or that your teacher has written. Few of us teaching AP classes have the breadth of experience, the expertise, or the time to write questions like the ones that make it into the examination.

The questions are written by AP teachers and by university and college faculty from all over the

country. Specialists at the Educational Testing Service examine the questions. The questions are evaluated after they appear on tests given to college and university students in introductory comparative government courses. The test development committee (college and university faculty, AP teachers, and ETS specialists) chooses questions from a large number of those items.

The choices are made in order to

- ask questions about all the topics in the AP curriculum (see the previous chapter)
- ensure that students of similar abilities taking different forms of the test will receive the same scores
- include questions of varying difficulties
- allow comparisons between scores from this year's exam and scores from previous years' exams
- (in the free-response questions) allow you, the test taker, to use your "powers of analysis to build logical structures with supporting arguments and interconnected elements"
- (in the free-response questions) allow students to present uncommon yet correct responses

HOW THE EXAM IS SCORED
Think of this as an exam with 120 possible points.

The First 60 Points:

- Half of your exam score is based on how well you answer the 55 multiple-choice questions. Each question is worth 0.55% of your exam score.

- You indicate your choice of "best answer" by filling in the appropriate bubble on the machine-read answer sheet with one of your #2 pencils. You don't get any points for questions you don't bubble in a choice for, but there is no penalty for incorrect answers.

- Let's say you chose the best answer for 46 of the 55 questions. Your score would be 46. That would be a very good score. That raw score will be magically transformed by the statistical wizards at the Educational Testing Service (ETS) into an adjusted score on a 60-point scale. The magical transformation probably involves percentiles.

The Second 60 Points:

- You'll be asked to define or describe five concepts or terms and offer examples of them. These five items account for a fourth of your free-response score. In other words, each item will be worth 3 points. The test creators suggest you spend up to 30 minutes on these short-answer concept questions.

- You will be asked to do a "conceptual analysis" using a major comparative politics concept. This analysis will involve identifying and explaining political and institutional relationships, causes, effects, and likely feedback. (See the sample question in the last chapter or online at *www.collegeboard.com/student/testing/ap/compgov/exam.html*

  This analysis is worth 25% of the FRQ section or 15 of the free-response section points. The test preparers suggest you spend no more than 30 minutes on this task.

- Finally, you'll be asked to respond to two questions which will ask you to apply comparative politics concepts to countries you have studied. Since this is a comparative government and politics course, you should

expect to be asked to compare at least two of the AP6 in each question.

These two questions are worth 50% of the FRQ section or 15 points each, and the test constructors suggest you spend about 20 minutes on each one.

Overall

- The time allowed for you to work on the multiple-choice questions is 45 minutes. You'll turn in that answer sheet at that point. You cannot begin the free-response section or return to the multiple-choice section once that time is up.

  How you divide up your time during the 100-minute free-response section is up to you. Use the time where you need it.

  Don't agonize over details on a 3-point short-answer concepts question if that takes away time you need to think about a 15-point conceptual analysis.

The Composite Score

- If you earned a 46 out of 55 on the multiple-choice section (and that translated to 53 of 60 points); if you did very well on three of the short-answer concepts questions (9 points) and sort of well on two of them (3 points); if you analyzed the concept pretty well (13 points); if you did very well on one of the application questions (14 points) and not very well on the other (5 points), your total score would be 90 out of 120.

  If past results can be used as predictors, a score of 90 would probably be in the range to earn a 5 (extremely well qualified) on the AP exam.

Want a Less Sanguine Example?

- If you chose the best answer for 26 of the 55 multiple-choice, your score would be 26.

  If your first short-answer concepts response was good (3 points) and three others were okay (7 points), and the fifth was wrong (0 points); if your conceptual analysis was good (14 points); if your first application answer was pretty good (10 points), and if your second application response was off the mark (2 points), your composite score would be 62 out of 120.

That might seem appallingly low, but this is an AP exam. A score of 62 would probably be in the top half of the range to earn a 3 (qualified) on the AP exam and college credit at many institutions of higher learning.

ACADEMIC GAMES, PART ONE: IT'S POLITICAL SCIENCE, NOT HISTORY

In spite of my earlier advice to avoid academic games, there are strategic decisions that could affect your scores on this exam.

Many of the students in AP Comparative classes I've taught have previously been successful in AP history classes. Some of them are startled when their earlier successes are not equaled in political

---

rule of thumb: a method or procedure derived entirely from practice or experience, without any basis in scientific knowledge; a roughly practical method. Also, a particular stated rule that is based on practice or experience

— *Oxford English Dictionary*,
quoted in Douglas Adams,
So Long and Thanks for All the Fish

Dear Mr. ESL — What does the expression: "take with **a grain of salt**" mean?

Mr. ESL answers — To "take something with a grain of salt" is to be cautious about accepting or believing the thing; to be skeptical.

— Ask Mr. ESL,
www.gepc.org/ESL/grain.html

---

science (like comparative government and politics).

One of the primary factors, I think, is the way they approach the topics in political science. (I know the following is oversimplified, but bear with me. Even simplistic things can be helpful sometimes.)

---

dynamic, adj.
1 relating to an object, or objects, in motion; opposed to **static**

— *Webster's
New World
College Dictionary*

Political science deals with more dynamic topics than does history. History requires analysis of events that have happened. Even though new information regularly comes to light about past events and historians argue about what past events really were, the topics are static. Political science deals with current situations, actions, and relationships. The topics are **dynamic**. Political scientists can't deal with the events of last month without taking into account the events of yesterday.

It's sort of like the difference between analyzing a book and analyzing a never-ending film. If history students have to analyze printed material, political science students have to analyze videos.

It may be a subtle difference, but it's important. Some people catch on to the difference without thinking about it. Others have to work at making the shift to dynamic analysis. Successful history students taking political science classes sometimes focus too much on the background and long-term causes.

Here's my rule of thumb: Don't discuss anything more than 20 years old unless you're specifically asked about it. To add another cliché to the mix, you must take this advice with a grain of salt. You must use your own judgment about the validity of the advice based on the context of the free-response question you're asked. (Ambiguity again!)

ACADEMIC GAMES, PART TWO: GUESSING

Be very careful when leaving a blank space on the multiple-choice answer sheet. If you intend to leave a blank space, be very sure you do. If you intend to skip #4 but fill the space for #4 with your answer for #5 and fill the space for #5 with your answer for #6, etc., etc., you're hurting your score much more than simply guessing on #4. In fact, this is a good argument for answering every multiple-choice question.

Since there is no longer (beginning with the 2011 exam) a penalty for incorrect answers, there's no good reason to leave a blank on the answer sheet. If you want to come back and reconsider an answer after you've completed all the others, fill in your best guess, circle the question on the **test** (not on the answer sheet), and then review the circled items if and when you have time later.

ACADEMIC GAMES, PART THREE: DON'T CHANGE YOUR MIND (USUALLY)

Research tells us that your first thought about the best answer is more likely to be correct than your second thoughts. "More likely" doesn't mean always, but it means you shouldn't change an answer unless you're really **sure** you goofed. I'd probably have $300 or $400 if I had a dollar for every time I heard someone say, while going over the results of a multiple-choice test, "Why did I erase that?"

Vague thoughts, memories, or confusions aren't enough to motivate a change in an answer you already put on the answer sheet. Vivid and sudden recall of something you read or heard **is** enough. So is a phrase from another question that rings a loud bell about a specific concept.

But don't do it often.

ACADEMIC GAMES, PART FOUR: BE AN INTELLIGENT TEST TAKER

- Read every word of every question.
- Circle words like "except" and adjectives like "best," "many," and "least."
- Cross out obviously incorrect choices.
- Guess on questions you're not quickly able to answer (and circle the question on the test).
- Watch the clock.

THE FREE-RESPONSE QUESTIONS

The College Board's description of the AP exam names the first part of the free-response section **"Short-Answer Concepts."** You will be asked to "provide brief definitions *or* descriptions of five concepts or terms, noting their significance…" You might be asked for an example or to compare one concept with another.

Your responses to these items should be short and direct. You do have up to 30 minutes to write about these five items. Think first. Then write. Follow the instructions. All of them.

In the grading of the 2007 exams, a contextual requirement was added to the grading rubrics for some questions. In other words, test takers were required to describe the topic or nature of the definitions or descriptions they provided.

Since this requirement is likely to be applied to future exams, it's essential that you introduce each of your **"Short-Answer Concept"** questions with a restatement or paraphrase of the question.

If you're asked to identify policy goals common to free market and command economies, your identification must include a statement that the "things" you identify are policy goals common to free market and command economies. The easiest way to meet this requirement is to begin your response with a restatement of the question.

The second part of the free-response section is titled **"Conceptual Analysis."** You will be asked to explain relationships, identify causes and effects of political decisions, and identify likely implications of political actions.

A contextual introduction to these responses is also wise. Examples are crucial when responding to this item, even if you might be able to answer abstractly or theoretically. Think about whether you're being indirectly asked about prominent examples from the countries you've studied. In other words, pay attention not only to the concept, but also to the context. Respond appropriately to everything you're asked to do.

You have 30 minutes for this section. Think and plan what you want to say. Make sure your statements are relevant to the question. Don't' ignore any part of the question.

The final part of the free-response section is called **"Country Context."** That means there are two questions asking you to specifically apply ideas you've learned to two or more countries you've studied.

Do the easier of these questions first. Think and plan what you want to say. Then say it clearly and directly. Don't neglect any part of the question. Be sure to explicitly compare the political systems you're asked about.

How Should You Approach These Questions?
My students who have taken these exams agree that one of the best pieces of advice I gave them was: "Read the verbs! Read the verbs and do what they ask you to do."

When we're confronted with a test question, we all pay attention to the nouns, so we know what we're being asked about. But some people ignore the verbs and instantly begin writing anything they know about the topic of the question. That's not a smart way to deal with any of these free-response questions.

Look at the verbs. Figure out what you're being asked to do as well as what the topic is. Make sure your responses are relevant to the topic **and** the task.

Here are the verbs in order of decreasing frequency of use in the free-response questions asked between 1999 and 2010. Most of these questions are available at the AP web site (see the URL at the beginning of this chapter).

- describe (used 83 times)
- explain (used 62 times)
- identify (used 50 times)
- define (used 21 times)
- discuss (used 10 times)
- compare (used 8 times)
- select (used 5 times)
- demonstrate (used twice)
- assess (used once)
- contrast (used once)
- support/refute (used once)

Describe, identify, and define have moved up the rankings in the past few years.

The game-playing question is "What are these words asking me to do?" Below are my answers. Remember, the exact meaning has to be derived from the context. (Ah, there's that ambiguity again.) What I'm suggesting in these "definitions" is what you probably ought to emphasize in responding freely to these verbs. "Thing" in these definitions refers to features — processes, institutions, traditions, etc. — of any governmental or political system or the environments within which they function.

describe — This verb, while similar to "explain," emphasizes the static nature of the "thing" asked about rather than the dynamic nature of its operation (unless you're asked to describe a process)

or you might think of it as a broader version of "identify" where you need to illustrate the prominent features of a "thing" more than distinguishing the differences between "things."

Describe does require some explanation; paint a word picture of the characteristics, qualities, and features of the "thing" asked about.

explain — This verb is usually asking you to describe a variety of features and their relationships to one another of the "thing" asked about

or to put that "thing" into a broader context

or to describe the dynamics of how that "thing" works.

Explain asks you by implication to deal with some cause and effect relationships; you might do well to start with a thesis and offer logical and factual support for the thesis in response to this question; be explicit about your explanation (implications won't get you any points).

identify — This verb is usually asking you to distinguish between the "thing" asked about and other, perhaps similar, things

or to choose one or more "things" from an environment or a political system

or to describe the characteristics of something.

Identify can be very concise; it does not require a lot of explanation; it might simply be a list.

define — This verb is often used as an introduction to a multi-part question; stick with a textbook definition as best you can. Sometimes examples can help.

discuss — This comes as close to asking you to "tell all you know" as any of these verbs; look closely at the context and see if you can narrow the scope of what you're being asked about; "discuss" may refer to some very specific "thing."

Discuss probably means you need to identify, describe, and explain; be concise, you don't have all day to do that; if it really does ask you to do all that, a thesis and careful support are going to be your best guides.

compare — When you're asked to do this in a free-response question, the topic is going to be pretty specific (you don't have all day); but you have to show your knowledge and good judgment by limiting your comparison to what's relevant to the question; identify and describe similarities (and differences where relevant); don't simply write separate paragraphs about the topics you're asked to compare; emphasize differences if the verb is **contrast**; going off on tangents will not earn points.

select — This one asks for something even simpler than identify; you'll probably be asked to choose one or two topics or examples from a list; be sure to name the thing(s) you select.

demonstrate — This verb is asking you to describe and explain a process or a cause and effect relationship. Make sure your logic is sound. You might be surprised to know how often test takers confuse cause and effect.

assess — This verb will probably be followed by a noun telling you what to assess; the question might also tell you what standards to use in evaluating the "thing" asked about; be careful about including value judgments in your answer — stay as objective as possible; a thesis would be very useful and logical; factual support is vital; this is a good place to use examples.

support/refute — These verbs are asking you to make and support a judgment about a situation, a hypothesis, a quotation, or about a set of data; you don't have to be formal, but a thesis and support is vital in questions that ask you to do this. Once again, do what's necessary to support your thesis; don't try to include everything.

There's always a chance that other verbs will show up on future exams. Verbs like:

list — This verb asks for a concise list of "things"; whole sentences are unnecessary unless such informality distracts you; no explanations or justifications are necessary.

analyze — This verb usually is asking you to identify the components of the "thing" asked about and describe their interrelationships;

or to describe the interactions of several "things."

You might be asked to compare or contrast "things" by analyzing their operation.

evaluate — In other words, how valid is a statement or conclusion? Your evaluation might be a simple phrase, but you must offer support for your conclusion — data, examples, correctly interpreted expert testimony.

If you think the distinctions between some of these verbs are fuzzy, you're right. You have to discern exactly what you're being asked about. Look at the whole question and determine

- What big idea (generalization or bit of theory) is the question about?
- What institutional or procedural comparison is at the heart of the question?
- What topic from the AP course outline is the question asking about?

You have to determine from the context what to emphasize in your response, what to minimize, and what to omit.

Remember those lines from the stated goals of the test development committee: Questions are chosen, in part, to allow students to present uncommon yet correct responses and to allow them to demonstrate their "powers of analysis" by building "logical structures with supporting arguments and interconnected elements."

The "Conceptual Analysis" and "Country Context" questions **do not** require formal five paragraph essays. They don't **always** require thesis statements. Your responses might be combinations of lists of phrases and explanatory paragraphs. Or they might be a one-sentence thesis statement and a list of supporting facts.

But be sure to introduce your responses with a contextual identifier, i.e., a statement or phrase that identifies the topic you're writing about.

JUST BECAUSE THEY'RE NOT FORMAL ESSAYS...

ONE: Just because they're not formal essays doesn't mean you shouldn't plan them out.

If you have 20-30 minutes to write these answers, you should take at least 5 minutes to plan how you're going to respond. Write yourself a little outline alongside the question. Be sure your outline responds to **all** the verbs in the question. (Remember each of the things you're asked to do is worth credit on the grading guidelines.)

TWO: There are no points awarded for parroting or paraphrasing the words in the exam question, BUT, sometimes such an introduction provides a required context for your response and writing such an introduction might help you get started.

THREE: Don't leave your best line for last.

If you plan, you may well come up with a great opening line for your response. If you don't plan, you may write a bunch of disjointed things (some irrelevant) and tack on a good line at the end when you've thought the whole thing through. That good line, if used at the beginning of your response, might create a frame of reference that makes your whole answer more coherent (and worth more points). Just to be on the safe side, leave a few lines blank at the beginning of your response. If you come up with a great introduction after you've written everything else, you can add it at the top, where it belongs.

Writing Strategies

Write down the time you begin the free-response section. Write down the time intervals for the three parts of the free-response section. Stick with the deadlines.

Start with outlines and plans to answer questions. Do whatever works for you: create a plan as you begin work on each question or create plans for all of them before you begin writing any of the responses. Do what works for you.

Once again, it's a good idea to respond right away to the questions you perceive as easiest. It's not necessary to answer the questions in the order they appear on the test. But, be sure you **number them correctly in your test booklet.** You should wait to work on questions that look difficult or confusing. Just remember not to get carried away with the easy questions. Keep your eye on the clock.

Don't struggle for exactly the right words. Use the ones that come to mind. You're not writing an essay, a research paper, or a book.

Write as legibly as you can. Test readers are a remarkable bunch. They can and do read nearly everything that students put on paper. But, they cannot evaluate illegible scribbling anymore than they can grade an essay in Russian or Chinese. (Everything has to be in English.)

Don't waste your time trying to erase. Just quickly cross out words you don't want as part of your answer. Crossed out words are ignored by test readers. They get to read 100+ free-responses or over 500 short-answer items a day. They don't have time to read extra words.

In Summary

You should keep in the back of your mind an image of the nature of the exam and the nature of the questions on it. It helps to recall the way in which the exam is scored.

You should be aware of the essence of the discipline and the AP curriculum.

You should be an intelligent test taker. That means using the available time well and guessing intelligently. Plan your reading, ideas, words, and time.

You have to work to understand the questions by taking into account the curriculum, the discipline, and the contexts created by the questions.

Use intelligent writing strategies.

Advice from a Former Chief Reader of AP Government and Politics Exams

"Tell your students, the key to earning points on AP GOPO FRQs is to answer the question that is asked (not the one they want to answer or the one they imagine was asked)! ...I suspect the students who are most surprised with their scores are those who write beautiful 5-paragraph essays, perfect in form, but never address any part of the question asked. That's a 0 or a dash. ...Some of the questions will call for an essay; others will be more amenable to other forms of response, including diagrams and charts.

"'Free response' does not mean that all forms of response would be equally likely to earn students points on each question. As long as the students can communicate their knowledge that addresses the question asked and as long as they carry out the tasks assigned... they will earn points. But those tasks will vary from question to question. The 'best' way of addressing the question is question specific."

— Joseph Stewart, Jr.
Professor and Chair
Department of Political Science
Clemson University
Clemson, SC

REVIEW EXERCISE

This exercise is meant to get you thinking about some of the basic facts and point out areas you might have to review more thoroughly. My responses follow.

1. The AP exam for Comparative Government and Politics
   (A) includes Document Based Questions (DBQs)
   (B) is written by high school AP teachers
   (C) allows test takers 45 minutes to answer 55 multiple-choice questions
   (D) includes questions about the United States
   (E) requires thesis based essays

2. The AP exam for Comparative Government and Politics
   (A) offers opportunities to earn points by demonstrating your powers of analysis
   (B) requires correct answers from specific textbooks
   (C) is structured so each year's test scores are unique
   (D) is identical for all students
   (E) asks question only about select parts of the course outline

3. You would probably earn a 3 (out of 5) on the AP exam if your score was about
   (A) 40%
   (B) 55%
   (C) 70%
   (D) 85%
   (E) 90%

4. In comparison to AP history exams, the AP Comparative Government and Politics exam
   (A) requires more thorough, long-term analysis
   (B) includes more formal thesis and argument questions
   (C) assesses knowledge of background conditions
   (D) focuses more on dynamic, current topics
   (E) asks more questions about cause and effect than about institutions

5. The penalty for an incorrect answer on the multiple-choice section of the exam is
   (A) a quarter point
   (B) a half point
   (C) three-quarters of a point
   (D) one point
   (E) there is no penalty for incorrect multiple-choice answers

6. The reason you are advised not to change answers in the multiple-choice section frequently is that
   (A) you probably don't have enough time during the exam
   (B) erasures on the answer sheet are usually read by scoring machines as incorrect responses
   (C) unconscious impulses can nearly always be trusted
   (D) the stress of taking the exam can cause you to doubt your choices
   (E) your first responses are most often based on things you've learned

7. It's a good idea to restate or paraphrase the FRQs as you begin your responses because
   (A) that will help you begin the writing process
   (B) you need to label the topics you are writing about (even if that's not explicitly asked for in the question)
   (C) an introduction that includes a restatement or paraphrase will help keep you focused on what you need to say
   (D) exam readers (graders) will be better able to identify which question you're responding to
   (E) all of the above are good reasons to introduce your responses with a label for your topic

8. The nouns in the FRQs tell you
   (A) how to structure your responses
   (B) what you should write about
   (C) the kind of analysis you should do in your responses
   (D) whether to write definitions or lists in your responses
   (E) how often to restate the question in your introductions

9. The verbs in the FRQs tell you
   (A) what the topics of the questions are
   (B) which countries to write about
   (C) the concepts that should be the focus of your responses
   (D) what you should say about the topics
   (E) which topics can be omitted from your responses

10. You will be penalized in an FRQ for
   (A) mentioning more than the required number of examples
   (B) misspellings (even if they do not change your intended meaning)
   (C) writing in a language other than English
   (D) small factual errors that do not detract from your main idea
   (E) grammatical errors (that do not affect the meaning of your response)

(For responses, see below)

4: Know ... THEORY

Unlike economics or psychology, comparative government and politics theory is in its infancy. All social scientists want to develop accurate generalizations and correlations about the topics under consideration. Those conclusions should help us better understand how things work. And, if research can demonstrate how some things cause others, people with power might find ways to bring about changes they desire.

Some scholars work diligently at constructing a meaningful theory built around fundamental concepts like "legitimacy" or "justice." But most contemporary theory used is just now moving beyond description.

The comparative process begins by being quite descriptive. After all, how can you do analysis without adequate description? **However, even description must be done within a theoretical framework.**

It is theory that answers questions like

- What should be studied?
- How should those things and processes be described?
- What questions should we ask?
- How can we evaluate answers to those questions?
- How much correlation is required to demonstrate causation?
- What data is needed to support generalizations or confirm apparent similarities?

Theories are based on concepts like legitimacy, justice, sovereignty, and democracy. The glossary at the end of this chapter offers definitions of many important concepts and useful labels, but it's not comprehensive. You should recognize that there are hundreds of concepts used in the study of comparative politics. Check your textbook's glossary, index, and end of chapter summaries for more help in preparing for the AP exam.

Most often comparative analysis begins with the definition of government as an institution that makes policy decisions and implements those

One Common Aim, Methods That Vary

Governments have many aims and functions in common. How they accomplish those goals differs widely, however. For instance, leaders of every political unit want to be seen as legitimate holders of authority. The ways they achieve legitimacy vary widely. The Iraqi regime of Sadaam Hussein used repression to maintain social order. His Baathist Party used near-totalitarian methods to distribute everything from food to electricity and their version of national pride. The level of legitimacy they earned was pretty low.

In industrial democracies, leaders depend largely on competitive elections and the rule of law to earn legitimacy. The provision of public goods like education, law enforcement, social security, and transportation are also part of the system that wins and maintains public trust.

policies for the people and territory within the jurisdiction of the government. The answers to the questions of what should be studied and described, then, are the **people, institutions**, and **processes** by which policy decisions are made and implemented for what's commonly called a "nation-state."

If all governments make and implement policy, then we can compare the ways they do that. What we need to do is find the people, processes, and institutions that decide on policy in one nation-state and compare them with the people, processes, and institutions that make policy in other nation-states. For the purposes of the AP exam, you can do that with carefully defined concepts like "interest articulation" and "interest aggregation" or you can do it with generic labels like "lobbying" and "political participation."

But you should be a bit more sophisticated in your responses than the simplistic idea above. You might refer to Locke's idea that there are three functions of legitimate government, i.e., one that represents the people: legislation (making policy), administration (implementing policy), and adjudication (resolving conflicts peaceably). These three functions turned into the legislature, executive, and judiciary in the US regime. How are those functions performed in other political systems?

Did you notice what I did there? I just asked a conceptual comparative question and provided you with a theoretical context in which to answer it. As an example, it makes a general point. Comparative government and politics promotes the description and comparison of analogous features of different systems. Identifying

and naming those analogous features is the beginning of comparative theory.

Speaking of systems, we can make these ideas a bit more sophisticated by expanding our focus from government to include the **environments** within which governments operate and the **resources** that governments have.

If government is the **place** where policy decisions are made and put into action, what does the government have to work with? Does it matter if the country is resource rich like the USA or resource poor like North Korea? Does it matter if the country has a huge population like China or a small population like Canada? Does it matter whether people value fairness and justice, as they do in the UK, or whether they value religious or ideological purity, as many people do in Iran?

I hope that you're now saying something like, "Those are blatantly obvious questions. Of course, those things matter." What I'm trying to get you to think about are governments' **environments** and the **inputs** to the governmental **system**.

Another way to think about the environments within which nation-states function is to distinguish between **domestic environments** and the **global environment**. A major part of the domestic environment is what political scientists call **the state**. The state includes the government and all the other actors in the nation-state that wield power and influence. So it's not only the natural or demographic features that make up a government's environment, but it's the people and organizations in the nation.

The global environment includes all those other nation-states in the world, international organizations like the UN and the EU, military and economic alliances like NATO and NAFTA, and non-governmen-

> ### Be Sure to Compare the Environmental Factors, Too
>
> The mineral resources, the talents and education of the people, international organizations, climate, and many other things are all part of the environment within which a government operates. Some of those things empower a government; other things impinge on its operation. They are valuable to consider when making comparisons.

tal organizations (NGOs) like Amnesty International, Doctors Without Borders, and the Internet Corporation for Assigned Names and Numbers (ICANN). The global environment also encompasses the conflicts between nations and other organizations, the general state of economies and trade, and any other situation to which governments must respond, like global warming or terrorism.

A POLITICAL SYSTEM

What do we have so far? A government that makes policies and puts them into practice. This government operates within a domestic environment and an international environment. Do you have an image of that? Here is my image. How does it correspond with yours?

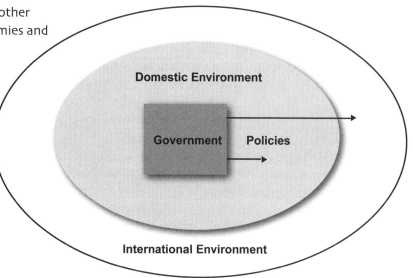

Initial Political System Model

If we're close to having the same images, then we can proceed (and you can skip the rest of this paragraph). If we're not on the same page with this model, let me explain mine. The international environment includes everything outside the nation-state. Everything! The domestic environment includes everything in the nation-state except the government. The government is made up of all those organizations, institutions, and offices (and the people who hold those offices) involved in making and implementing public policies. It is also all those public laws, rules, regulations, standards, and red tape.

> **public**: "of, belonging to, or concerning the people as a whole; of or by the community at large"
>
> — *Webster's New World College Dictionary*

If you're confused about the arrows representing policy, there are two because some policies affect only the nation-state and others affect the world beyond the nation-state. In a rich and powerful country, many affect both. If you're still having trouble with this, think about it and hang in here.

I'm going to elaborate. And that may actually help make sense of this idea.

ELABORATION

Newton's Third Law of Motion states that for **every** action there is an equal and opposite reaction. As much as some social scientists would like to, none of us has found universal laws like that for political science.

> **Universal Laws of Social Science**
>
> Justice is one of the values most discussed — especially by philosophers — as a candidate for a universal law of social science.

We are, however, able to state emphatically that effective policy will produce results. If policy is effective, the consequences will change the environment within which the policy maker resides. That means that policymaking in the future will take place in an environment different from the one in which previous policymaking took place. Right! Huh?

In other words, if three countries (say Canada, Mexico and the USA) choose, in 1993, to follow a policy of free trade between and among themselves (say a North American free trade association), then the domestic and international environments of all three nation-states would be altered. After the 1993 agreement, policymaking would be different. How do we include that in our model?

Borrowing what we can from other scientists, social scientists label those changes caused by policy decisions "feedback." The feedback becomes part of the environments for future decision making. So here's a new sketch.

Expanded Political System Model

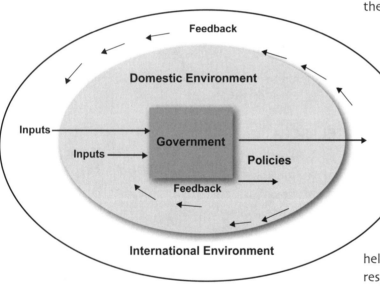

The final elements of the model are the inputs. Inputs are the political acts that can be identified as directly contributing to the policy-making process. This might (in the case of a US policy on petroleum) be interest aggregation and articulation like the lobbying of the Sierra Club and the Wyoming Independent Producers Association.

The effects of these inputs on the administration of the Energy Department or the legislative committee work of Wyoming Representative Cynthia Lummis are direct. As you can see, the model is

designed to show that some inputs come from the international environment and others come from the domestic environment. Make sense?

So what? What do **you** do with this descriptive model of governing?

If theory tells us to compare analogous features of policymaking in various countries, a systems model should help you determine what is analogous to what.

If, as the 1999 AP test did, this year's test asks you to compare ethnic conflict in two countries and "how the government" in each nation-state "has dealt with ethnic conflict," you should be easily able to identify the environments within which the conflicts took place and the inputs that affected policymaking. That ought to make your comparison of differences between government policies in Russia, Mexico, and Nigeria clearer.

You probably won't use the words "environment" and "feedback" in your free response (though you could), but the theory will help you make sense of the question and frame your response.

Similarly this systems model might have helped you respond to the 2006 question about "how a decentralized unitary system differs from a federal system." You would focus on which policy-making elements of a unitary system are analogous to policy-making

Distractions

Some would argue that incidental acts with political consequences (the increasing use of low-mileage SUVs by American consumers, for instance) are also inputs. You can make a case for that in a free-response answer, but don't get distracted from your main point.

elements in a federal system. Then you could describe differences between, for instance, the devolved bodies in the UK and the states in the USA.

BEYOND SYSTEMS THEORY

Some years ago, comparative theory moved toward **behaviorism**, like most social sciences. This was a step beyond description. Behavioral studies focused on individual decision making within the institutional and political frameworks described earlier. It assumed that most people made rational, informed decisions in their own self-interests.

The focus of much comparative political science shifted from government to politics; from institutions to people's behavior. If you've studied economics, this should sound familiar.

This change in theoretical emphasis also made quantitative studies more realistic, since statistical analysis depends on large numbers of examples (i.e., people's decisions) for accuracy.

If making verifiable generalizations using descriptive comparisons was difficult, behaviorism also had its limitations. People don't always seem to make rational decisions. Sometimes they make choices that are more beneficial to others than themselves. And globalization began making it more and more difficult to be well informed about the consequences of choices.

More recently, some comparative political scientists have begun integrating descriptive and behavioral methods with **a cultural approach,** borrowed, in part, from anthropology. This theoretical approach to comparative politics is the most nebulous. How do you take into account institutional, political, behavioral, and global cultural variables when comparing political systems? The answers to that question are only beginning to appear.

Jean-Germain Gros, who teaches comparative politics at the University of Missouri-St. Louis, describes[1] three "schools of analysis":

inputs: the ways average citizens and the groups they form (interest groups and political parties) affect political life

policies: regulatory, redistributive, assertive, and symbolic, actions (and actions not taken) by government

environment: everything outside the political system

feedback: the ways in which people's reactions to policy help shape the next phase of political life

— Hauss, *Comparative Politics, Domestic Responses to Global Challenges*, 2003

legitimacy: "the sense that the political system in place not only has political power, but ought to have this power"

— Theen and Wilson, *Comparative Politics, An Introduction to Seven Countries*, 1992

1. Political economy, which focuses on the interface between politics and economics. Some scholars in this "school" emphasize systems analysis; others are behaviorists.

2. Modernization theory is much more of a cultural approach to comparative politics. Scholars look for "modern" and "backward" features of a nation-state and study the forces instigating and resisting change in those features. From a normative perspective, modern is usually seen as preferable to backward.

3. Dependency theory is also a cultural approach, but it integrates many aspects of systems theory. The focus of these studies is on the global political-economic system and how countries are empowered and enriched or weakened and impoverished by globalization. There are pretty obvious normative judgments in dependency theory, too.

COMPARATIVE METHODOLOGY

All of these theoretical approaches rely on comparative case studies.

If you compare events in different political systems using case studies, you're looking for causes and effects. The effects are like the results of experiments (i.e., dependent variables). The causes are like the experimental processes (independent variables).

If you choose events carefully (say the promotion of private enterprises in Russia and China), you can identify the results, label some causes as constants (because they're the same in both countries), and label other causes as independent variables that account for the differences in outcomes.

However, if you don't choose carefully and try to compare essentially disparate events (say an ideological and social revolution in China with a theocratic revolution in Iran), there may be so few constants and so many independent variables that coming to any reasonable conclusions about the causes of results is virtually impossible.

There are two basic approaches to case studies: most similar systems (MSS) comparisons and most different systems (MDS) comparisons.

In MSS analysis, you want to look at similar governance systems and look for correlations between differences in the systems and differences in policies and/or government actions.

In MDS analyses, you seek correlations between system similarities and policy similarities when governance systems are quite different from one another.

Both approaches are valuable for descriptive, behavioral, and cultural theories. Quantitative and qualitative approaches also use either approach or systems theory.

Case analysis might be very useful in the AP exam's "free-response" section. Questions will ask you to make comparisons and the topics are likely to imply some similarities as well as some differences.

If you can limit the **independent variables** (the differences between the causes in one country and the causes in another), you might have a nifty outline of a response to the question.

Be sure you're not overlooking any significant details or minimizing political, economic, or cultural differences.

A CLASSIFICATION SYSTEM

Another bit of theory you should master is part of the process of making generalizations. What systems have in common is as important as how they differ. When generalizing, we try to put countries into meaningful categories that describe how members of a category are similar. None of the variety of attempts to sort nation-states into groups is entirely satisfactory, and people use different systems for different purposes.

The old classifier, Aristotle, probably began this process. In fact, if we can agree on how many is a "few" or a "many," the categories at right may still be useful theoretical tools.

The modern standard system has deep historical roots. In Europe and the USA, it began as "us and them." Before World War II, there were the Western and non-Western Worlds. At the beginning of the Cold War there were democracies ("the First World") and communist countries ("the Sec-

Sorting Out the Categories: The Aristotelian Model

Number of Rulers	Rule in the General Interest	Rule in Self Interest
one	monarchy	tyranny
few	aristocracy	oligarchy
many	democracy	ochlocracy

ond World"). Both of those classification systems, based on politics, were loaded with ethnocentric assumptions — something political scientists strive to avoid.

Even without the biases, such a static and simplistic view of the world was doomed.

- In 1948, India became an independent country with an elected government. Did that it make it part of the First World?

- In 1949, China switched from "us" to "them" and became a Second World country.

- In 1955, Indonesian President Sukarno hosted the Bandung Conference of Non-Aligned States in part to assert that there was more to the world than "us and them."

- In 1957, Ghana became the first of Europe's former African colonies to become an independent nation. The number of nation-states grew rapidly in the 1960s.

Politicians and political scientists responded by adding a new category, "the Third World," to the "us and them" categories.

By the 1970s, it was obvious that the assembly of Third World nation-states was pretty diverse. Industrialization happened rapidly in some Asian countries. In the 1990s, democratization was an identifiable trend in Asia and Africa. Some people began using an additional category, "Fourth World," to identify countries that were desperately poor and distinguish them from those Third World countries that were a bit better off.

The collapse of communism in the Soviet Union and Eastern Europe made the communist countries category obsolete. Some political scientists

Composition of Economies (as percentages of GDPs)

	Agricultural Sector	Industrial Sector	Service Sector
Iran	10.9%	45.2%	43.9%
Mexico	4.1%	34.5%	61.3%
Nigeria	33.4%	34.1%	32.5%
PRC	10.9%	48.6%	40.5%
Russia	5.2%	31.9%	58.1%
UK	1.2%	23.8%	75.0%
USA	1.2%	21.9%	76.9%
Canada	2.0%	28.4%	69.6%

Data from *2010 CIA World Factbook*

have continued to talk about communist and former communist countries because those nation-states do share some important characteristics.

(As a sidelight, the AP Comparative Government and Politics curriculum has gotten beyond including "the former Soviet Union." However, because it is the direct ancestor of contemporary Russia, you'll need to know some basics about the USSR.)

MORE COMPLEXITY

The recognition of more and more complexity led to new ways of categorizing nations. One popular categorization put nation-states into groups based on descriptions of their primary economic activity: post-industrialized, industrialized, industrializing, non-industrial. Other people tried labels like developed and developing or underdeveloped categories. You will see labels like LDC (less developed countries) or the G8 (the Group of Eight most industrialized) countries. In other contexts you'll see the labels north and south applied to "developed" and "developing" countries.

India

PRC

Indonesia

Ghana

None of these systems has proved totally satisfactory for describing groups of nations. Nonetheless, the terms are still used because in certain contexts, they're useful descriptions. (Ambiguity. Remember?)

The primary implication is that if you label a nation-state, you're telling your audience something about it. If someone tells you that Singapore and Sudan are Third World countries, they're not communicating much of anything. In fact, such a statement would cause confusion since Singapore and Sudan have so little in common. If they say that Sudan, Somalia, Laos, and Nicaragua are Third World countries, you should be able to understand several possible messages (ambiguity raises its head again) and to be able to ask for clarification.

What you have to do is become conversant with these labels and their limitations. You must understand what the test writers mean when they use them. If you use them in a free response, you must use them properly. Otherwise, you'll not get credit for your ideas.

If you look at your textbook, you may well find some categorization. Here's what it probably means.

**First World Countries /
Industrialized Democracies /
Durable Democratic Regimes /
Early Developers**

When authors or test writers use these terms they are usually talking about rich, Western countries with relatively long histories of political development. The countries have some form of representative government. That means there are regularly scheduled competitive elections. The elections are run and broad policymaking is done transparently. In other words, there is relatively meaningful political accountability and reliance on the rule of law.

These countries also have an active civic society. People are free to form and join public and private organizations which contribute to the communities they are part of. There is also in these countries, a general sense among citizens that the government and the elites who wield political authority legitimately have power.

Nearly all these countries have mixed economies that rely on markets and private property to greater or lesser degrees. All the governments exert power over private economic activity and all provide at least basic public and social services. The social services and the taxation to pay for them usually have the effect of reducing class-

Causes and Results: Keep Them in the Right Order

One of the biggest problems AP test takers have is maintaining clear, logical relationships between causes and results. Given the pressures of testing situations, the complexity of cause and effect relationships, and the desire to show they know "things," test takers regularly confuse causes with results and vice versa. It doesn't matter whether it's sloppy thinking or sloppy writing, you probably won't get any points for describing a public policy as causing public opinion in a republican system. In a republican government, policy is usually a result of public opinion.

However, the nature of feedback implies that a policy might cause the aggregation and articulation of opinion. If you're going to assert such a relationship, you must describe it completely.

It's ambiguity again. Keep your thoughts clear and your writing precise. Describe relationships fully — especially if that relationship goes beyond the common sense simplicity of the obvious.

based cleavages and increasing social mobility. The governments of all of these countries provide subsidies to agriculture and to other "desirable" industries.

The economies may be called industrial, but post-industrial is more accurate. The service sector is becoming more and more important. They are becoming "post-industrial." The transition from industrial to service economy is creating problems of structural unemployment in many of these countries. In addition, post-materialist values are becoming more important as awareness of environmental and other quality of life issues grows.

Second World Countries / Communist and Former Communist Regimes / Middle Developers

Most of the countries in this category share authoritarian/totalitarian political histories. Politics was open only to self-perpetuating elites. These countries also shared command economies, where planning the use of publicly-owned assets substituted for markets and private ownership. They also shared systems that provided relatively high levels of social services and promoted egalitarian economic and social policies. These countries also have relatively old infrastructure and industrial capital.

Today, these countries are at various stages of change. People in all these countries are trying to establish stable, legitimate regimes. Some might be called transitional democracies. Others continue to be ruled by small, closed elites. Nearly all are giving market-oriented forces more legitimacy. Many of these countries are faced with large-scale social and economic problems ranging from ethnic warfare to shrinking economies and high inflation. People are trying to find ways to adjust to an economic/political system that does not guarantee jobs, housing, health care, and security. Two of the world's remaining communist countries, China and Vietnam, are actually confronting the problems of economic growth.

Third World Countries / Less Developed Countries / Newly Industrializing Countries / Late Developers

Test writers and textbook authors usually are talking about countries that were once colonies of Western industrialized countries when they use this category. The variety of regimes and economies among this group is great. Generally, the dependency of colonial status continues for these countries. Their economies are dependent upon exports and foreign investments, which limit the choices of governments and states. The power of multinational corporations (MNCs) in these countries is great. So is the power of international organizations like the IMF, the World Bank, and the World Trade Organization.

If the power of outsiders is great, the power of governments is weak. Regimes tend to be unstable and relatively short-lived. Some of these states are called "failed" states. The institutions of the state are ineffective and inefficient. Those characteristics together with dramatic poverty mean that there is a lack of even basic public services (clean water, law enforcement, schools, roads). There is also the absence of rule of law. Elections, if they take place, and policymaking are not likely to be transparent.

Political scientists would say these countries have to deal with a low level of political integration. That means there's little sense of national identity. People identify themselves primarily by their ethnic heritage or religion rather than their citizenship. There is likely serious ethnic conflict (even if it's not violent). In these countries there is likely to be a relatively wide gap between the elites and the rest of society in wealth, education, and attitude. All these characteristics and non-democratic politics are encouraged and facilitated by patron-client relationships that are prominent features in these countries. Patron-client relationships are important in all political systems, but in these countries the unequal linkages dominate politics.

Besides poverty and dependency, countries usually placed in this group are facing the problems of rapid population growth and environmental degradation. Greater resources must be allocated to feeding people, and the resources of these countries are limited. Thus there's even more temptation to make long-term ecological sacrifices for short-term economic gains.

POLITICAL ECONOMICS

One of the major areas of policymaking governments must deal with is economics. Even for countries with powerful economies and strong states, domestic economic issues have global implications. And those policy decisions are also made within the context of global politics and economics, which limit the choices of all sovereign nation-states.

In order to be prepared for the AP exam, you'll have to have a grasp of basic economic policies, how economic policy decisions are made, the implications of those policies, and limitations imposed on policy makers by the global economy. If you need to review this in detail, check out the "macroeconomics" article in a good encyclopedia or at Wikipedia.com.

Domestic economic policies center on taxation and government spending, usually referred to as **fiscal policies**. The highest level policies have to do with how much government should spend and how much of the money to be spent should come from taxes, how much should come from the sale of state resources, and how much should come from borrowing. Debates on these issues center on what effects fiscal policies will have on economic stability, growth, prosperity, efficiency, trade, and often how much "profit" will be returned to those in power.

The underlying issues, often decided before the highest level ones, have to do with things like who is taxed, who is subsidized, and at what levels, who loans money to the government, what goods and services are public, and who benefits from government spending — legitimately or not. Debates on these issues focus on winners and losers as well as on the larger issues of stability, growth, prosperity, efficiency, and trade.

Other domestic economic policies center on money and interest rates. These are usually referred to as **monetary policies**. While all the issues mentioned above are part of debates about monetary policies, international trade becomes an issue since the value of a nation-state's money is directly related to trade issues.

In addition, governments make **trade policies**, which affect their own and other nation-states' economies. They also make **regulatory policies** that affect the efficiencies and trustworthiness of their domestic economies.

All of this domestic policymaking is done within an environment that includes global markets for goods and services, global markets for currencies, over 200 nation-states, cartels that distort markets (like OPEC), international trade pacts (like NAFTA and the WTO), supranational organizations (like the EU), and global interest groups (like the Center for Global Justice).

In spite of the fact that economists and politicians don't agree on exactly what effects result from economic policies, you probably need to know that

- fiscal policies affect economic growth
- monetary policies affect economic growth and trade
- trade policies are limited by global markets, international treaties, and supranational organizations
- regulatory policies affect growth, efficiency, and trade

Review the economic terms in the glossary. Make sure you have a clear idea of what they mean and how they're related to each other and to politics.

The distinctly economic terms are agricultural sector, balance of trade, budgetary deficit, capitalism, command economy, currency markets, distributive policies, economic liberalization, extractive policies, fiscal policy, foreign exchange rates, gross domestic product, import substitution, industrial policy, industrial sector, Keynesian economics, monetary policy, national debt or surplus, parastatal, political economy, post-industrial, privatization, redistributive policies, regulatory policies, rent seeking, service sector, social democracy, social welfare, socialism, structural adjustment, supply side economics, and welfare state.

> **jargon**: 1 incoherent speech ... 4 the specialized vocabulary and idioms of those in the same work, profession, etc.
>
> — *Webster's New World College Dictionary*

JARGON

The word "jargon" carries pejorative implications. Perhaps we should use the label "scientific terminology." The idea is that by using carefully specified names for carefully identified features, communication will be facilitated. In other words, telling someone to "watch out for the yucky green stuff in the woods" may not be adequate warning about poison ivy. And telling him not to "let the oleoresin urushiol from *Toxicodendron radicans (L.) Kuntze* contact your epidermis" might be equally ineffective. However, there are contexts in which each warning might be appropriate.

The grand theory ideas above are aimed primarily at the general-to-specific thinkers. This bit is aimed at the specific-to-general specialists.

There is a bit of scientific vocabulary in the study of comparative politics, and using it correctly means you are knowledgeable. It also helps communicate within the context of an AP exam. Outside of class, the textbook, or the exam, this vocabulary might appear to be jargon. Once again, context helps determine what's best.

WHAT VOCABULARY DO YOU NEED TO KNOW?

Begin with the index of your textbook and the lists of terms at the ends of chapters. Many of the words in those parts of the book that are not proper nouns are valuable terminology.

My incomplete list of comparative concepts and terms are noted on the pages that follow. If you're not sure what they mean, look them up in your textbook. If you don't find them in your textbook, do a search on the web for the words in a political science context.

You don't have to know all of these terms. You should at least know the ones your textbook uses.

accountability: the concept that government officials are responsible to and serve at the pleasure of constituents or elected officials (and that they may be removed from office by those electors or officials) (see **collective responsibility**)

adjudicate: to resolve a matter in dispute; when backed up by the authority of government the decision can be enforced

agricultural sector: that part of a country's economy that is involved in the production of farm products

autarchy: complete self-sufficiency

authoritarianism: a system of governance based on coercion rather than political legitimacy

authority: the legal right to exercise power on behalf of the society and/or government

autocracy: a system of governance in which a small group has absolute power

autonomy: the degree to which a state can implement policies independent of the populace or the amount of sovereignty a nation-state can exercise in the global environment

balance of trade: comparison between the value of exports and the value of imports for a nation-state; usually figured by subtracting the value of imports from the value of exports (a positive balance of trade means that exports were worth more than imports; a negative balance of trade means the value of imports exceeded the value of exports)

bicameral: describing a legislative body with two houses

budgetary deficit: the result of government spending in any one fiscal year exceeding the government revenue in that year (national debt is the total of yearly deficits)

bureaucracy: a hierarchically structured organization charged with carrying out the policies determined by those with political authority

cabinet: in a parliamentary system, the group of ministers who direct administrative bureaucracies (ministries) and make up the government, which is responsible to the parliament (see **accountability**); in a presidential system, the administrative directors responsible to the president

capacity: the degree to which a state or government is able to implement its policies

capitalism: an economic system that emphasizes private property rights and market mechanisms

catch-all party: a political party whose aim is to gather support from a broad range of citizens through a de-emphasis of ideology and an emphasis on pragmatism, charismatic leadership, and marketing

causation: a correlation in which a change in one variable results in change in others

checks and balances: a system of governance in which divisions of government can restrain the political authority of other divisions

citizen: a member of a state who is legally entitled to full civil rights and is legally obliged to perform defined public duties

civic culture: a political culture in which citizens widely share a belief in the legitimacy of their regime and a trust in the government; therefore the citizens demonstrate restraint in their demands on the government

civil servants: employees of the government who administer (not make) policy; expected to serve all governments (see **civil service**)

civil service: a system of carefully describing the tasks involved in performing government jobs, evaluating applicants for those jobs (civil service examinations), and hiring people from among those applicants based on skills and experience rather than political factors; civil service also protects incumbents in civil service positions from politically based retribution

civil society: all those organizations outside of government and (according to some authorities) commercial arenas, which provide avenues of public participation in society

class: the divisions of society into groups according to economic roles and status attributes (also called social class); see **cleavage**

cleavage: factors that separate groups within a society; may be cultural, historic, geographic, economic, ethnic, racial, etc.; the wider and deeper the cleavages, the less unified the society; cleavages which coincide with one another can reinforce each other; cleavages that don't coincide can weaken the divisions between groups

clientalism: an exchange system in which clients offer support and loyalty to patrons who offer material and intangible benefits

coerced participation: political action organized by ruling authorities rather than by interest groups or civil society groups

collective responsibility: in a parliamentary system, the concept that all cabinet members agree on policy decisions and that all will be responsible for the results (see **accountability**)

command economy: an economic/political system in which government decisions rather than markets determine resource use and output

compromise: a decision-making (policy-making, law-making) process in which all parties concede some of their goals in order to reach other of their goals through agreements with other political actors

conflict: a situation in which values, goals, or policies are contradictory or incompatible with each other

consensus: a decision-making (policy-making, law-making) process that emphasizes win-win outcomes while seeking to avoid zero-sum or win-lose situations by seeking unanimous agreement

constant: any of those things in comparative case analysis that are essentially identical in studied examples

constitution: a supreme law that defines the structure of a nation-state's regime and the legal processes governments must follow

co-opt: win support by granting special favors to an individual or a group (clientalism or corporatism); there is often an implication that those receiving benefits abandon important goals when offered less-important benefits

corporatism: a system of governance in which the government is dominated by representatives of groups within society; may or may not be democratic to some degree

correlation: an apparent association between variables

coup d'état: the forceful replacement of a regime or a government by a small elite group or groups

currency markets: markets in which traders buy and sell currencies; the values of currencies set in these markets have a powerful influence on **foreign exchange rates**

decolonization: the process by which colonial powers (mostly European) divested themselves of empires (not always voluntarily)

demand: pressures from people and interest groups on the government and state for change

democratization: the spread of representative government to more countries and the process of making governments more representative

dependent variable: a result of political decision making which is determined by the inputs, institutions, and processes (independent variables)

developed countries: nation-states which have industrial and post-industrial economies

developing countries: nation-states which are industrializing

devolution: a process in a unitary system of delegating some decision making to local public bodies

distributive policies: government policies that allocate valuable resources

economic liberalization: policy designed to remove political controls over economic activity (see **Keynesian economics** and **supply side economics**)

empirical analysis: consideration of agreed-upon facts gathered by observation or experiment

ethnic group: a group of people seen by themselves and/or others as belonging together because of ancestry, religion, linguistics, and/or other cultural features of the group; often the basis of a nation

ethnic identity: cultural and social characteristics that distinguish one nation from another — especially in the minds of the members of the ethnic group

executive: the people and agencies, which implement or execute government policy (from the head of government to the lowest bureaucrat)

extractive policies: government efforts to gather valuable resources for public use (think taxes)

extractive sector: that part of an economy which involves making use of natural resources for economic purposes (e.g., mining)

faction: a group organized on the grounds of self-perceived common interest **within** a political party, interest group, or government

failed state: a state within which the government has lost the ability to provide the most basic of public services or implement its policies

federalism: a regime in which political authority is shared between a central government and local governments

feedback: the reactions of people, organizations, and other factors that shape political environments for future policymaking

first past the post: see **plurality system**

fiscal policy: government decisions about total public spending and revenue that result in **budgetary deficits** or surpluses

foreign exchange (ForEx): the rates at which the currency from one nation trades with others; affected by **currency markets**, balances of trade, and domestic government policies

function (public): the actions taken by a government to decide upon, implement, and enforce policy decisions (private functions would, of course, be those things done by individuals and private organizations to further their goals)

fusion of powers: a system of governance in which the authority of government is concentrated in one body (see **separation of powers**)

generalization: a description of common features of a chosen group or category of examples

global warming: a well-supported theory that certain human-produced gases in the atmosphere are causing the earth's climate to warm

globalization: the increasing interconnectedness and interdependence of people, cultures, economies, and nation-states facilitated by technology, trade, and cultural diffusion

governance: the characteristics of a regime or a government

government: the part of the state with legitimate public authority; the group of people and organizations that hold political authority in a state at any one time (for Americans this would be a synonym for administration)

grassroots politics: locally-organized activism; as opposed to top-down, hierarchical organizing

gross domestic product (GDP): the total value of goods and services produced by an economy (very similar to gross national product or GNP)

head of government: the office and the person occupying the office charged with leading the operation of a government

head of state: the chief public representative of a state

identity politics: political activity and ideas based on the shared experiences of an ethnic, religious, or social group emphasizing gaining power and benefits for the group rather than pursuing ideological or universal or even state-wide goals

imperialism: the practice of one nation-state taking control of nations and territory of other countries

import substitution: a government policy that uses trade restrictions and subsidies to encourage domestic production of manufactured goods

independent variable: any one of the inputs, institutions, or processes that shape the results of government decision (policy) making

industrial policy: a government's decisions and actions, which define goals and methods for the manufacturing sectors of an economy (see **economic liberalization**)

industrial sector: that part of the economy which manufactures finished and secondary products

inputs: demands and support by individuals and groups upon the decision (policy) making process of government

interdependence: a situation, brought about by specialization and/or limited resources, in which nation-states rely on one another for economic resources, goods, and services and political assets such as security and stability

interest aggregation: ways in which demands of citizens and groups are amalgamated into proposed policy packages (e.g., leadership, political parties, etc.)

interest articulation: the methods by which citizens and groups can express their desires and make demands upon government (e.g., political participation, lobbying, protest, etc.)

interest group: any organization that seeks to influence government policymaking to better serve the self-perceived wants and needs of its members

international: describing organizations or events that involve more than one nation-state

intervening variable: a factor influenced by an **independent variable** that affects the changes in a **dependent variable**

interventionist: describing an activist government and/or state that is involved in a wide range of political, economic, and social arenas

iron triangle: mutually-beneficial relationships between private interests, bureaucrats, and legislators; sometimes called an "integrated elite" (see also **patron-client relationships**)

judicial review: the power of courts to modify or nullify the actions of legislatures, executives, and lower courts

Keynesian economics: the ideas of John Maynard Keynes that governments can manipulate macro-economic demand through taxation and spending policies in order to foster stable growth (see **economic liberalization** and **supply side economics**)

legitimacy: the belief that a regime is a proper one and that the government has a right to exercise authority

monetary policy: domestic government policies affecting interest rates and the supply of money available within an economy

multiple causality: the simultaneous effects of a number of independent and intervening variables that bring about changes in dependent variables

nation: a group of people who identify themselves as belonging together because of cultural, geographic, or linguistic ties

nation-state: a territorial unit controlled by a single state and governed by a single government

national debt or surplus: the historic total of yearly government budgetary deficits and surpluses for a nation-state

nationalization: the process of making the government the owner of productive resources

neo-imperialism: a pejorative label given to a variety of attempts to achieve hegemony over other nations; some people tend to use the term to describe the use of corporate power and wealth to gain influence in Third World countries; others use it to describe attempts by international organizations to impose change upon rich and powerful nations (e.g., the Kyoto Treaty or the International Court of Justice)

newly-industrializing countries: nation-states that began developing economic industrial sectors relatively recently

non-governmental organization (NGO): private (often membership) group that pursues self-defined goals outside of government; common activities are publicizing issues, lobbying, making demands on government, and providing direct services

normative analysis: consideration based upon preferences and values about what things should be like

oligarchy: a system of governance dominated by a small powerful group in the state

parastatal: a government-owned corporation to compensate for the lack of private economic development or to ensure complete and equitable service to the whole country (can be anything from a national airline or railroad to a postal system or manufacturing and marketing operations)

parliamentary government: a system of governance in which the head of government is chosen by and serves at the pleasure of the legislature

particularistic party: a political party that does not attempt to appeal to voters beyond an identifiable group within a population

patron-client relationships: a usually informal alliance between a person holding power and less powerful or lower status people; the powerful patron provides power, status, jobs, land, goods, and/or protection in exchange for loyalty and political support (related terms: clientalism, patrimonialism, **prebendalism**)

peak association: an interest group organization whose membership is other organizations with parallel interests and goals; frequently a nation-wide organization of specialized or localized smaller organizations (e.g., Trades Union Congress in the UK)

plurality system: an electoral system in which election winners are determined by which candidate receives the largest number of votes (regardless of whether or not a majority is received)

police powers: government powers to regulate public safety and enforce laws

policy: decisions made by an organization defining its goals and actions (public policies are decisions made by government)

political communication: the flow of information from and about government to its constituents and feedback from constituents to people in government

political culture: the collection of history, values, beliefs, assumptions, attitudes, traditions, and symbols that define and influence political behavior within a nation-state

political economy: the interaction of political and economic systems and policymaking of a state

political participation: the actions by citizens which involve them in the process of selecting leaders and making policies

political party: an organized group of people with the primary purpose of electing its members to government office (alternatively, some parties exist to represent and promote a point of view or ideology regardless of electoral successes)

political recruitment: the processes by which people are encouraged and chosen to become members of an elite within a political system or state

political socialization: the institutions and methods of developing and reinforcing significant public beliefs, attitudes, and practices (How does a culture get its people to be good political citizens or subjects?)

politics: the processes through which groups of people govern themselves or are governed; activities associated with the exercise of authority

post-industrial: describing an economy in which the service sector has become more important than the industrial sector

post-materialist values: beliefs in the importance of policy goals beyond one's immediate self interest (e.g., environmentalism and cultural diversity) as well as one's prosperity and security; sometimes labeled "postmodern" values

power: ability to direct the behavior of others through coercion, persuasion, or leadership (see **authority**)

prebendalism: the form of patron-client politics that legitimizes the exploitation of government power for the benefit of office holders and their followers

private: interests, activities, and property of individuals and groups not part of government

privatization: the process of putting ownership of productive resources into the hands of non-governmental organizations and people (see **economic liberalization** and **nationalization**)

proportional representation: an electoral system in which voters select parties rather than individual candidates and parties are represented in legislatures in proportion to the shares of votes they win

public: actions, policies, institutions (and the people in them) supported by, of concern to, and open to the community at large

qualitative research: case studies of historic and cultural aspects of political systems

quantitative research: statistical studies which seek correlations and causations between data

realignment: a significant change in the party or policy loyalties of substantial groups within a nation-state

redistributive policies: government policies that take valuable resources from one or more groups in society and allocate them to other groups

reductivism: the attempt to explain complex correlations and causations using a single independent variable; oversimplification

regime: a pattern of organization for a government (often described in a constitution or supreme law)

regulatory policies: government policies designed to control practices and behavior of citizens and organizations and prevent harmful results and/or ensure civic benefits of those behaviors

rent seeking: the practice of political leaders who, for the purposes of remaining in positions of power, "rent" public assets (resources or tax supported services) to patrons who profit from those public assets

republic: a political regime in which government citizens choose leaders directly or indirectly

revolution: a process by which a political regime is overthrown and replaced because of broad popular support and participation in the process

rule of law: constitutionalism; a governance system operating predictably under a known and transparent set of procedural rules (laws)

run-off elections: an electoral system that requires winners to earn a majority of votes cast; in cases where no candidate wins a majority in the election, least successful candidates are removed from the ballot and another election is held

separation of powers: the system of governance in which government power is divided into several bodies with the ability to check the power of the other bodies (see **fusion of powers** and **checks and balances**)

service sector: that part of the economy which organizes and provides services at an economic cost

single-member district: an electoral system in which voters choose an individual running for office in each legislative district (also called "first past the post" if the winner is chosen by a plurality)

social change: alterations in the characteristics of a group or in the relationships among and between group members

social contract: the basic agreement between group members and the group as a whole as to rights, privileges, duties, benefits, and costs; often partially explicit in a constitution; usually implicit, in part, in the history and politics of a group

social democracy: a political philosophy centered on electoral politics, egalitarian social policies, and the creation of social welfare systems

social movement: collective political action by a section of society outside the realm of established parties, interest groups, and power elites; social movements' goals are often adopted by parties and interest groups; social movements and their leaders can be **co-opted** by power elites

social welfare: the material condition of the members of a group; may also refer to the group-supplied material benefits in a society (e.g., health care)

socialism: a political/economic system in which the government plays a major role (usually ownership) in determining the use of productive resources and the allocation of valuable goods and services; may be democratic or authoritarian

soft power: a term credited to Harvard professor Joseph Nye, who defines it in international relations as "co-opting people rather than coercing them."

In domestic politics it's often used by political leaders as a justification for limiting the activities of dissidents and foreign and international NGOs who are seen as introducing non-traditional values. References are often made to the 2004-2005 Orange Revolution in the Ukraine, the Rose Revolution in Georgia, the ousting of Slobodan Milosevic in Serbia, the Tulip Revolution in Kyrgyzstan, and the 1989 Velvet Revolution in Czechoslovakia. All of those regime changes involved mostly grassroots, non-violent movements funded and encouraged by NGOs, many funded by the United States.

sovereignty: independent legal authority over a population in a particular place; the degree to which a state controls its own territory and independently make and carry out policy

state: the assembly of all those people and groups within a nation-state that have power to effect change at some level of society through direct action or political participation

strong state: a state with extensive capacity to carry out policies adopted or a state in which there are few limitations on the actions of one or more parts of the state

structural adjustment: World Bank programs which offer financial and management aid to poor countries while demanding privatization, trade liberalization, and governmental fiscal restraint

structure (public): an organization or process by which a government carries out its public policies (private structures would, of course, be those organizations and processes by which individuals and private organizations further their interests)

supply side economics: the economic theory

1. that markets are the most efficient and fair way to allocate productive resources and valuable products;

2. that government should interfere in the production of goods and services as little as possible;

and 3. that economic actors will negate any actions by government to manipulate demand by anticipating the actions and taking counter measures (see **economic liberalization** and **Keynesian economics**)

supranational: organizations or events in which nations are not totally sovereign actors (e.g., the European Union or global warming)

system: an organization of interdependent, interacting features bounded by limits, which interacts with its setting or environment

technocrats: highly-educated bureaucrats who make decisions based on their perceptions of technical issues rather than political ones (often contrasted with patron-client politics)

unicameral: describing a legislative body consisting of one house

unitary state: concentration of political power in a central government as opposed to federalism

vote of confidence: a vote in a parliament expressing support for a government; a government losing a vote of confidence is often expected to resign

weak state: a state with little capacity for carrying out policies adopted or a state in which the powers of the state are limited

welfare state: a state which provides a wide array of social services to its members

win-win outcome: a resolution to a situation in which all parties benefit

zero-sum game: a resolution to a situation in which one side wins and others lose

FOOTNOTE

[1] Gros, Jean-Germain, Comparative Politics Made Simple, AP Comparative Government and Politics Homepage, AP Central, *apcentral.collegeboard. com/apc/members/courses/teachers_ corner/52085.html*, retrieved 3 February 2010.

REVIEW EXERCISE

This exercise is meant to get you thinking about some of the basic facts and point out areas you might have to review more thoroughly. My responses follow.

1. Comparative theory does NOT tell us
   (A) how to describe things we study
   (B) what conclusions we should arrive at
   (C) how to evaluate the information we come up with
   (D) what data to look for
   (E) what questions we should ask

2. A basic comparative method is to
   (A) decide which public policies we approve of
   (B) find out how democracies are superior to other regimes
   (C) look for the flaws in political regimes
   (D) identify analogous political institutions in diverse systems
   (E) look for evidence to support conclusions

3. The environment within which governments function includes
   (A) natural resources within a country's borders
   (B) political parties that contend for power
   (C) the global community of nation states
   (D) a country's political culture
   (E) all of the above

4. In systems analysis, feedback includes
   (A) the results of previous policy decisions
   (B) discovery of new natural resources
   (C) policy making
   (D) policies that are made now
   (E) innovations made by bureaucrats

5. In comparative politics, behavioral theory
   (A) emphasizes the actions of large public and private institutions
   (B) assumes that people act on training received in early childhood
   (C) takes for granted that people don't know what's best for them
   (D) focuses on the analysis of individual decisions
   (E) questions the validity of representative government

6. Normative assumptions in dependency theory include
   (A) the exploitation of poor countries' resources promotes wealth for everyone
   (B) an assumption that basic values vary from country to country
   (C) an explanation for why poor countries cannot improve their statuses in a globalized world
   (D) the advocacy of change
   (E) the idea that industrialized countries deserve the wealth they have

7. Independent variables are usually thought of as
   (A) those things that cause changes in dependent variables
   (B) actions that can be taken by anyone or any country in a case study
   (C) things that are totally beyond the control of governments
   (D) liberty, human rights, and democracy
   (E) minor factors in a comparative case study

8. The First World, Second World, Third World classification system doesn't offer a good description of countries today in part because
   (A) there are more than three countries
   (B) there are many more than three kinds of countries
   (C) so many countries are now considered "First World"
   (D) globalization has made countries so much alike
   (E) democracy has spread to so many countries

9. Fiscal policy is concerned with
   (A) how healthy countries' populations are
   (B) the rate of monetary expansion in a country
   (C) foreign exchange rates
   (D) imports and exports
   (E) public taxation and spending levels

10. A distributive policy
    (A) is a law about how much land people can own
    (B) concerns what individuals, corporations, and foundations can give to charity
    (C) deals with allocating valuable resources in a country
    (D) is a law that determines how much people owe the government
    (E) forces government to privatize public resources

(For responses, see below)

5: Know ... THE UNITED STATES

The USA is not mentioned anywhere in the AP Comparative Government and Politics curriculum. Students in other countries take an AP comparative course and don't learn much of anything about the government and politics of the USA.

Why mention it here? Why do many comparative textbooks[1] include chapters on the USA?

Here's another question for you: Do fish know what water is?

Okay, okay, enough indirectness. Let me try to answer my questions for you.

We all have several frames of reference. They consist of the familiar things and ideas we refer to when we try to make sense of something new. We grow up in a family with characteristics we probably come to assume are normal. We get used to the appearance of the landscape around us and come to think of it as normal. The normal things we're used to become the standards we use to evaluate and understand things that are unfamiliar.

I grew up in Minnesota. To me it's normal that temperatures in January and February are regularly below zero and that things outside my window are covered with snow. I have to think beyond my frame of reference to realize that my cousin living on the west coast of Australia sees no snow in January and does not have a Monday holiday in January to honor Dr. Martin Luther King, Jr.

Unless I think a bit, I'm like the fish that lives in water and doesn't even know there is such a thing.

The political frame of reference most of us in the USA share requires that we give some thought to the ways our political culture, political values, institutions, traditions, and assumptions differ from those in other countries.

> **frame of reference** (pl. frames of reference)
> 1. a structure of concepts, values, customs, views, etc., by means of which an individual or group perceives or evaluates data, communicates ideas, and regulates behavior
>
> — Dictionary at Fact Monster.com,
> www.factmonster.com/ipd/A0448202.html

What do we need to know about ourselves? In comparative terms, what makes the USA stand out?

1. LIMITATIONS ON THE STATE

In order to persuade enough people to adopt the US Constitution, the creators of the regime had to agree to a series of 10 amendments to the proposed constitution that would limit the power of the government. This was pretty revolutionary in an 18th-century world where some Europeans were just beginning to think beyond divine monarchies.

Our system limits the regulatory powers of the government. It limits the police powers of the government. It took another amendment to the US Constitution to allow the government to collect a graduated income tax.

These limits don't exist because of the results of an election; they are built into the system of government.

The American system limits other actors in the state as well. Companies are not allowed to discriminate on the basis of race, religion, or gender when hiring employees. Property owners are limited in what they can do on their land or in their buildings by zoning laws. The United States Supreme Court has made decisions affecting the ability of universities to set their own admissions standards.

Limitations on public and private powers are controversial issues in the USA. If people perceive that crime rates are rising or the threat of terrorism is growing, they may accept or even call for increases in government power. If people perceive that the power of government threatens their liberties without cause, they are likely to try to reduce government powers or resist them.

These limitations are greater than those in most other democratic countries. In 2003, the Bureau of Citizenship and Immigration Services (BCIS) was in the news because of its inability to locate students and legal residents who are not US citizens. There is public discussion about the need for efficiency and greater powers for the BCIS to keep track of foreign nationals. In Austria, however, the law requires a residence permit for **everyone**. Imagine what kind of political uproar a proposal for such a requirement would have in the USA.

In the United Kingdom, you must have a license to own a radio or television. The license fees help fund the BBC. In the USA, there is opposition to the funding for PBS because of the perception that it is competition for private broadcasters. In France, you must have a residence permit. With one, you're automatically registered to vote. In the USA, same-day voter registration is a rare and controversial thing.

Over a century ago, "Progressives" promoted initiative, referendum, and recall as ways of limiting the power of government to accede to the ministrations of large, private interests to use public authority for their own advantages. But it's not just public power that is limited.

When private actions are seen as threatening, even generally conservative politicians seek greater public power. George W. Bush's 2004 budget included large increases for funding the Securities and Exchange Commission (SEC). That budget even included proposals for increased spending by the Internal Revenue Service (IRS). Why? Because of the perception that companies (like Enron) had not been policed adequately and that too many individuals were evading income taxes.

The point of all this is to make you aware that a typically-American attitude toward limiting the power of government is not universal. Many if not most, other countries accept greater government power than we do. The British Official Secrets Act is much more restrictive of private speech than anything similar in the USA. (And there are many fewer "leaks" from official sources than there are in this country.)

Similarly, the typical American attitude against regulating private behavior is not universally shared. Americans usually accept such regulation grudgingly. In the UK almost everyone accepted the creation of the National Health Service and the limits on individual choices the NHS required. Of course, states without a democratic tradition, like China, regulate individual behavior dramatically. (The 1989 Tiananmen Square demonstrations and the occasional dissident are outstanding exceptions to the widespread acceptance of such control.)

Judicial review limits the power of government and the private sectors of the state. Neither the US Congress nor the president can operate without an eye to the attitudes of federal judges. A large-scale, private lobbying effort may ultimately be unsuccessful if the law or regulations the effort supported are found by a court to be unconstitutional.

Federalism also limits the power of government.

2. FEDERALISM

The USA, Russia, Mexico, and Nigeria are all formally federal systems. To some degree, political authority is shared between the national government and units of local government. The UK, Iran, and most other states are not federal systems.

That doesn't mean you should assume that Russian or any other federalism works like the system we have. The USSR was a federal system, after all. Even in a more democratic Russia, the power of local units of government depends upon much more than constitutional provisions. In 2004, the president was given the power to appoint officials resembling regional governors in Russia. States in Nigeria, even those with rich oil resources, have very little power. In Mexico, the centralization of politics around the presidency turns the states into "the minor leagues" of politics. In Iran, the constitution calls for local provincial governing councils to be elected by local citizens. But local elections were not held until 20 years after the revolution. And when reformists were elected in those 1999 elections, the Expediency Council ensured that no significant policymaking powers devolved to local governments.

American states have considerable powers to implement their own policies and resist the imposition of national standards. If you want an example, review what you know about the administration of Medicaid or unemployment programs in the USA. The lengths to which Congress went to establish a nationwide legal drinking age demon-

> ### Protection? Or Intrusion?
>
> Zoning laws are government regulated restrictions on how a particular piece of land can be used... These laws are at least partially an attempt to solve a very real problem. If people buy a house in a residential area, they do not want a loud or polluting factory to be opened next door to them... A house becomes unusable if the sound, smell, or air quality around it is suddenly changed.
>
> Zoning laws are a heavy-handed remedy for this problem, though... [They] are merely a method of increasing power in the hands of bureaucrats. They are a direct violation of property rights. Through the use of force, they can specify how people can or cannot use their property.
>
> — From the "Bloody Politics" section of "The Importance of Philosophy" web site www.importanceofphilosophy.com/ Bloody_ZoningLaws.html

strate how difficult national policymaking is. And, one of the controversies about the NAFTA treaty is the extent to which its provisions might invalidate state policies.

Don't assume the American kind of local government power (especially in providing social services like welfare and education) is normal. It's not.

The devolution of some political authority to legislatures in Scotland, Wales, and Northern Ireland may look like federalism, but be careful about drawing that conclusion. The local legislatures have only those powers that the British Parliament in Westminster is willing to give them. Even those can be taken back any time the government decides to do that.

Unitary governments are more normal than federal ones are.

Yes, there are local authorities in the UK. They perform the functions the parliament assigns them. There's no Tenth Amendment reserving powers to the states and citizens.

3. SEPARATION OF POWERS

Constitutional prohibitions and federalism aren't the only things reining in the power of government in the USA. There's this structural thing called separation of powers. (I hinted at this earlier with the comment about judicial review.)

The heart of this is what James Madison (in *Federalist 10*) described as creating centers of power which would pursue their own self interest. The resolution of those competitions would prevent tyranny, Madison asserted.

We have an executive with specified and implied powers. We have a legislature with specified and implied powers. And we have a judiciary with specified and implied powers. In addition, we have a bureaucracy, nominally under the control of the president, which wields power by making choices in how to administer the mandates it receives from Congress and the executive.

But who is head of government in the UK? Well, it's the prime minister, who is chosen by the legislature (and can be voted out by the legislature). How can they function without separation of powers? Why haven't they long ago turned into a tyranny? A better question is why did the British system become a liberal democracy without separation of powers?

Russia has a president. The Russian president's power is basically unchecked by the legislature. China has a president. The Chinese president's power depends upon his support within the Communist Party. Vicente Fox, as Mexico's president, found that he could do little without the support of the legislature. Nigeria's president relies on military leaders and economic forces more than his constitution, the legislature, or his party. Iran's Supreme Leader serves for life and controls who can be elected to lower offices.

You have to understand that the American system, which we assume is so normal, is not normal. In fact, you have to have a good handle on parliamentary, unitary systems to have a good understanding of most governments.

4. DEMOCRACY = LEGITIMACY? LEGITIMACY = DEMOCRACY?

Americans assume that republican (representative) regimes are legitimate. The government represents the people and the people's interests. If the people are displeased, they can elect a new government. In fact, the progressives of the late 19th century argued that government can be more legitimate if people can (by popular vote) make laws, invalidate laws, and unseat government officials.

Americans also generally (at least in theory) think that limited government is legitimate. We also think pragmatic government is legitimate — which is why there are so many exceptions in practice to the beliefs mentioned here.

However, even in these days of Three Represents and Harmonious Society, many Chinese cling to the belief that a government is legitimate if it raises standards of living, promotes egalitarianism, and prevents exploitation. The closest Americans come to a belief like that is when it comes to national defense. A government that didn't protect the country could not be legitimate.

The Soviet government earned a sense of legitimacy during World War II by playing a vital role in defeating Germany. Today, a Russian regime that does a good job of organizing the economy can earn legitimacy even if it limits democracy. In Iran, to many people legitimacy of the regime means maintaining *sharia*. To many others in Iran, a regime that fails to create economic growth and protect personal freedoms cannot be legitimate.

Legitimacy is a product of public opinion. Public opinion is a fickle thing. One generation may accept the leadership of a strong dynasty (as in Iran). But a couple of generations later, the secular, interventionist themes that were associated with the Pahlavi dynasty are not acceptable.

There are many ways for a regime or a government to achieve legitimacy. Republican government is one very successful way. It's not the only one. Protecting the nation-state from outside powers is another. Providing services to people works sometimes. So does promoting egalitarianism. What works in any place is what best fits the political culture there at that point in time.

5. ELECTORAL SYSTEMS

Who wins elections? Why, the person with the most votes, of course. Of course? Who won the US presidential election of 2000? Why, the person with the second highest number of popular votes. If that election had taken place in France, it would have been settled by a second, run-off election between the two top vote getters. In the USA, it was settled by arguing procedural law in front of the Supreme Court.

Plurality elections (where the candidate receiving the most votes wins) may be normal in the USA and the UK, but they're not normal everywhere. Russian candidates must win majorities.

And voting for candidates is not the norm everywhere either. In Russia, the Duma is elected by a proportional system. In that system, people vote for a party, not a candidate. The party chooses the candidates who get elected based on the popularity of the party.

Even in the UK, where plurality voting and single-member districts are the norm, parties select candidates. Parties assign rookie candidates to districts where they have little or no chance of winning. The loyal party supporter, who returns to run again, may well be assigned to a district where she or he has a better chance of winning. The big shots in the parties are of course assigned to districts where they can't lose.

The primary election, which in the USA is becoming more and more important as a way of selecting candidates, is practically unique. It's not normal.

Neither is the two-party system that characterizes American politics. The UK almost has a three-party system, but the plurality system sidelines even the popular Liberal Democrats. (That system has the same effect on minor parties in the USA.) Almost every other democratic system has multiple parties. Nigeria tried at one time to create a two-party system by allowing only two parties, but without government coercion more than 30 parties were organized for the most recent national elections.

6. POLITICAL PARTICIPATION

In the USA, we know well what political participation is. It's voting, writing your representatives, and organizing for your causes. What else could there be?

In fact, political participation is any action that has a political aspect.

- If a Beijing family shows up in Tiananmen Square on October First, they are participating politically in the life of China.
- If a Mexican farmer accepts a gift from a political party, he's participating in the politics of Mexico.
- If an Iranian mother goes to a meeting of other women to learn about birth control, she's participating.
- If a British worker joins a union, she's participating.
- A Russian retiree who protests cuts in pension benefits is participating.
- If a Nigerian goes to Friday prayers and listens to a sermon by the Imam, he may be participating in politics.

Put aside the closed definitions that are so comfortably familiar. Participation takes many forms. Learn to "recognize the water" in which you swim and recognize that other people exist in other environments.

Why is it that British voter turnout of just under 70% is seen as scandalously low, while a voting rate of 50% in presidential elections in the USA is average? Are there other forms of participation in the US that compensate for that low turnout?

The emphasis in our political culture on individual responsibility extends to voting. In the USA, most elections are held on Tuesdays. And before you vote, you must register — often three weeks before the election. In many countries, voting is done on a Sunday or a holiday. And registration is seen as a responsibility of the government, not the individual.

7. A LITIGIOUS SOCIETY

Curtis Dyer, a Texas lawyer, asserts in his advertisement for legal insurance that "In today's litigious society, did you know that you are three times more likely to be embroiled in some type of legal issue than you are to have a need for medical attention at the hospital?"[2]

The Corrosion Club asserts that "In the introduction to his very popular book *Corrosion Engineering*, Mars G. Fontana observed 'we are indeed a litigious society today.' The need for awareness of legal liability in the corrosion engineering domain was emphasized in this book. ...

"According to [his] figures the number of lawyers in the United States (622,000) exceeds the combined total of materials engineers, chemical engineers, mechanical engineers, civil engineers, chemists and physicists."[3]

A Presbyterian minister in Indiana preached that "... ironically, one of the odd twists of life in our free land has been the evolution of a litigious society. We have more lawyers than any other country because we are most conscious of the law that spells out our freedom, our rights."[4]

Is this normal for a political system? Not by a long shot.

We see it every day, but people in most political systems do not settle as many issues in court as we do. It's no more normal that primary elections or two-party systems.

Participation takes many forms and holds meaning only within the context of the actions. Ambiguity raises its head again. Don't be satisfied with simple answers.

The Wacky Warning Label Contest, now in its 13th year, is sponsored by the Foundation for Fair Civil Justice, in order to reveal how lawsuits and concern about lawsuits have created a need for common sense warnings on products.

In 2009, the winner was a label attached to a portable toilet seat for outdoorsmen called "The Off-Road Commode" because it is designed to attach to a vehicle's trailer hitch. The warning label reads "Not for use on moving vehicles." A runner up entry was a label on a very small LCD panel that read, "Do not eat the LCD panel."

www.foundationforfairciviljustice.org/ news/in_depth/wacky_warning_labels_ 2009_winners_announced/

People find many different forms of politics legitimate. And they do so for many different reasons. Are you open to those possibilities?

Many people live perfectly satisfactory lives in states without separation of powers or a constitution. And most people live in nation-states governed by regimes where governments act like or are unitary, not federal. Stay aware of the contexts in which these political systems exist.

Most people live under regimes that are not limited like the US regimes (federal, state, and local) are. And they live in states where private activity is more constrained than it is in the USA.

The value judgments are yours to make. But if you're responding to questions on the AP Comparative Government and Politics exam, you must support those judgments with objective information, clear reasoning, and open-minded awareness.

You can think better than a fish. You can recognize the water you swim in. When you do, it will help you succeed on the exam.

Keep your eyes and your mind open.

FOOTNOTES

1   For example, Almond and Powell, et al.,
    Comparative Politics Today; Hauss, *Comparative
    Politics;* and Kesselman, Krieger, et al., *Introduc-
    tion to Comparative Politics* all contain chapters
    on the USA

2   Curtis Dyer, Attorney at Law,
    www.curtisdyer.com/odds.htm

3   Corrosion-Club.com, *www.corrosion-club.com/
    litigious.htm*

4   Stuart D. Robertson, "Life in a Litigious
    Society," *dcwi.com/~faithch/sermons/
    2001/01.11.11.htm*

REVIEW EXERCISE

*This exercise is meant to get you thinking about some
of the basic facts and point out areas you might have to
review more thoroughly. My responses follow.*

1. Our frames of reference can mislead our analysis
    (A) if we assume that things outside our frame of
        reference are irrational
    (B) when it limits our definition of normal
    (C) if we study only those political institutions
        that are like the ones we know
    (D) when we assume that what we know is better
        than what is unfamiliar
    (E) in all of the above examples

2. Limitations on governments in the USA
    (A) are regularly voted on by members of Congress
    (B) strengthen the government in areas where it's
        allowed to take action
    (C) make it possible for candidates for public of-
        fice to campaign on more substantive issues
    (D) are greater than the limitations on most other
        regimes
    (E) prevent the government from offering ad-
        equate public services

3. Federalism limits the power of government in the
    USA by
    (A) holding the threat of secession "over the
        heads" of the national government
    (B) reserving some powers to the states
    (C) centralizing policy-making power, thus creating
        a complex system that is very difficult to manage
    (D) giving state and local governments power
        over the national government in some areas
    (E) adopting the British form of devolution

4. Separation of powers in the USA
    (A) means that each part of the government has
        potential authority to limit the power of other
        parts of the government
    (B) is similar to most parliamentary systems
    (C) allows interest groups to concentrate their
        persuasive arguments in a single part of the
        government
    (D) requires all parts of government to maintain
        public approval
    (E) amplifies the importance of elections

5. Legitimacy can be obtained and maintained
    (A) only when everyone is satisfied with the poli-
        cies of the government
    (B) by an authoritarian government if it meets the
        needs of the ruling class
    (C) by competitive elections
    (D) through government control of domestic media
    (E) if citizens are kept in subservient statuses

6. Which of the following pairs most accurately
    identifies the primary source of legitimacy for the
    nation-state mentioned?
    (A) Russia: free and fair electoral competition
    (B) USA: provision of social services
    (C) China: raising standards of living
    (D) Iran: guaranteeing civil liberties
    (E) UK: strictly maintaining law and order

7. A plurality electoral system
    (A) encourages multiple parties
    (B) requires majorities for electoral success
    (C) promotes single party systems
    (D) is one in which winners receive more votes
        than other candidates
    (E) guarantees representation from minority groups

8. A proportional electoral system
    (A) requires primary elections
    (B) is one in which voters choose among parties
        not individual candidates
    (C) resembles the one in the USA
    (D) guarantees legislative majorities
    (E) is a political environment favorable to two-
        party systems

9. Which of the following would NOT be considered
    political participation?
    (A) attending a national day rally
    (B) meeting with a city council representative
    (C) participating in a government-sponsored edu-
        cational program
    (D) attending a birthday celebration for a
        neighbor
    (E) writing a letter to a legislator

10. Lawsuits are
    (A) often used to expand the powers of
        governments
    (B) more common in the USA than in most
        countries
    (C) universally desirable features of the political
        environment in the USA
    (D) unknown in most countries
    (E) usually won by plaintiffs (i.e., those who bring
        the suits)

(For responses, see below)

6: Know ... THE UNITED KINGDOM

PREFACE

Remember the six main topics in the course outline? I'm going to use those topics to organize the country chapters that follow. (If you don't remember the topics, you can review them in Chapter 2.) I'll begin, like most comparative government and politics textbooks, with the UK and then consider the other countries in reverse alphabetical order.

If you're in need of categories that are absolutely mutually exclusive, this organizational structure may make things difficult for you. For instance, concepts related to political culture appear in three of the topics. However, this will give you many chances to practice tolerating and appreciating ambiguity.

I think you ought to use the notes that follow as stimulus. Your responses ought to be thought and research (if necessary). Some of the terminology may not match what you're familiar with, but you need to be able to figure out the comparable concepts or topics. (After all, the AP exam may not use the same "jargon" as your textbook's author did.) The glossary in Chapter 4 will be helpful.

1. INTRODUCTION TO COMPARATIVE POLITICS

You've probably never wondered why the UK comes first in comparative government textbooks because you haven't read many. I've noticed, but I've always assumed that was only right (from an American perspective). British values like accountability and legislative supremacy shaped our own system. The Westminster model of parliamentary government influenced regimes around the globe.

If Britain was the model of representative government in the past, it may be the model of adaptation to a post-industrial world now. How do governments innovate in established regimes? Is there, as Tony Blair suggested, a "third way"? Does such a third way de-emphasize the importance of centuries' old class divisions? Are new gender roles a vital part of a third way?

So Britain becomes the standard to which other countries are compared. Is it ideal? No. Is it unique? Not quite. But, in the context of world

political systems, much about the UK is unusual. You have to keep that in mind as you examine other systems, other cultures, and other governments. Keep your eyes and ears open.

2. SOVEREIGNTY, AUTHORITY, AND POWER

The UK is a small island country off the northwest coast of Europe. There are two islands: Great Britain and Ireland. There are three kingdoms (England, Wales, and Scotland) plus Northern Ireland. Some authors identify five nations: the English, the Welsh, the Scots, the Protestants of Northern Ireland and the Catholics of Northern Ireland. Immigrants from former colonies may be another nation, but they make up only 7% of the population and many of them identify themselves as British. The English make up over 80% of the population.

HISTORICAL TURNING POINTS

1215	Magna Carta	1867	Second Great Reform Act
1265	First parliament	1911	Supremacy of Parliament (Commons) Act
1532-1536	Reformation	1914-1918	World War I
1642-1649	Civil War	1918	First women's suffrage
1649-1660	Cromwell's "republic"	1928	Universal suffrage
1660	Restoration	1929-1939	Great Depression
1688-1689	Glorious Revolution and Bill of Rights	1939-1945	World War II
1721-1742	First prime minister	1945-1979	Collectivist consensus
1750s	Beginnings of Industrial Revolution	1979	Election of Margaret Thatcher; End of Collectivist consensus
1832	Great Reform Act	2010	First coalition government formed since WWII

The British Isles are very densely populated and have been for a long time. The UK has a history of agricultural, industrial, and imperial successes. Brits can brag about an impressive record of political, artistic, literary, technological, and commercial achievements.

In the 19th century, Great Britain was a global power. Since the end of World War II, the British state and its people (like the rest of the world) have been adjusting to new circumstances. Today, the main foreign policy concerns are less about empire and more about European integration, global competition, and terrorism.

The GDP per capita is about $35,400. That puts the UK among the richest countries in the world. However, that figure is only 75% of the GDP per capita of the USA.

Traditions are a major part of the political culture. Ritual plays a very visible role in politically important events. Without a written constitution, precedent plays a vital role in defining the proper behavior of government, politicians, and citizens.

The country's long political history has not always been peaceful. The Magna Carta originated in war. There was a War of the Roses. And neither the Enclosures, the Luddite movement, nor the women's

suffrage movement were without casualties. But many aspects of political development have been based on pragmatism and conciliation. The voting reforms of the 19th century and the ongoing work at resolving the conflicts in Northern Ireland are good examples.

The UK has been fortunate in that political developments there have come sequentially rather than simultaneously. Creating a nation-state did not occur at the same time as resolving the relationships between church and state. Sorting out the relationship between the monarch and the parliament did not come at the same time as the Industrial Revolution. While the creation of a liberal democracy did overlap with the Industrial Revolution, the economic changes allowed for a certain amount of flexibility outside the political realm. At the present time, the British are dealing with Europe, minorities, and post-industrial adjustments, but not (as in Russia and Eastern Europe) with the creation of new political systems.

Another bit of fortune for the political culture has been the prominence of *noblesse oblige* and "deference" among political values. These relics of feudalism, along with a healthy regard for pragmatism, helped resolve many of the political and social transitions of the past 200 years.

The question today is whether these old values and the gradualism usually ascribed to political change in the UK can survive the rapid pace of change in a global, post-industrial world. The debates about civil liberties and immigration that followed the July 2005 subway bombings are signs of those pressures.

The British believe in their political system. The history and the generally successful resolution of problems and conflicts have created a strong sense of legitimacy. The belief that the government is accountable through Commons continues. The prime minister does have to stand up and directly answer (on live television) questions from elected representatives every Wednesday, doesn't he?

In his final years as prime minister, Tony Blair was accused of being too presidential. He led the country into war with Iraq in the face of disapproving public opinion. However, the criticism has been of the prime minister, not the regime. There may be arguments about the role of the monarch in the 21st century, about the desirability of "union" with Europe, or about which immigrants to tolerate. But the biggest debate about regime change is over whether or not to have proportional elections.

3. POLITICAL INSTITUTIONS

The regime in the UK has been called a constitutional monarchy, a parliamentary democracy, legislative (as opposed to presidential), and a system of collective responsibility. Each of those labels highlights an aspect of the system.

There is a monarch. The queen gives a speech at the opening of each session of the parliament. In the speech she clearly outlines the goals of "my government." The leaders of the government write the speech. The queen has no input into its contents. Parliamentary bills are given "royal assent" before they become law. If the queen refused to give assent to a bill, the British Parliament would quickly find such assent unnecessary. They might also find an allowance for the Royals (as

the royal family is familiarly called) unnecessary.

The queen and the Royals are popular celebrities. Gossip and large-scale photo magazines about the Royals are consumed avidly by large numbers of people. In London one day, my wife and I had a terrible time getting a cab because the queen was hosting tea for couples who had been married more than 50 years. The elderly couples were all taking cabs to the "do."

The British regime is a parliamentary democracy. It's **the** prototype of legislative government. The executive is part of the legislature. The executive is chosen by the legislature. There is no separation of powers between them. A powerful consensus about what is right and proper restrains the actions of the majority in the British Parliament.

Until recently, there was little separation of powers between the legislative and judicial powers.

POLITICAL TURNING POINTS

1945	First Labour Government
1948	National Health Service created
1957	Beginnings of African colonies' independence
1973	UK joins European Economic Community
1979	End of collectivist consensus with election of Conservative government led by Margaret Thatcher
1982	Falklands War
1997	Labour government led by Tony Blair elected
1998	Northern Ireland Peace Agreement
1999	Welsh, Scottish, and Northern Ireland Assemblies created
2003	Iraq War
2010	Coalition government elected

Judges were independent and the government didn't interfere in court cases. But judges were appointed by the monarch upon recommendation of the Lord Chancellor, who was a member of the Cabinet and a judge.

The highest appellate court was a committee of the House of Lords made up of the Law Lords. The Appellate Committee could rule on procedural and evidentiary matters, but it could not overturn a law passed by the Parliament.

Once the UK joined the EU, there was pressure for change. The European Convention on Human Rights did not allow the fusion of powers exhibited in the legislative, executive, and judicial powers of Parliament.

The Constitutional Reform Act of 2005 created a new Supreme Court and a new cabinet position to administer the judicial system. That minister will also hold the position of Lord Chancellor, but will not recommend judges for appointment. Appointments will be made by a Judicial Appointments Commission chaired by the President of the Supreme Court (like the Chief Justice in the USA).

The new court officially began work on 1 October 2009. The 12 judges of the Supreme Court will no longer be members of Parliament. The court has it own headquarters outside of Westminster. In cases involving human rights, decisions by the UK's Supreme Court can be appealed to the European Court of Justice.

The executive, called the government, is chosen by a majority of the House of Commons. The majority all sit together in Commons on the speaker's right. The government is made up of ministers who have specific responsibilities (foreign policy, treasury, transport, trade and industry, education, etc.) and are appointed by the prime minister. The prime minister (PM) is usually the leader of the largest party in Commons. If that party does not hold a majority of seats, it must seek coalition partners from smaller parties to form a majority (as the Conservatives had to do after the 2010 election). Leaders of the smaller coalition partners usually demand and receive ministerial appointments in the government. The ministers as a group are also known as the cabinet. They sit together during sessions of Commons in the front row on their side of the House. The loyal opposition's leaders sit in the front row opposite the government. (That's why they're known as front benchers. Their supporters, who sit in the rows behind them, are known as back benchers.)

The system hinges on the PM and the government maintaining the support of a majority of the Members of Parliament (MPs). The government maintains this majority support through a system of party discipline (parties choose candidates for each constituency and have a major role in formulating the PM's program), patronage (the PM appoints about 25% of the MPs to government jobs), and collective responsibility. Roughly 90% of the votes taken are ceremonial in the sense that all the MPs vote for their party's position. Public dissent within the government is virtually unknown. It was big news when two cabinet members resigned because of their disagreement with the decision to go to war with Iraq. Collective responsibility means that once a government decides on a policy, everyone shares in that policy's success or failure. (On narrow, technical

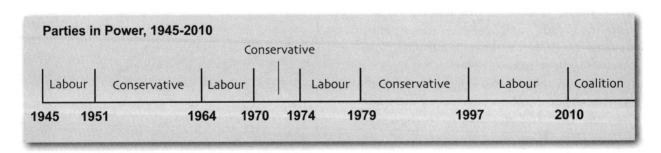

Parties in Power, 1945-2010

1945	1951	1964	1970	1974	1979	1997	2010
Labour	Conservative	Labour	Conservative	Labour	Conservative	Labour	Coalition

issues, a minister may have to assume individual responsibility.)

The bureaucracy has the job of administering government policies. The British civil servant is perhaps the prototype of government bureaucrat. The civil service has powerful traditions of political neutrality and excellence. While politics is not seen as a good career choice for a young man from the upper class, civil service is.

The Whitehall bureaucracies recruit from the brightest and the best of university graduates. Alumni of Oxford and Cambridge are vastly over-represented in the ministries up the street from Parliament's Westminster meeting place. The civil servants actively seek to carry out the plans of the elected government. They also seek to shape those plans in ways deemed acceptable to the policy experts in the bureaucracies. It's not unlikely that a new minister is greeted by civil servants with "schemes" for the policies his government promoted during a recent election. The schemes are likely to suggest alternatives to methods deemed less workable by the technocrats.

There are two major parties: Conservative on the right and Labour on the left. A third party, the Liberal Democrats, on the center-left attracts considerable support, but rarely elects many members to Commons (see notes on plurality elections below). All three parties today strive to be "catch-all" parties seeking votes from the great center of the British political spectrum. The Conservatives' core support comes from the upper classes, the suburban middle and upper-middle classes, and traditionalists among the working classes. Labour's core support comes from urban middle and upper-middle classes, the unionized working class, and progressives.

The political elite is characterized by political experience, high levels of education, wealth, and testosterone (i.e., it is mostly male). The Labour Party's policy of putting women on the ballot in electable districts brought about the doubling of

women in Commons in '97. Nonetheless, the percentage of women in the British legislature lags behind the percentages in many other European countries.

The leaders work their way up through local offices and party organizations (including unions, in the case of the Labour Party). The parties' control of nominations ensures loyalty and makes collective responsibility the norm for political behavior. The leaders succeed on their way up the political ladder with pragmatic rather than dogmatic approaches to issues. People from London are over-represented among the political elite.

Parliamentary elections are held at least every five years. That "at least" is one of the things that puzzles Americans. The "at least" is there because elections might "be called" less than five years after the last election. The queen officially calls for an election, but she only does so at the behest of the prime minister.

The 2010 Conservative-Liberal Democratic coalition has proposed a five-year definite term Parliament as a way to guarantee continued cooperation. Under the proposal a new election could only be called by a super-majority that neither the Conservatives nor the opposition could muster on their own. Its passage was not assured when I wrote this. Did it become law?

In extreme and rare cases, the request for a new election might come because a government loses support of its party in Commons. It's more likely that a government perceives some political advantage to an early election. Americans are likely to ask: Why would the leader of a majority in the parliament call for a new election? Maybe the government is riding a crest of extraordinary popularity three or four years after the last election. Capitalizing on that success guarantees at least five more years in power, even if the government's popularity declines later.

Elections for Commons, like those for the House of Representatives in the USA, choose one legislator for each district. The contests are plurality elections: The candidate with the most votes wins the seat. When preparing for an election, party leaders will evaluate their chances for winning in each of the 650+ districts. Since there are no residency requirements or primary elections, anyone can apply to be a candidate. Local party committees screen applicants and members choose candidates. But the recommendations of the national party are usually followed. Parties want their leaders and senior members to run in districts they're sure of winning. Younger candidates run in marginal districts where they have a chance to win. The least senior aspirants will become "sacrificial lambs" in districts where they have no chance of winning. (This loyal sacrifice may pay off later in a chance to run in a winnable district.)

As they do in the USA, plurality elections marginalize minor parties. It's not unusual in the UK for the Liberal Democrats to win 10-15% of the vote. But they rarely win more than 3% (or 20 seats) of the places in Commons. They come in second in many constituencies.

The organized interests that want to influence policy decisions operate quite differently than in the USA. Lobbying MPs won't be worth much, since they are predictably going to vote with their parties. So interest groups have to lobby party leaders, government members, and bureaucrats. They also make efforts to sway public opinion.

These interest groups don't throw money at politicians as much as they do in the US either. Official election campaigns are only four to six weeks long (although the maneuvering by politicians may go on for a year before an anticipated election), and neither candidates nor parties can buy advertisements on television or radio. "Instead, before elections [broadcasters] have to give the candidates free broadcasting time, outside of the segments reserved for commercials. The format of these free time slots, which usually use old-fashioned formulas such as a direct speech or prearranged Q & A, is very different from paid political advertising in the United States."[1] However, in 2010, leaders of the three main parties debated on live TV, much like presidential candidates in the US.

Most of the lobbying is done by ad hoc groups which exist for a single purpose. Some groups focus on local issues, others on topics of a national scope.

The most powerful interest groups (peak groups) are organized nationally around economic issues. The biggest are:

- Confederation of British Industry
- British Employers' Confederation
- Association of British Chambers of Commerce
- Trades Union Congress
- National Union of Teachers
- National Farmers Union

CBI is closely associated with the Conservative Party while the TUC is a major sponsor of the Labour Party.

Another important way that interest groups are involved in policymaking is through "quangos." Quasi-Autonomous Non-governmental Organizations are created by Parliament to put government and private interests together on a policy-making board. Quangos do things like developing safety regulations for factories, creating proposals to improve race relations, and maintaining railway infrastructure.

Civil servants, lobbyists, and sometimes even members of government serve on quangos. The purpose is to get all interested parties together to agree on policy decisions. Quangos sometimes implement as well as make policy.

Since 2000, quangos have come in for a lot of criticism and are less frequently used than in the past. However, government agencies — like the Office of Communications (popularly known as

Ofcom), which is an independent regulatory body — use procedures that resemble quangos when deciding on new or revised regulations.

It's probably no surprise that some interests are not adequately represented in the halls of government. That doesn't mean those interests are not considered by leaders when making policy. It simply means they don't have much of a voice in representing themselves. As is true in most places, people at the bottom of the socio-economic hierarchy are not proportionally represented. This means that the UK north and west of London is politically peripheral. Ethnic and racial minorities as well as women are under-represented in policy-making bodies.

The UK has a long history of government activism. For over 200 years, the government has played a leading role in the economy. None of us should be surprised that John Maynard Keynes was British. His theoretical work offered 20th-century rationales and methods for government stabilization of economies.

After World War II, Britain was faced with expensive reconstruction, loss of empire, and relative economic decline. The response was a "collectivist consensus" to make public (government) spending a vital part of the economy. The social security system, large-scale public housing programs, and the National Health Service were the centerpieces. Everyone would be guaranteed health

---

'Spending Way Out of Recession' Derives from Theories of John Maynard Keynes

Keynesianism is named after John Maynard Keynes, a British economist who lived from 1883 to 1946.

Keynes described an economy as a circular system of money flow. Simplistically, people spent money that became income for businesses. Businesses used income to employ people to produce products and provide services.

In normal times, there is a high level of employment and spending, earnings and production. If consumers lose confidence in the future, they may spend less. If businesses lose confidence in the market spending of consumers, they may cut back on production (and employment). Either or both of those actions reduce the money flow and cause the economy to shrink. This is a recession: less spending, less production, fewer jobs, and a smaller economy.

The cure, said Keynes, was for a national bank to "expand the money supply." If there was more money in the system, interest rates would decline, consumers and businesses would have more money to spend and their confidence in the future would return.

A depression is a drastic recession that can't be cured by an increase in the money supply. In a depression, the recessionary cycle can't be simply broken. In those crisis times, government should increase spending to create jobs and incomes for people. The people will use their new incomes on new spending, thus reversing the recessionary cycle. The government spending will have to be done with borrowed money, creating a fiscal deficit.

Keynes noted that in times of prosperity, government should spend less and reduce the deficit. This would have the added advantage of reducing the likelihood of inflation.

Massive government borrowing and spending in the USA during World War II is credited with ending the depression of the 1930s. That demonstration of the success of Keynes' ideas convinced nearly all public policy makers in industrial countries to adopt some form of Keynesian economic philosophy.

Adapted from an unsigned article, "Review of Keynesian Theory,"
www.korpios.org/resurgent/Keynesianism.htm

care, a place to live, and a minimal income. And the government could exercise enough influence in the economy to prevent the recurrence of a 1930s'-style depression.

What Keynesian economic policies did not do is guarantee people jobs. Nor did it offer guidelines for adapting economies to new circumstances (especially in the face of powerful interest groups dedicated to preserving the status quo).

The problems created in the 1970s brought an end to the period of collectivist consensus and led to the success of a decidedly non-Keynesian Margaret Thatcher. She was not opposed to big government, and she didn't reduce government spending as a share of the economy. But, she did oversee large-scale privatizations of the coal industry, railroads, public housing, and municipal water suppliers.

Tony Blair came to office in 1997, promising to create economic growth and fix the problems of social security and National Health System. He advertised his as the "Third Way." Government is still a major actor in the economy.

Blair was successful in many ways because of economic growth and his personal popularity.

Blair's successor, Gordon Brown was neither as lucky nor as charismatic. Tory leader David Cameron, PM of the government elected in 2010, is not proposing reductions in the size of British government, but to "restore trust and accountability" and promote efficiency in government. What has he done to fulfill those pledges?

In addition to economics and the government social welfare programs, Britain's relationships with international organizations are major issues. Margaret Thatcher resigned primarily over the issue of the UK's relation to the European Union and the EU's monetary union proposals. The political system is still dealing with those issues. Monetary union is so controversial that Prime Minister Gordon Brown proposed a national referendum

on it. The British monetary system is seen as a sign of independence and the pound sterling is a symbol of national pride. The Euro is seen by many as a sign of European **hegemony**.

> **hegemony**, noun: the position of being the strongest and most powerful and therefore controlling others (esp. of countries)
>
> — *Cambridge International Dictionary of English*

There's even argument about the EU's policy on human rights. As presently framed, it would become a virtual "Bill of Rights" in the UK. Not everyone is enthusiastic about a written constitution-like document. Even some advocates of a written constitution aren't sure about one written by Europeans.

Britain's relationships with the USA, NATO, and UN are also issues to be watched. The debate about war with Iraq and its aftermath continued into 2010.

4. CITIZENS, SOCIETY, AND THE STATE

The name of the country, the United Kingdom of Great Britain and Northern Ireland, implies some politically important cleavages. Except for Northern Ireland, the implication is misleading.

Nationalistic parties in Scotland and Wales are forces to be reckoned with, but they are not decisive. The Labour Party initially won pluralities in both local assemblies. In 2007, the Scottish National Party won a plurality (by one seat) in the Scottish Parliament and formed a minority government with support from the Scottish Green Party. The Bank of Scotland circulates currency which is interchangeable with the English pound and public signs in Wales are in Welsh and English, but the ethnic or nationalistic impulses are not national issues.

Northern Ireland is made up of two nations: one Catholic and Irish and the other Protestant and

Scotch-Irish. Residential segregation, historic discrimination against Catholics, and the resulting economic disparities reinforce the divisions. General economic difficulties exacerbate the problems.

There's still a hereditary aristocracy in the UK. Class divisions are still recognized and there's greater class-consciousness than we find in the USA. Historically, these divisions have been recognizable by residence and speech (see *My Fair Lady*). However, the class divisions have not had the political effects you might predict. There have been avenues for social mobility (colonial service, union organizing, entrepreneurship — especially in industry and high tech, for example) and successful political representation of the working class by the Labour Party.

The importance of *noblesse oblige* on the part of many aristocrats appears in the prominence of upper class liberals. The existence of deference by many workers shows up in the third of working class voters who cast ballots for the Conservative Party. The social security system and the National Health Service provided safety nets that reduced class conflicts to some degree. Another factor ameliorating the cleavages between social classes is the growing importance of the middle class and post-industrial values.

Technology and education were keys to the expansion of the middle class. After World War II, governments brought about changes in the educational system. Government high schools got better. The opportunities for university schooling

increased dramatically with the establishment of post-secondary polytechnic institutes. While a degree from a polytechnic did not carry the weight or prestige of a degree from a research university, it was a route for social mobility. In the 1990s, the polytechnics, because of their expanding research activity and economic importance, were given university status and allowed to award academic degrees.

The benefits of these developments are not uniform. The south of England is richer and offers more opportunities than the old industrial north, Scotland, Wales, or Northern Ireland. This geographic divide is very evident in elections. The Conservative Party rarely wins parliamentary seats in Scotland, Wales, or northern England.

The religious cleavage so prominent in Northern Ireland is not a major factor in the rest of the UK. A third of the population identifies itself as non-religious. In London and larger cities, the religion of immigrants may be politically relevant on local issues.

The ethnic divide that separates immigrants (virtually all non-European) from other Brits is greater and more politically difficult. Racism and intolerance are political issues for local officials and for national parties.

People in the UK begin their political education at home, just as they do in every other country. The attitudes, values, knowledge, and skills learned at home are important.

Culturally, Rank Has Had Both Privileges AND Obligations

The English Common Law evolved as a formal set of precedents and named relationships earlier grounded in *noblesse oblige*, the foundation of feudalism as a valuing culture.

Noblesse oblige, poorly translated into today's English as "the nobility is obliged" or "obligations of nobility," characterized the inter-relationships then prevailing from King to lowliest serf.

The Magna Carta of 1215 C.E. is a codification of essential principles within *noblesse oblige*. That we have been conditioned to regard feudalism negatively may say more about the interpretations we are taught than the actualities of feudalism.

— Clark, Milo, "A Dry Critical Perspective on Today: Job Property Rights and the Magna Carta of 1215 C. E.," *www.swans.com/library/art3/ mgc031.html*

While learning at home is quite individualistic, public education is a common one. Schooling is universal up to age 17, and what we in the US would call civics is part of the curriculum. Nonetheless, interest in politics is quite low compared to the USA, while voting rates are higher (though perhaps falling). Less than a fifth of the populace does anything more than vote.

On a local level, people are more willing to organize around specific issues, but the participation of the active 20% is sporadic. Historic exceptions to that are the nationwide women's suffrage movement in the first decades of the 20th century and the Campaign for Nuclear Disarmament during the Cold War. Environmental issues have attracted some support and activists, but less than in Germany.

Social Movements: Most visible in recent years have been

- the women's movement: it is decentralized and locally active on health and children's issues; organizations of professional women in many fields are also active on specific issues

- the "counter culture:" anti-poverty events like Live 8 (2005) and Rock Against Racism (2004) have raised awareness and money for specific causes; groups protesting globalization, genetically-modified food products, and the war with Iraq have also been sporadically active

- at the height of the "mad cow" epidemic in 1996, farmers organized to ensure that they were compensated for the millions of cattle destroyed

Labor unions are active politically in the Trades Union Congress, one of the primary sponsors of the Labour Party. Even union activity is sporadic. Large numbers of union members vote for parties other than Labour, and short-term strikes (which are sometimes political as well as economic) in specific industries are the most likely form of activity beyond voting.

> **History of 'Peaceful' Change Began with Coerced Concessions at Runnymede**
>
> The Magna Carta is a series of concessions wrung from the unwilling King John by his rebellious barons in 1215. ... [It] established for the first time a very significant constitutional principle, namely that the power of the king could be limited by a written grant.
>
> ... In January 1215 a group of barons demanded a charter of liberties as a safeguard against the king's arbitrary behaviour. The barons took up arms against John and captured London in May 1215. By 10 June both parties met and held negotiations at Runnymede. ... The concessions made by King John were outlined in a document known as the "Articles of the Barons."... Meanwhile the royal chancery produced a formal royal grant, based on the agreements reached at Runnymede, which became known as Magna Carta, the "Great Charter."
>
> — The British Library
> *www.bl.uk/collections/treasures/*
> *magna.html*

The continued operation of a liberal democratic system without a written constitution suggests some areas of broad consensus. Those areas include

- a devotion to justice and fair play
- human and civil rights for all
- acceptance of class distinctions and social mobility
- equal representation
- civilian government
- pragmatism and cooperation
- tolerance
- both community and individual responsibility
- honesty and transparency in government and business and

- acceptance of an activist government (see the "collectivist consensus" for examples)

Mass media in the UK are primarily national media based in London.

If government is divided into "dignified and efficient" sectors, newspapers are divided into to undignified and efficient. Most people read papers like American super market tabloids (some of which are really British). They're full of gossip and sensationalism. The major journalistic papers are published in London and available throughout the country. They tend to be editorially aligned with one of the major parties and offer straightforward news. Local newspapers cover local issues almost exclusively.

There is little local television or radio. Every once in awhile, the BBC is criticized for its coverage of a specific issue, but the news is considered reliable and thorough. In times of fiscal belt-tightening, the public media are always targets of budget cuts. There is growing competition from cable and satellite broadcasts, but they haven't had noticeable political effects like they have had in the USA.

5. POLITICAL AND ECONOMIC CHANGE

The stereotype is that political change in Britain has been peaceful and gradual. Well, that ignores a lot.

The Women's Social and Political Union staged a campaign of arson and destruction of property during the years before World War I to force the government to allow women the right to vote. Terrorism and murder have characterized the struggle between Catholics and Protestants in Northern Ireland.

Recognizing this, you have to realize that, in a comparative sense, political change in the UK has been relatively peaceful. (There's that ambiguity again.)

The extension of voting rights during the 19th century came about peacefully as did the redrawing of electoral district boundaries (to eliminate the "rotten boroughs"). The parliament did not have to raise an army to make the government responsible to the parliament (1911). Workers did not have to stage a revolution to put the Labour Party in power.

Political change looks gradual, in part, because not all changes have taken place at the same time. However, depression, war, the loss of empire, and the adjustment to a post-industrial, global economy have been taking place nearly simultaneously. There have been cushions to the change: an improving educational system, a tradition of technological innovation, North Sea oil to replace dwindling coal reserves, and straightforward trade with Europe to replace the unequal trade with the empire.

The post-World War II adoption of the policies that made up the "collectivist consensus" was peaceful. Labour and Conservative governments promoted the basic plans. Even the end of the consensus with Thatcherism and the transition to Blair's Third Way have been peaceful and gradual.

Violence was common in the disputes over Northern Ireland. The British army finally withdrew from the counties in the summer of 2007, but the thrust of government policy all along has been to find accommodation. The 1998 Good Friday agreements appear to have haltingly led to resolution when the IRA finally agreed to "decommissioning" (i.e., disarming) and all parties endorsed it in 2006. That opened the door for new elections in the spring of 2007 and a new assembly.

In early 2010, the Irish and British governments oversaw negotiations that resulted in the devolution of police powers to the Northern Ireland government. Most observers saw this as the last step in implementing the Good Friday agreements.

The Thatcher — Blair Transition

After wining office in 1979, [Margaret Thatcher] pursued several key economic policies. First she set about reducing the power of labor unions. ... Second, the ... administration lowered taxes. ... Third, Thatcher sold off publicly owned companies. ... Finally, Thatcher encouraged competition. ...

The free-market philosophy had become so popular and institutionalized that when Tony Blair became leader of the Labour Party in 1994, he immediately set about ... committing it to the maintenance of some of the more popular aspects of Thatcherism, most notably privatization. Indeed ... elements of the Labour manifesto [of] 1997 ... included a balanced budget, greater independence for the Bank of England, efforts to reduce welfare dependency, promotion of the work ethic, close ties to business, and a rejection of special deals for labor unions ... [an emphasis on] the need to deal with the problems of the underclass and to pay greater attention to improving education and health care.

— McCormack, John, *Comparative Politics in Transition*, 2001, pp. 112-113.

One of the big issues to be settled in the future is the exact nature of British involvement in the European Union. It hardly seems possible that the UK could remain even marginally on the outside of such a powerful economic bloc. But it also seems unlikely that the British will quickly embrace the multinational governing features of the EU.

The resolution of economic issues also remains. Thatcher, Major, and Blair pursued policies to reduce government's role in the economy and "improve" the welfare state. The primary difference between the Conservative and Labour government's improvements was that Blair's proposals involved increased funding. The economic situation of the early 21st century has demanded adjustments. A recession or global energy crisis could force quick decisions on the government. It's too early to analyze successes or failures. Go look for recent evidence on the British economy, government economic policy, and public opinion.

The global recession led the Labour government to Keynesian stimulus spending. That drove up deficits and offered the Conservatives issues on which to base their 2010 electoral campaign.

6. PUBLIC POLICY

As you know, policy development in the UK is a top-down process. The elite respond to popular sentiment — like the Labour Party's decision after the 2001 elections to improve the NHS and schools and raise taxes to fund the improvements.

But, most of the time policy is developed by the very top civil servants and the very top government leaders in consultation with lobbyists from the peak associations. Party manifestoes are created by party leaders with an eye to members' view and public opinion, but it's not a democratic process.

Parliamentary reform is widely discussed. After many proposals, hereditary Lords lost their votes in Parliament when Blair's government decided to act. There are proposals to replace the House of Lords with an elected body, but the advantages over simple abolition are not clear.

Devolution is a "constitutional" reform in a state without a constitution. Local assemblies in Scotland, Wales, and Northern Ireland now have limited authority to legislate on local matters. While devolution is a response to local elites and some grassroots sentiment, it is carefully directed by the government and clearly frees Commons from dealing with many local issues. In fact, there are proposals being floated in Commons for the creation of an English assembly to deal with issues that involve only England. Similarly, the creation of city councils frees Commons from dealing with many municipal issues.

In the 1990s, general prosperity made some reforms easy. Unemployment, inflation, and budget deficits fell. The responses to the economic downturn have been predictable. Consumption taxes and interest rates were lowered. Social safety net spending rose. Banks were bailed out. Unemployment rose to nearly 8% (lower than the US rate of 10%). Because recovery was so slow, Labour's opponents had ammunition with which to attack

Without a Bill of Rights, Britons' civil liberties have been in the hands of Parliament. However, Blair's government adopted the European Convention on Human Rights as British law and established an independent supreme court. That gives citizens access to British courts as well as the European Court of Human Rights.

There were scattered incidents of racist violence in the summer of 2005 in the wake of the terrorist bombings. Government and civic authorities from the PM and the Archbishop of Canterbury on down condemned them and the terrorism. In spite of a low level of background racism, tolerance remains a British value in law and in practice. The issues will be apparent in debates about immigration and free speech as Britain responds to radicalism among immigrants and citizens. You should be up to date on recent events.

Similarly, environmental issues are mostly in the background. They tend to be local — near historical or prehistoric sites and former industrial areas. As such they are generally dealt with by local officials (mostly civil servants). The failure of the Green Party to elect many MPs is indicative of the local nature of these issues.

FOOTNOTES

1   Pantin, Laurence, "Fifty Years Of Political Ads," *www.mediachannel.org/arts/perspectives/ pol_ads/index.shtml*

REVIEW EXERCISE

This little exercise is not meant to be comprehensive. It's meant to get you thinking about some of the basic facts and point out areas you might have to review more thoroughly. My responses follow.

1. In the Western academic tradition, the UK is a common beginning point for studying comparative politics because
   (A) nearly all countries have parliaments like the UK
   (B) the regime is unlike any other
   (C) the British idea of rule of law has been so influential
   (D) it has the world's oldest constitution
   (E) political change has been peaceful throughout British history

2. Which of the following is NOT part of the United Kingdom?
   (A) England
   (B) Scotland
   (C) Northern Ireland
   (D) Ireland
   (E) Wales

3. Which nation is NOT part of the UK?
   (A) the English
   (B) the Britons
   (C) the Scots
   (D) the Welsh
   (E) the Protestant Scotch-Irish

4. Which political reform in the UK was accompanied by significant violence?
   (A) the Great Reform Acts
   (B) the Supremacy of Parliament
   (C) creation of the National Health Service
   (D) the acceptance of the European Convention on Human Rights
   (E) women's suffrage movement

5. Which of the following does NOT contribute to the legitimacy of the British regime?
   (A) the limitations on freedom of the press by the Official Secrets Act
   (B) the monarch as head of state
   (C) a history of successfully resolving social conflicts
   (D) the accountability created by free and competitive elections
   (E) public question time of ministers in the House of Commons

6. The creation of a Supreme Court in 2009 is a change from
   (A) royal prerogatives influencing court decisions
   (B) the inquisitorial system of justice
   (C) aristocratic adjudication of disputes over points of law
   (D) fusion of powers
   (E) reliance on the European Court of Justice

7. The British parliamentary system is functional, in large part, because of
   (A) bipartisanship
   (B) transparency of policy making within parties
   (C) collective responsibility
   (D) the requirement of Royal Assent
   (E) separation of powers

8. The British multi-party system is in fact a two party system because of
   (A) the "first past the post" electoral system
   (B) federalism
   (C) the extremism of all but the two major parties
   (D) the charismatic popularity of Conservative and Labour leaders
   (E) the near absence of difference between the preferred policies of the two largest parties

9. Interest groups in the UK focus their efforts on
   (A) voters
   (B) elected leaders in local councils
   (C) local party organizations
   (D) party leaders
   (E) financing campaigns for crucial candidates

10. In the UK, there is less public interest in politics than in the US, and voting rates are
   (A) lower
   (B) higher
   (C) about the same
   (D) more variable from election to election
   (E) higher among minority groups

(For responses, see below)

7: Know ... RUSSIA

1. INTRODUCTION TO COMPARATIVE POLITICS

One of the topics political scientists focus on when studying Russia is change — political and economic change. How will a new political-economic system emerge from the statist heritage of Tsarist and Soviet Russia in the environment of a global, free market economy? Will it be democratic? How will such a multi-faceted change take place? Will simultaneous economic, political, legal, and social changes be easier or more difficult than sequential changes? Are the changes revolutionary? What role with oil markets play in the political process? What role will traditions of centralization have? What role will personalized leadership have? How will the presidential succession take place? (Of course, if you're reading this after the election, you will have the answers in your head.) Think about those things. Each one is a potential topic for a free response question.

Another area to pay attention to is the role of actors outside the government. In Tsarist and Soviet regimes, the government monopolized power as much as possible. Now, the government's legitimacy rests, in part, upon votes as well as orderly government and prosperity. In spite of Vladimir Putin's consolidation of power, there are the surviving oligarchs and the empires they have created. There is a significant organized crime "industry." There are thousands of small businesses. And there are millions of property owners. All are actors in the state. How will they affect future developments?

Comparisons between changes in Russia and Eastern European countries will be another subject for study. Since the political and economic backgrounds have some commonalties, the successes

and failures of change will be topics for academic studies and future textbooks. Similarly, for this course, comparisons between the Russian situation and the changes in China need to be considered. Remember the comments about case studies? And prepare yourself to clearly distinguish between correlations and causation.

2. SOVEREIGNTY, AUTHORITY, AND POWER

Russia is a huge country in northern Europe and Asia. It spans 11 time zones (there are only six between New York City and Honolulu). Half the country is north of the latitude of Anchorage, Alaska (60°). Most of the country is north of 49° latitude (the western Canadian-USA border). There is an abundance of natural resources, but it exists in inhospitable environments. It's a multi-ethnic country. Government policy (Tsarist and Soviet) was to promote Russian emigration to the frontier ("Go east, young man!"). Policy also demanded the "Russification" of the non-Russian groups. (Chechnya demonstrates one of the more tragic failures of that process.)

Russia is a very poor country. Its GDP per capita is $15,200, a figure that is only 70% that of the EU's poorest country, Portugal ($21,700) and less than half the EU average ($32,700).

Ecologically, Russia is a dangerous disaster area. Scuttled atomic submarines litter the Arctic ports in the north. Factories whose only goals were high output poured lethal chemicals into the air and on the ground when they were functioning. Many have now been abandoned. The disaster at Chernobyl created a dead zone in the Ukraine. Similar atomic power plants continue to operate. Air and water pollution threaten people throughout the country.

This is a country with a political history as least as long as the UK's. What do you need to know?

For centuries, many people in Russia, from the elite to the peasants, have felt that their country was the last custodian of real civilization and Christianity. Civilization and Christianity spread from Rome to Byzantium and to Russia. Then Rome was destroyed. The Muslims conquered Byzantium. As many saw it, that left only Russia as the bastion of true civilization and true Christianity: The West lost the real meanings of these treasures during the Renaissance and the Enlightenment, but Russians held on to their essence throughout a long Mongol despotism.

We can make a neat historical analogy by extending that sense of global mission from Tsarist Russia to the Soviet Union. Then the sense of mission became the preservation and spreading of true Communism (the Third International).

Where does that leave Russia and the Russians today? Perhaps in a place that reflects another theme of Russian/Soviet history.

The interface between Russia and the West has been an issue since the Russians finally got free of the Mongol invaders. If Russia was the custodian of truth, then following the example of the West would be a betrayal. But, even for Peter the Great the technological accomplishments of the West were models to follow. The push and pull between the *zapadniki* (who want to modernize Russia by following Western models) and Slavophiles (who hold higher the genius of Russian culture) continues. The *zapadniki* held Catherine the Great's attention while the Slavophiles cranked out rumors of her depravity. Gorbachev and Yeltsin's economic *zapadniki* advisors pushed their leaders toward Western-inspired reforms while the

HISTORICAL TURNING POINTS

1690	Peter the Great begins establishing a Tsarist empire
1861	Emancipation of the serfs
1917	Revolution
1918-1922	Civil War
1921-1928	New Economic Policy
1924	Death of Lenin
1927	Ascendancy of Stalin to head of USSR
1929-1939	Great Depression Collectivization and famine, 1929-1933; Purges, 1934-1938
1941-1945	World War II
1945-1989	Cold War
1953	Stalin dies
1956	Russian army crushes Hungarian democracy movement; Khrushchev's secret speech denouncing Stalinism
1962	Cuban Missile Crisis
1964	Khrushchev ousted as Soviet leader
1968	Russian army crushes Czechoslovakian democracy movement
1979	Invasion of Afghanistan
1980-1982	Solidarity Movement in Poland
1982	Brezhnev dies

Slavophile Communist traditionalists fomented revolution.

You need to have a good grasp of the recent past, especially Yeltsin's rise to power after decades of economic, ideological, and social stagnation and after Gorbachev's doomed reforms.

Do you remember the themes of *glasnost* and *peristroika*? And why was it that *glasnost*, which let people know more about what was going on, made Mikhail Gorbachev less popular? (Think about finding out how government industrial policies had polluted your neighborhood and the air you breathe.) And what were the results of *demokratizatsiia* (attempting to create more democracy within the Communist Party)? (Think coup d'etat and Boris Yeltsin.)

Then remind yourself of how the USSR fell apart (see **Political Turning Points** sidebar, below) and how Yeltsin worked to keep some of the pieces together. And how he reacted to a coup attempt. (I keep things straight by first imagining Yeltsin

manning the protective barricades in front of the "white house" or parliament building in '91 and then recalling his loyal artillery blasting the "white house" with point blank barrages in '93.)

Then there is the new constitution (see the section on Political Framework) and the transition from Yeltsin to Putin. Putin? Where did he come from? (Think KGB.) Then there was the election of Dmitry Medvedev. He worked in the St. Petersburg mayor's office with Putin.

While you're thinking along these lines, you need to recall the basics of the privatization of the Russian economy. There was the "spontaneous" privatization that began in the *glasnost* years and

---

POLITICAL TURNING POINTS

1985 .... Gorbachev becomes General Secretary of CPSU; beginnings of peristroika, glasnost, and de-mokratizatsiia
1989 .... Collapse of communist regimes in Eastern Europe
1990 .... Yeltsin elected chairman of the Russian Congress of Peoples Deputies and resigns from CPSU
1991 .... Yeltsin elected president of Russia; Attempted coup d'état: Yeltsin organizes opposition; USSR dissolved; CIS formed
1992 .... Russian Federation created and it joins the IMF
.... Shock therapy and privatization vouchers issued
1993 .... Yeltsin convenes constitutional convention, dissolves Congress of Peoples Deputies and calls for elections and referendum on new constitution; Attempted overthrow of Yeltsin's government;

Referendum approves new constitution; Elections for Federal Assembly
1995 .... Communists win one-third of seats in Duma
1996 .... Yeltsin reelected president of Russia
1998 .... Economic collapse; IMF rescue with structural adjustment conditions; Russia defaults on loan payments; Three prime ministers in one year
1999 .... Duma tries unsuccessfully to impeach Yeltsin; Terrorist bombings in Moscow; war renewed in Chechnya; Yeltsin resigns
2000 .... Putin elected president of Russia; .... Putin reorganizes regional government
2004 .... Putin's reelection
2008 .... Medvedev's election

continued into the '90s. There was no legal basis for it, but managers and workers in small and mid-size state enterprises (especially in the service areas — restaurants, gas stations, beauty shops) began transforming their workplaces into private businesses. The managers and workers remained the same. The state-owned equipment and buildings were used to produce private profits.

If you don't remember the outline of the large-scale privatizations of the '90s, go back to your textbook and review. There were the vouchers given to Russian citizens. (They caused as much confusion and fraud as they did chances to invest.) There were the "fire sale" prices of stock offered to the managers of state enterprises. Often 51% of the stock was "sold" this way. Much of the money to buy that stock came from company treasuries. Some of the money came from Communist Party assets. The Communist Party became the owner of banks, stores, and tourist agencies. Finally came the sale of shares to foreign investors.

There was capital flight. It seems that some people in Russia were making huge deposits in Swiss banks at the same time that the IMF was making massive loans to the Russian government and some foreign companies were investing. At the end of the '90s came the economic crash. The government defaulted on loans. The stock market crashed. The ruble crashed. The IMF made more loans and imposed a Structural Adjustment Policy

Burger King Sold at 'Fire Sale' Price

United Kingdom-based drinks giant Diageo has finally sold its Burger King fast food chain to a consortium of US investors for $1.5 billion — a third less than the same buyers had previously offered, on account of a slump in the chain's sales.

16-Dec-02
www.quickfrozenfoods.com/news

on Russia. Economic recovery has been evident since 2000, especially with rising oil prices.

As Russians struggle to create a new political culture (as well as new economic and social arrangements), we need to remember where they're coming from. In Tsarist times government legitimacy came from divine designation of the Tsar as the creator of society and protector of the faith. During Soviet times, whatever sense of legitimacy could be achieved came through ideology, egalitarianism, technological, industrial, and military achievements. A rising standard of living until the 1980s helped too. Today, hopes for legitimacy ride on the creation of a rule of law and representative government as well as the promise of economic prosperity. All three are works in progress.

And how does a nation create a political culture that is different from what existed in the past? Neither the Tsars nor the Communist leaders recognized such things as civil liberties. People were not citizens, they were subjects. The Tsar was the representative of God and his centralized state was the creative and motivating force in the country. Communism was the truth, and the party was its vehicle. The primary characteristics of those states were an oligarchic autocracy, strict censorship, secret police, an enforced uniformity of thought, and an intrusive state.

Today the beginnings of civil society are being threatened by the centralization of state power. Non-political groups focused on local issues are common and tolerated. But, any group, especially those with international connections with hints of politics (for instance, human rights or environment) is likely to find itself investigated, restricted, or banned if its goals come into conflict with those of the government.

What do Vladimir Putin and the reformers work on now? The tasks appear to be overwhelming. And are we even sure Putin is a reformer? We do know his power is limited by domestic and international economic forces and organized crime.

Appearances CAN Be Deceiving

Potem'kin vil'lage, a pretentiously showy or imposing façade intended to mask or divert attention from an embarrassing or shabby fact or condition.

— InfoPlease.com,
www.infoplease.com/ipd/A0597811.html

Cruising along the banks of the Volga River in the late 1700s, Queen Catherine of Russia viewed what appeared to be a picturesque setting of well-built, tidy houses and shops with villagers happily engaged in commerce and other pursuits. She was oblivious, however, to the poverty and misery existing just beyond her sight. Unknown to the queen, the setting was all a sham. Known as a "Potemkin Village," these false buildings were a moveable, fake village, set up along Catherine's carriage or river route to give her a satisfying but false experience of her dominions.

— CommentMax Stiff Right Jab:
A Model Potemkin Village,
Steve Montgomery & Steve Farrell,
Oct. 1, 2001,
*www.newsmax.com/
commentarchive.shtml?a=
2001/10/1/143126*

What you need to know is that the political culture is in flux; that changing political culture is a long, laborious process. The efforts in Russia have only been going on since 1993 (or 1991 or 1985). Context matters. (Ah, that ambiguity again.)

Another bit of context that matters is economic. Will growth be adequate to support political stability? Will the distribution of income contribute to a growth of the middle class? Will economic decline put an end to political reform or will it be ended by centralization of Putin's power? Will the rule of law become powerful enough to guarantee property and contract rights?

3. POLITICAL INSTITUTIONS

Nomenklatura: Let's get this out of the way if you don't already know about it. In the old Soviet days, there was a special section of the Communist Party bureaucracy that kept track of everyone worth keeping track of. If they didn't have a file on you, you weren't important.

The people who kept the records were supervised by the Politburo. They gathered information about people from teachers, principals, supervisors, military officers, Party cadres, and anyone else in a position to evaluate a person's abilities and loyalties. If the information in your file was favorable enough, your name could be placed on one of the *nomenklatura* lists. People's names were selected from these lists for important jobs with the Party, in government, or in a government "enterprise." Having a "patron" who could choose your name from a *nomenklatura* list helped a lot too. So, in the Soviet system, you not only wanted to keep your record exemplary, but you wanted to have friends in higher places. You made those friends by being a loyal follower (client). What we saw in that system was a combination of authoritarian control and patron-client politics.

A 1998 paper titled *How Russia Is Ruled* by Donald N. Jensen (associate director of broadcasting at Radio Free Europe/Radio Liberty) explains that system's relevance today. It may be a little dated, but in spite of elite "turnover," the people running most things in Russia today, including Putin, are "products" of the *nomenklatura* system. (The bold face emphases in the quote below are mine.)

> "Studies of the new Russian elite show that the majority of its members are drawn from the second rank of the Soviet-era *nomenklatura*. According to one study, **19% of the 1988 elite were in leading positions of private business in 1993; 48% of the 1988 group were still in the political elite in 1993.** A large proportion of today's ruling class [is a product of the same recruitment process] that spawned the Soviet leadership or worked in the Communist

Party's youth branch, the Komsomol… Still others — industrial managers, ministers, enterprise directors — came to power by "privatizing" their public sector economic ministries during the waning Gorbachev years… they continued to profit from their official contacts. This core group has been **joined by new elements — entrepreneurs** without government money and contacts and **people with links to organized crime** — comprising about one-third of the total, who did not occupy leadership roles in the Soviet system."

It appears that the new Russia is being run by the people selected by the old Soviet system that valued obedience and loyalty to those above you. Putin's government has reinforced that theme and moved against those entrepreneurs and criminals who resisted government power. Patron-client relationships become more important as the *nomenklatura* system becomes less important. Whether or not those people and those values can succeed in creating a viable political system remains to be seen.

The 1993 Constitution

In the midst of 1993's political/economic crisis, Yeltsin dissolved the legislature and called for new elections. After a month-long struggle, the opposition leaders were arrested, and Yeltsin proposed a referendum on a new constitution to follow the new elections.

The new constitution was approved (even though Yeltsin's opponents won a majority in the new legislature). The new constitution created what Yeltsin called a "presidential republic." While it resembles the French Fifth Republic in some ways, it is dramatically more "presidential."

The Executive

The president is directly elected for a six-year term in a two-ballot system. A candidate must win a majority to be elected. If no one gets more than 50% of the votes, a second round of voting is held. The top two candidates from the first round compete in the second round. The last election in 2008 saw Medvedev win a four-year term (constitutional amendments in 2008 extended the president's term to six years). Most observers expect Vladimir Putin to run for president in 2012 with hopes of serving two consecutive six-year terms (the constitutional limit).

The president appoints the chairman of the government (often informally called the premier or prime minister) and the cabinet with the approval of the Duma. There are constitutional limits to the Duma's power to reject the nominees. In the incumbent political situation, United Russia's dominance makes it highly unlikely that the Duma will reject a nominee in the near future.

The president has his own staff of advisors (much like the Executive Office of the President in the USA). The president can issue decrees that have the force of law unless countermanded by the Duma and can declare a state of emergency when the country is in dire straits. The so-called "power ministries" (defense, foreign affairs, interior, and the KGB's replacement, the State Security Bureau or FSB) are responsible to the president, not the prime minister. These power ministries are the core of the president's "security council" that includes the prime minister, the finance minister, and the heads of the legislative bodies.

The president can dissolve the Duma and call for new elections and can veto acts passed by the legislature. Given the disunity in the legislature, Yeltsin was the primary actor in policy formation. Putin has played the same role, both as president and prime minister.

Until Putin took the office, the prime minister served the president. As prime minister, Putin has been at least the political equal of President Medvedev. The prime minister administers the dozen "non-power" ministries of the regime. Bureaucrats, not politicians, run most of those ministries. Many of the bureaucrats are holdovers from the Soviet regime. They got into their positions through the *nomenklatura*/patron-client process. Newer government workers have been hired through connections to United Russia rather than the old *nomeklatura* system.

The very top people in the Soviet system (many of whom went on to lead newly privatized businesses) lost their jobs, but the second-level people moved up. They gained positions from which to appoint their loyal clients to higher positions. *Nomenklatura* may no longer function as a formal system, but its effects are going to be around for a long time.

The Legislature

The Federal Assembly (Federalnoe Sobranie) is a bicameral legislature. The upper house is called the Federal Council (Soviet Federatsii) and represents the local governments in the Russian Federation. It has little power, except to delay legislation. Its power of consent to the appointment of judges has helped to politicize the judiciary. The members are local officials, which means they have little time to devote to their legislative duties.

The lower house is the State Duma (Gosudarstvennaya Duma). There are 450 seats in the Duma. Originally, half of them represented single-member districts and half were chosen in proportional elections for four-year terms. In 2005, the Duma followed Putin's recommendation and eliminated the single-member districts, so the whole Duma was chosen in a proportional election. Putin said he wanted to strengthen the party system. Outside observers noted that many local "favorite sons" were winning single-member district seats and their loyalties were not with any party. As predicted, the Duma elected under the new rules in 2007 was dominated by United Russia, which won 70% of the 450 seats.

Another change helps account for United Russia's sweeping victory. Parties had to win at least 7% of the total vote to be eligible to elect any deputies to the Duma. In earlier elections, that number

had been 5%. In 2007, only four parties reached that threshold.

In 2008, the Duma extended legislative terms to five years.

Before these developments, the parliament was never in an equal bargaining position with the president. It had constitutional powers, but exercising them would have required more unity and party discipline than existed. The Federal Assembly could pass laws, but it couldn't force their implementation. It could override presidential vetoes, but the two-thirds vote of both houses was a practical impossibility until United Russia's success.

The Duma can pass a resolution of no confidence in the government by a simple majority, but the president can reject it. The president must respond only if the Duma passes a second no confidence resolution within three months. Then the president must replace the government or dissolve the Duma and call for new elections. Deputies don't like the prospect of campaigning and losing legislative perks like Moscow apartments.

The president holds all the highest cards in this political poker game. His powers are not unlimited, but he can almost always achieve his policy goals. He cannot dissolve the Duma during the year following an election. His power to call for new elections is also limited when he's exercising emergency powers or when he's under impeachment. Those limitations are minor compared to the president's powers.

The Judiciary

The Soviet judicial system (like the Tsarist system) centered on the procurator general. The position and structure was created by Peter the Great as "the eyes and ears of the government."[2] The procurator general's office was to ensure the observance of law by all government and private entities, investigate criminal cases, bring charges against criminals, supervise the courts and evaluate their decisions, and supervise the operation of prisons.

The general assumption was that an investigation by the procuracy would uncover all the facts and identify criminals. In other words, the presumption was that only guilty people were brought to trial. The purposes of trials were to make public a record of the facts and to impose sentences. Combined with the power of secret police (in both Tsarist and Soviet regimes), the procurator general's office was a powerful institution.

Along with the absence of a presumption of innocence, there was no presumption of civil liberties or civil rights.

If one key to creating a system deemed legitimate by Russian citizens is to create the rule of law, you can see what a long road Russia has to travel. Participants in the legal system have almost totally new roles to play. Imagine the differences for judges, prosecutors, defense lawyers, criminal investigators, and jury members. An adversarial,

transparent system that runs by rules rather than politics requires sets of professional skills that were far from normal 15-20 years ago.

In the Soviet system, judges were on the lowest rungs on the bureaucratic ladder in the procuracy. Even so, they got their jobs through the *nomenklatura* system. Today, the criminal court system is structured to look like those in industrialized democracies. There are even appellate courts and a Supreme Court to make final decisions. But can the judges perform? Can they be protected from politics and graft? How about the attorneys? And the juries?

There are commercial courts to deal with issues of business law and private property. Once again, this legal field is a novelty in Russia.

The 1993 constitution also created a Constitutional Court. Its 19 members are appointed by the president and approved by the Federation Council. This court has the potential for ruling on the constitutionality of legislative acts and executive actions. It has shown a great deal of hesitancy to challenge the president. As in the "contest" with the legislature, the president holds the power.

Local Governments

Local government in Russia is a cobbled-together "crazy quilt." Some bits have feudal roots, others are creatures of the expansion of the Russian state 300-400 years ago, and still others are remnants of Soviet attempts to recognize local ethnic groups.

It's almost as though each of the subdivisions has a unique status in relation to the Russian government. Such situations made it easy for many of these local "governments" to become the personalized "kingdoms" of local leaders. Autocratic (sometimes criminal) bosses ran many of the local areas. And since those local leaders were represented in the Federal Council, their powers were magnified somewhat. The demands of local leaders inundated the government in Moscow.

That situation is partly what led Putin to get new laws passed in 2000 to reduce the power of the Federal Council and to create seven federal districts. Presidentially appointed governors head the new districts. The governors supervise the local governments in their districts, and the Russian president is now allowed to remove local leaders if they are not following national law. In the summer of 2005, local legislatures were given the power to nominate candidates for these appointments. But, given the growing power of United Russia in local legislatures, this is unlikely to limit Putin's power. Keep your eyes open for developments in this area.

Does this simply mean more centralization and power to the president? Or, does it mean more assurance that local tyrants can't abuse Russian citizens? Like the election reform laws, the results seem both promising and worrying. Both of those are reasons to know what's going on.

Political Parties

Political parties in Russia have been, for the most part, vehicles for individual leaders. Between elections, most parties are almost invisible. At every election so far, ambitious politicians have organized new parties. People don't join them because there's no real point. The exception is the Communist Party. Like so much else about the politics of Russia, party politics are in a formative, ever-changing stage.

In the Duma, politicians appeal more to popular dissatisfactions by criticizing the government rather than supporting it. Patronage networks are centered on government, not on parties, except in the case of United Russia, which is so integrated with the government that it's difficult to distinguish between them. (Remember *nomenklatura* and patron-client relationships?)

> A **crazy quilt** by definition is "a quilt made of pieces of cloth of various colors and irregular shapes and sizes."
>
> — *www.ksu.edu/ humec/atid/historic/ crazy.html*

Given the rapid evolution of parties (United Russia, put together in the three months before the 2003 election, won the most seats in the Duma), there are only a few to pay close attention to: United Russia, the Communist Party, the Liberal Democrats, and Fair Russia.

United Russia is the party of the ruling elite. The Communists campaign for a state-controlled economy and a more secure social welfare system. The ultra-nationalist Liberal Democrats promise to revive the glorious and powerful Russia of the past. Fair Russia was created by Putin allies to compete for the votes of supporters of the Liberal Democrats.

Political Elites

Shall we make a list of groups from which the elites come?

First, there's the *nomenklatura* elite. These people seem to occupy positions in the government — especially in the security ministries. The government's role has declined since Soviet days, but businesses still need permits, licenses, and access to public resources.

Then, there are the oligarchs. Call them whatever you wish, they are incredibly rich and powerful. They used their wealth and media properties to prop up Yeltsin during his last election and Putin during his first. They own businesses controlling most natural resources, industrial production, and media. Putin has acted against any of them who showed signs of political independence. Several emigrated and some are in jail. Putin's government has effectively taken control, if not ownership, of Russian broadcast media and the oil industry.

There are small groups of people powerful in limited environments: young elected officials; entrepreneurs of small and mid-size businesses;

technical and scientific experts who can cash in on their expertise.

There are now several routes to power and influence, although only one that leads to the very top. The system is changing.

4. CITIZENS, SOCIETY, AND THE STATE

Young people in Russia might well look on the present situation as an opportunity to do exciting work shaping the future. Young people holding all these perspectives can be found in United Russia's elite youth group, Nashi. Modeled on the Soviet Komsomol, Nashi is the most visible form of mass participation. It is funded by corporate supporters of United Russia. Activists are rewarded with government jobs and business internships. There's a summer camp, military training, and religious instruction. Members are organized to protest the political opposition and cheer for Putin. Besides comparing Nashi to Komsomol, some observers have compared it to the Iranian Basij and even the Hitler Youth.

For most people politics is framed by poverty, although growing oil wealth ameliorated that to some extent in the 1990s. The global recession has kept the issue at the forefront of politics since then.

And the Winner Is ...

Duma Elections: December 2007 (almost 64% of the electorate voted)

Party	% of vote	Seats Won (out of 450)
Edinaja Rossija (United Russia)	64.3	315
Kommunisticeskaja Partija Rossijskoj Federacii (Communist Party of the Russian Federation)	11.6	57
Liberalno-Demokraticeskaja Partija Rossi (Liberal Democratic Party of Russia)	8.4	40
Spravedlivaya Rossiya (Fair Russia)	7.7	38
Agrarnaja Partija Rossii (Agrarian Party of Russia)	2.2	0
Jabloko – Rossijskaja Demokraticeskaja Partija (Apple, Russian Democratic Party)	1.6	0
Grazhdanskaya Sila (Civilian Power)	1.1	0
Sojuz Pravych Sil (Union of Right Forces)	1.0	0
Patrioty Rossii (Patriots of Russia)	0.9	0
Partiya Sotsial'noy Spravedlivosti (Party of Social Justice)	0.2	0
Demokraticeskaya Partiya Rossii (Democratic Party of Russia)	0.1	0

— Election World, *en.wikipedia.org/wiki/Russian_legislative_election,_2007#Official_results*

Poverty is still there for older people. Non-Russian minorities and pensioners have been the hardest hit. Laid off or unpaid factory workers share the fate of the pensioners. Alcoholism is rising; life expectancy for men is falling.

We in America may see televised scenes of Moscow streets full of BMWs and Mercedes and the openings of Hugo Boss and Naf Naf stores. An American network news program did a story on Moscow's new shopping mall and the Russian "mall rats" who now hang out there. It's a "Potemkin village." Behind that facade is the reality of life in Russia. Be aware of Potemkin villages in your images of Russia both past and present. Homeless and unemployed people along the streets and outside the malls outnumber the wealthy 2% and the 10-15% middle class.

There are 15 major ethnic groups in Russia. The ethnic cleavages coincide with geographic, linguistic, and cultural (and often religious) divisions. Russians account for over 80% of the population. Because of long-standing government policies, there are significant Russian minorities in areas of non-Russian ethnic group concentrations.

The Soviet revolution promised to create a classless society. However, after some initial enthusiasm for drastic egalitarianism, a new class system developed. Workers, peasants, and intellectuals were recognized as distinct groups. Within each group, differences were recognized and rewarded, especially for Communist Party workers, economic managers, and ideological theorists.

The class differences appeared less as differences in income or wealth and more as differences in power and access to public goods (like vacation homes and imported items sold only in stores restricted to the elites).

Smaller material perks were handed out to encourage desired behavior and thought. The use of coercion and rewards usually went hand in hand, the amount of each varying over time.

Today, there's the tiny class of really rich. Most of them are former high-level (not highest level) Party bureaucrats and industry/factory managers. Nicknamed "oligarchs," they usually achieved their positions by manipulating the privatizations of state enterprises that took place in the last Gorbachev and early Yeltsin years. The notoriety of their excesses in wielding power and wealth has grown so great, they've hired publicists to persuade media not to use the term "oligarch." Putin's pressure on anyone contesting his power has sent a couple oligarchs (like Khodorkovsky) to jail, forced some to leave the country, and others to avoid politics.

The middle class is small by Western standards and is made up mostly of successful entrepreneurs, people with technical educations, and people lucky enough to be employed in successful privatized companies.

For most people, maintaining their economic position is a full-time task. Some workers still get paid only sporadically. It was only as oil prices rose, for instance, that most teachers were paid regularly and even received some of the wages they were owed for the past.

The political consequences of this developing class system are unclear. Pensioners, veterans, and older people are most closely associated with the successors to the Communist Party. Many other people support local leaders who most realistically promise them benefits.

The Soviet heritage of participation was one of obedience. There was voting, but there were only Communist candidates. Voting was a duty of citizenship, but (especially in the 1970s and '80s) many people avoided voting by requesting absentee ballots and never returning them.

Following the Communist Party line was important for success in almost any endeavor. That meant knowing the line and demonstrating your knowledge publicly. If you wanted to get the best education, you joined the Young Pioneers in grade school and Komsomol (Young Communist League) in high school or college. Eventually an ambitious young person would join the Communist Party. Membership in the Party was never much more than 10% of the population. The organization and activities of United Russia appear to be modeled on those of the Soviet Communist Party.

Other "civic" groups were official or underground. Even the Russian Orthodox Church fell under government control. (Perhaps that wasn't too different from Tsarist days.) There were underground religious groups, but they were observed, infiltrated, and obstructed as much as underground political groups.

If you were a stamp collector or a soccer player or a glee club baritone or amateur baker, there was an officially sanctioned group organized for your participation. To try to organize something outside the purview of the state was suspect. (See Big Brother in George Orwell's novel *1984*.)

Beginning with Gorbachev's *glasnost* campaign in the '80s, people began identifying other people with interests similar to their own. There was enough freedom for people to begin communicating with each other outside of official channels. *Peristroika* offered some reforms within the Communist Party that loosened controls. People began forming groups on their own. The process sped up dramatically after 1991.

Some groups were "insider" groups. Industrial managers organized to preserve their positions and their advantages in privatizations. Government workers organized. Military officers organized. The state-sponsored unions worked to keep their members loyal.

Other groups were "outsider" groups. For instance, some workers organized independent unions in competition with the old official ones. Environmental groups organized. Women's groups were prominent. Soldiers' mothers orga-

nized. In 1993, a women's political party was a major force in the elections. Professional groups formed as lawyers and doctors recognized the opportunities or needs of representing themselves. The successes and influence of these groups varied widely. The Women of Russia party that made such a big splash in the '93 elections has all but disappeared. The environmental groups are active in localized campaigns, but haven't had much national influence. Most have been overshadowed by the success of United Russia.

Fewer than 20% of Russians report belonging to any kind of civic group. (See references to Nashi, above, for an example.)

If civic participation is difficult to perceive, political culture and values are even more difficult.

It's probably fair to say that in modern times Russia has never had a government perceived as legitimate. Does it have one now?

On one hand, public opinion polls repeatedly report that Russians hold many basic liberal democratic values. People apparently value representative government, private property, and civil liberties. (The younger and better-educated Russians report higher loyalties to these values than older and less-educated Russians do.)

The same polls report a very low level of satisfaction in the present regime. Falling voting rates parallel those reports. Voter turnout in the first real democratic elections was quite high. Voting rates have been gradually falling since. In 1993, Yeltsin's constitutional proposals almost failed because of low voter turnout.

Perhaps suspicion of people in authority is a feature of political culture that has survived since pre-Revolutionary times. Russian literature is full of examples, from Gogol to Dostoyevsky. A satirical newspaper *eXile* published "baseball cards" featuring, not athletes, but the political elite. Many of them were described on the cards as "Stealing: left and right." Their official positions identify the "teams" or oligarchic "clans" they played with.

In spite of, or perhaps as a result of, the low confidence people have in the regime and its leaders, public opinion polls report that many people (more older than younger) express the desire for government ownership of major industries and for government direction of the economy.

One other bit of culture, organized crime, sometimes becomes political. Prominent people, including politicians, have become victims of organized crime. In Soviet times, criminals were the capitalists. They organized and operated secretly. With reform, they continued to operate lawlessly. With the transition to a more market-oriented economy, some of their businesses became legitimate. But some of the old methods of operation persisted. When government officials or politicians come into conflict with the "gangs," they are in danger. Bodyguards are in high demand by government officials and the wealthy.

Putin's presidency marked a dramatic change in Russian media. Print, television, and radio grew more and more independent in the late 1980s. In the 1990s, oligarchs gained control of the broadcast (profitable) media. Most of them used their outlets to help Yeltsin get reelected and Putin to get elected.

However, beginning in 2000, Putin used a variety of means to take control of the national television and radio networks. None of them offer critical comments on government policies.

There are many newspapers and magazines, but the rising cost of newsprint has made them very expensive and their circulations are limited. The Internet is an independent source of news, but it's only available to a third of the population.

5. POLITICAL AND ECONOMIC CHANGE

It should be clear, from all the words that have preceded these, that change in Russia is ubiquitous, and that in recent years Putin's government has sought to gain control of the outcomes.

The process of change is not carefully planned — although wishful thinking may be involved in many policy proposals. Some changes like the "spontaneous privatization" of the late '80s and early '90s proceeded successfully. Other economic changes of the '90s were lurching, painful rides along the path to restructuring.

The political changes have been just as various and dramatic: elections, coups, and civil war. What more variety could you ask for?

The process is ongoing. There are signs that legal processes are becoming more important. But corruption along with the growing power of the government and organized crime should make you question those changes.

The expectation is that Putin will reclaim the presidency and that Medvedev will fade into the background, but observers can't know for sure what will happen. If Putin is elected to 12 more years as president, what kind of system will he create?

Economic change is also apparent, but hard to describe simply. Small businesses, as a percentage of the economy, play less of a role than in Western countries. The huge Soviet conglomerates may have been partially or mostly privatized, but more and more they take direction from the government. Corruption and uncertainties about business and contract law discourage foreign investment. The risks of investment are high and investors demand high rates of return. Without oil revenues, the economy would probably be a basket case.

Political stability and the rule of law are, ironically, beneficiaries of economic stability and growth and victims of economic recession. The historic foundation of stability and rule of law are weak in Russia. That suggests obvious "most similar systems" comparisons with China and "most different systems" comparisons with the UK.

When it comes to thinking about the role of government in the economy, you should be able to describe comparisons with any of the AP6 countries.

6. PUBLIC POLICY

If political parties are top-down institutions, policymaking is a top-down process in Russia.

The government commands the heights of the economy as it did in the Soviet regime, even if the conglomerates are partially private. That makes it easy to coordinate fiscal, monetary, and corporate policies. It doesn't guarantee wise decision-making. Since so much depends on oil revenues, Russia is dependent on world markets.

Structural adjustments and reduced government spending means that there are great pressures on social welfare programs. As with economic policy, Putin and his supporters in the Duma are in control of policymaking. The demonstrations by retirees, old veterans, and dissidents can almost be ignored. There are few ways for the grassroots to influence policy.

Russians want and enjoy civil liberties as never before. However, government control of media casts a shadow over other rights. Anti-terrorism policies might also threaten individual rights.

All policymaking is done within the context of new political institutions, a changing political culture, and a developing economic system. Decision-making is centered more and more on the executive. Look at recent policy decisions. Who made them? How were they implemented? What effect did they have on people's lives? What effect did they have on the country? What effect did they have on the power elite?

FOOTNOTES

1   The Russian interior ministry is not like the US Department of the Interior, which runs national parks, fights wild fires on public lands, administers Indian reservations, and conserves fish and wild life. The main job of Russia's interior ministry is to run the police force.

2   Theen, Rolf H. W. and Frank L. Wilson, *Comparative Politics, An Introduction to Seven Countries*, 1992, p. 332

3   Myers, Steven Lee, "Youth Groups Created by Kremlin Serve Putin's Cause," *New York Times*, 2 July 2007, *www.nytimes.com/2007/07/08/world/europe/08moscow.html, accessed 15 August 2007*

REVIEW EXERCISE

This little exercise is not meant to be comprehensive. It's meant to get you thinking about some of the basic facts and point out areas you might have to review more thoroughly. My responses follow.

1. One of the primary topics that comparative political scientists are interested in when studying Russia is the
   (A) changes in politics caused by a change from a market to a command economy
   (B) role of religion in power politics
   (C) competition between catch-all political parties
   (D) evolution of an authoritarian state
   (E) "capture" of political power by the incredibly rich oligarchs

2. Russian cultural ethnocentrism is based on
   (A) centuries of Mongol rule
   (B) a historical narrative that describes Russia as the custodian of true civilization
   (C) great advances in standards of living under the Soviet system
   (D) the rescue of the Soviet Union by the USA and the UK in World War II
   (E) the migration of Russians to the far reaches of its empire

3. The changes accompanying glasnost and perestroika were initiated primarily by
   (A) Khrushchev
   (B) Brezhnev
   (C) Gorbachev
   (D) Yeltsin
   (E) Putin

4. Privatization of the Russian economy
   (A) was not a smooth transition that benefited everyone equally
   (B) took place in the 1980s under Western supervision
   (C) has been a model followed by most countries in the former Soviet bloc
   (D) granted workers equal shares of the privatized "companies"
   (E) happened in planned, transparent ways

5. *Nomenklatura*
   (A) like other civil service systems, made promotions on the basis of job performance
   (B) removed corruption from government hiring
   (C) was the guarantee of a job for everyone
   (D) allowed people to apply for important government positions in the former Soviet Union
   (E) put career success in the hands of Communist Party officials

6. Abolishing single member districts for Duma elections was intended to
   (A) weaken political parties that opposed Putin's policies
   (B) make elections simpler
   (C) eliminate independent local political leaders from the legislature
   (D) focus more attention on constituent preferences
   (E) create nationwide constituencies

7. In order for the Duma to express "no confidence" in a government it must
   (A) circulate a petition in the country and obtain the signatures of at least 10% of the people who voted in the most recent election
   (B) obtain the resignations of a majority of its members
   (C) impeach one of the ministers in charge of a "power ministry"
   (D) enact a law requiring new elections
   (E) pass two resolutions within three months

8. A significant change in Russia from Soviet times has been
   (A) a reduction in the number of powerful positions in the elite
   (B) the development of new routes to positions of power
   (C) revitalization of Communist ideology
   (D) the aging of the leadership
   (E) a more open and fair competition for political power

9. Compared to the middle class in most Western countries, Russia's middle class
   (A) holds a much greater proportion of the country's wealth
   (B) has maintained its standard of living during the past decade
   (C) is about the same percentage of the population
   (D) is tiny
   (E) is huge

10. In examining rule of law, a "most similar systems" case study would probably compare Russia to
   (A) China
   (B) Iran
   (C) Mexico
   (D) Nigeria
   (E) The United Kingdom

(For responses, see below)

8: The Peoples Republic of China

1. INTRODUCTION TO COMPARATIVE POLITICS

There are several lenses through which we can study China.

How do the changes in China compare with the changes in Russia (and Eastern European formerly communist countries)? It seems logical to compare the attempts of Gorbachev and allies in *glasnost* and *peristroika* with the purely economic changes ongoing in China. Or, how do changes in China compare with changes in Putin's Russia? Putin's attempts to centralize power and bring more of the economy under the control of the government might be seen as imitations of the controls the Communist Party of China (CPC) and the Chinese government have maintained.

Another set of questions to answer revolves around comparisons between Chinese economic development and development in other Third World countries. How, for instance, do the economic development projects and political environments in China compare with those in Nigeria? or Iran? Or how do Chinese politics compare with politics in economic powerhouses like Korea and Taiwan?

We could ask why China has, in a Third World context, had so much success in providing education and health care to its people. In many Third World countries, efforts in both areas have been more difficult and less successful. What's been different about China? Have those differences disappeared as the economy has been opened up to entrepreneurs and foreign investment?

Similarly, we could ask about national unity. Why has China, in spite of some language problems,

had so few fractious cleavages in the last 50 years? The "Sinofication" of Tibet (analogous to the "Russification" of the near abroad in the Soviet Union) and the protests of Muslims in Xinjiang (the far northwest autonomous region) are major exceptions to Chinese unity. What factors have made such unity possible?

When we observe the Chinese model of attempting economic restructuring without political restructuring, we're curious. Westerners just have to ask whether economic freedom will lead to desires for political freedom. After all, that's one of the bits of political culture most Westerners are sure of. Will it be true for China as well?

In recent years, organizations that look like elements of civil society have appeared in China. There are professional associations and chambers of commerce and soccer leagues. Does the fact that organizational leadership for these organizations comes from the CPC mean they are not really civil society organizations? Or will the interests of the members of these groups be strong enough to influence policymaking? And what are we to make of active efforts by the Party and the government to prevent the formation of independent unions, peasant associations, and religious bodies? Do the extensive attempts to control e-mail and Internet communication mean that real civil society in China is a long way off?

Do you see any possible free-response questions in those topics? Think about potential comparisons to Russia, Iran, Mexico, or Nigeria.

HISTORICAL TURNING POINTS

ca. 551 BCE......	Kongfuzi (Confucius) born
221 BCE	Beginning of Qin Dynasty
1644 CE...........	Beginning of Qing Dynasty
1839-1842........	Opium Wars
1911.................	Revolution overthrows Qing Dynasty
1912	Founding of the Kuomintang (KMT or National Peoples Party) by Sun Yixian (Sun Yat-Sen) and Sung Chiao-Jen
1921	Founding of Chinese Communist Party
1927	Shanghai massacre (KMT attacks CPC) begins civil war
1931.................	Japan invades China
1934-1935	Long March
1937-1945	World War II
1945-1949	Continuation of civil war
1949	Peoples Republic of China established
1949-1953........	Land redistribution
1950-1953	Korean War
1976.................	Death of Mao Zedong

2. SOVEREIGNTY, AUTHORITY, AND POWER

China is a US-sized country in East Asia. Its population is more than four times the size of the US population, and it has only half as much arable land. The Chinese name for the country, *Zhong Guo*, means country in the middle of the world.

Until the early 20th century, China was ruled by emperors who fit into the Confucian system. Kongfuzi (Confucius) had taught that everyone had a place in society. They owed allegiance to those above them and were responsible for the welfare of those beneath them.

In the 19th century, advances in military technology gave Europeans tremendous advantages in dealing with China. The Chinese government lost sovereignty over many coastal regions. Western ideas and education spread among some of the elite, as did knowledge of the success of Japanese modernization (Meiji reforms). Discontent and imperial weakness led to revolution, civil wars, and invasion. The 1949 ascension to power by Mao Zedong and the Communist Party of China (CPC) was, in some ways, the culmination of this historical process.

New chaos followed as the Communists extended their power and tried to modernize and restructure society and the economy. Progress in feeding everyone was sometimes impressive. Failures in mass campaigns like the Great Leap Forward were horrific and tragic. The Great Proletarian Cultural Revolution was, perhaps, a last-ditch effort to create a communist society or the last phase of the 20th-century civil war. The on-going transition to a market-based system in a global economy is the subject for current events and future analysis by political scientists.

The growth of China's economic power has also led to China's ability to influence global politics. China has flexed its diplomatic muscles by negotiating with North Korea, arbitrating disputes between Iran and the West, and buying up American debt. All this makes domestic Chinese policy decisions more important globally.

The traditional political culture centered on paternalistic exploitation of usually obedient people by the elites. The Communist regime demanded obedience, but forswore exploitation, promising food and better living conditions.

Since the death of Mao in 1976, the leaders have worked at creating "socialism with Chinese characteristics." (It looks a lot like capitalism with an authoritarian regime.) Under the leadership of Deng Xiaoping, Jiang Zemin, and Hu Jintao the Communist Party elite has undertaken its own economic/social/cultural revolution. It's been good at many parts of the task, but especially at preserving its own power.

The imperial regimes claimed legitimacy through Confucian order and a "mandate from heaven" under which emperors were seen as pleasing the gods. The Maoist regime claimed legitimacy through egalitarianism and politicizing almost every aspect of life. Today, the Communist Party elite is hoping that a rising standard of living and promises of opportunities in the future will guarantee people's loyalties and not upset its monopoly on political power.

Since Confucian times, the economy has been a command economy. The first task after 1949 was to restore food production. Next, the command was to industrialize — the Chinese version of import substitution. During the Cultural Revolution, the economy (and nearly everything else) took a back seat to egalitarian ideology and intra-Party and personal power struggles.

Beginning with Mao's death, economic commands focused on growth. The irony has been that the Party and the government felt they had to encourage private enterprise and reduce their ability to command in order to achieve the desired growth. Still, control of banking, subsidies of new developments, and manipulation of markets give the political elite significant control. What they have given up is the control over many aspects of people's private lives.

There are glimpses of rule of law in China. The most visible signs are in commercial and contract law. While laws clearly tilt in favor of Chinese interests, the courts can be counted on to enforce the commercial laws as written.

POLITICAL TURNING POINTS

1949	Mao Zedong proclaims the Peoples Republic of China
1949-1953	Land redistribution
1956	Hundred Flowers Campaign
1958-1960	Great Leap Forward
1960-1966	Centralized planning and market-oriented economic rebuilding under Deng Xiaoping and Liu Shaoqui
1964	First nuclear weapons test
1966-1976	Great Proletarian Cultural Revolution
1971	China recognized by the United Nations and US begins process of normalizing relations with PRC
1976	Mao Zedong dies
1978	Deng Xiaoping becomes "paramount leader" and Four Modernizations Campaign endorsed Democracy Wall and "Fifth Modernization" essay
1986	PRC joins GATT
1989	Democracy Movement and Tiananmen massacre; Jiang Zemin becomes head of CPC
1997	Deng Xiaoping dies; Hong Kong reverts to Chinese territory
1993	Jiang Zemin becomes president of PRC
1999	Falun Gong demonstration outside of Zhongnanhai
2000	China joins WTO
2003	Hu Jintao becomes president of PRC

Criminal and civil laws are less developed. Lawsuits are more common than they once were but state interests are rarely on the losing end of decisions. Courts often deal with criminal cases swiftly. Political protest or dissent is usually seen as criminal and sometimes dealt with in extra-judicial ways.

Political legitimacy rests on economic growth and a rising standard of living. The Party has no fall-back position upon which to claim legitimate authority. It has abandoned the ideals of egalitarianism and has yet to adopt any features that would make Party leaders accountable to the citizens. If economic growth falters or if rural standards of living continue to fall behind urban levels, look for evidence of political responses.

3. POLITICAL INSTITUTIONS

As you work your way through this section, it will probably be helpful to look at the diagrams of the structures of the Chinese government and the Communist Party of China in your textbook. The textbooks I have looked at all had useful charts and diagrams.

The Chinese state and regime organizations are modeled on those of the Stalinist Soviet Union. Democratic centralism is the key concept, but there are traces of decentralization as well.

One of the key things to remember is that the CPC and the government are parallel institutions. For every people's congress (government), there's a Party congress. For every government ministry, there's a party office to oversee it. Many times the supervising CPC official and the supervised government official are the same person. Obvious examples are that the last three men to serve as president of the PRC also served as general secretary of the CPC.

In spite of the equality implied by parallel structures of government and party, there's no doubt about where the real power lies. It lies with the Communist Party of China. The CPC is huge, with

> **Core Values ...**
>
> The Chinese Communist Party is the core of leadership of the whole Chinese people. Without this core, the cause of socialism cannot be victorious.
>
> — *Quotations from Chairman Mao Tse-tung* (The Little Red Book), *art-bin.com/art/omao1.html*

over 70 million members (more members than most countries have people). But in China, that means that only a bit over 5% of the population belongs to the CPC.

One of the reasons people still want to belong to the Party (even entrepreneurs are allowed to join) is to exercise power. Another reason is to make contacts. Soviet-style *nomenklatura* is alive and well in China. While private enterprise may offer alternate routes to success these days, the connections people can make inside the Party can be invaluable.

Remember, you not only have to get your name on the *nomenklatura* list, you have to get someone to choose your name. Or you want to know people whose names are chosen in case you ever need a permit to stage, say, a concert by the Rolling Stones in Shanghai or start a taxi service in Jaingyan. The Chinese word for these patron-client relationships is *guanxi*. And as the importance of *nomenklatura* may be in decline, the importance of *guanxi* is rising. And the CPC is still the best place to develop the connections that can lead to advancement.

At a grassroots level, *guanxi* can help people obtain construction or business permits. At higher levels, it can facilitate bank loans and contracts with foreign investors. At the highest levels, it can determine who gets on the Politburo (several Politburo members are sons of former high-ranking

CPC officials.). Sometimes *guanxi* becomes nepotism. It might determine your children's futures. Deng Xiaoping's children and grandchildren are all doing very well for themselves, thank you. One of Deng's grandsons was even born in the USA and is eligible for US citizenship.

Another thing to remember about China is that there is official truth. It's called Marxism-Leninism-Mao Zedong Thought-Deng Xiaoping Theory. Jiang Zemin and Hu Jintao authored books on ideology appropriate for 21st-century China, so their names may yet be added to the awkward moniker of designated truth. Or, perhaps, the official name will be simplified to socialism with Chinese characteristics.

Until then, Hu's version of the "mass line" will have to suffice. The mass line is the Party's broad policy outline. The Four Modernizations was the name given to the 1980s' mass line. The Three Represents followed in the 1990s. "Creating a harmonious society" is the label most often applied to Hu's mass line announced in 2005. All actions and programs have to be made to correspond with the mass line or current version of the designated truth.

Hu's "Constructing a harmonious society" is a fusion of socialism, democracy, and social harmony. The announced goals are to make significant progress in narrowing the wealth gap, increasing employment, improving public service and protecting the environment by 2020.

The *People's Daily* summarized the methods that leaders must follow to create a harmonious society:

"1. Strive for sustained, rapid and coordinated economic growth

"2. Develop socialist democracy

"3. Actively enforce the principle of rule of law

"4. Strengthen ideological and ethical buildup

"5. Maintain social equity and justice

"6. Establish a fine-tuned social management system and well handle the people's internal contradictions

"7. And to beef up environmental protection."[1]

The Party Central Committee in 2006 officially adopted Constructing a Harmonious Society as the mass line. It was the culmination of a series of major changes. The party no longer proclaims itself the party of the proletariat. It is now the

(Re)Defining Democracy of a Different Kind?

We communists are bitterly opposed to the democracy practiced in capitalist countries, that is, to "bourgeois democracy" based on periodic elections with secret ballots for presidents and parliaments or congresses. Bourgeois democracy is an elitist system that guarantees the capitalists run things while workers have no real say in how society works...

The Party is organized on the basis of democratic centralism. The Party is divided into cells, or clubs, which meet regularly to evaluate members' work and to make suggestions about how to improve it, and to evaluate the Party's positions and make suggestions for change. These suggestions are taken by the club leader to section meetings made up of the club leaders and other leading comrades in an area, and by section leaders to the Central Committee. Based on the collective experience of the Party, the leadership decides on new positions (a new line) which all Party members are then bound to put into practice. Only if all of us put the same line into practice can we find out if the line works; if each of us goes our own way, we will never have the common strength of a united Party.

— On Democratic Centralism at the Progressive Labor Party web site,
www.plp.org/pl_magazine/democent.html

party of the "overwhelming majority." Entrepreneurs and business people can now join. Marxist ideology is being replaced as the guiding truth by the need to represent "development needs" and "advanced culture."

The effort to create a "harmonious society" is being reinforced by new teachings about Confucius. The CPC leadership may see the old messages about duty and loyalty as principles that support the legitimacy of their power the way that egalitarianism did for the Maoists. The government has encouraged the creation of private schools based on Confucian ideas and pedagogy.

The Executives

In the government, the top executives are the president and the premier (also referred to as the prime minister). The president is head of state and holds little constitutional power. Recent presidents have been the general secretaries of the CPC, so in reality they have been the leaders with power.

The premier is the head of the State Council, which resembles a parliamentary cabinet. The premier and the other ministers are in charge of the various "departments" of the government bureaucracy.

These executives are elected for five-year terms by the National Peoples Congress after being "nominated" by the CPC's National Party Congress.

The president, the premier, and the most powerful of the elite serve on the Central Military Commission, which oversees the Peoples Liberation Army.

In the CPC, the top executive is the general secretary. He's in charge of the Party bureaucracy, the top level of which is called the Secretariat.

There's also a Central Commission for Discipline and Inspection, which is to keep Party members in line and relatively honest. (In 2010, this group caught Liu Xinyong, a senior official in Chongqing, taking bribes that totaled more than $4 million. He was sentenced to death, but given a reprieve because he paid back over half of the money. It was good publicity for the CPC to oversee the crack down on such a high level crook, but it didn't restore most people's faith in the system. Most of them probably thought Liu had either not bribed the right people or somehow crossed the wrong ones.)

The Legislatures

It might help here to picture the Russian *Matrioshka* dolls. You know, those dolls which have dolls inside them which have dolls inside them which have dolls inside … That's because the Soviet-style legislatures are sort of constructed like that. "On the outside" is a national legislative body. "Inside" that legislature is a smaller, representative group that functions when the legislature is not in session. But "inside" that smaller group is an even smaller group that operates pretty much full time. Those smallest, inside groups are the ones that really have power.

Remember how the Russian president can make decrees with the force of law? These smaller legislative/executive bodies in China can do that, too.

The top legislative body in the government is the National Peoples Congress. Its nearly 3,000 members are chosen by provincial peoples congresses

---

Tiananmen Perspectives

The protests in Tiananmen were primarily focused on demands against corruption, greed, nepotism, and arbitrary bureaucratic rule. When students occupied the square, they created a focal point for the urban workers to vent discontent on these issues, which were also their primary concerns.

— 10 Years On:
Assessing Tiananmen Today at
www.marxist.com/Asia/tiananmen.html

from across the country. All those people show up yearly in Beijing to meet for a couple of weeks. Think for a minute about that. Three thousand people (most of whom serve only one term) from all over the country (some of whom can't even talk to one another) meet as the supreme legislature for a country of over a billion people. How much legislating can they do? It seems like it might take half a day just to take attendance. And then there's all the time it would take each day to file into and out of the Great Hall of the People.

Well, the solution is that the National Peoples Congress chooses a Central Committee of a

The National People's Congress: An Official Description

The NPC, the highest organ of state power in the PRC,... exercises legislative power, revises the Constitution and supervises the implementation of the Constitution; examines and approves national economic and social development plans and reports on their implementation; examines and approves state budgets and reports on their implementation; and elects... the members of the Standing Committee of the NPC, the state president and vice-president, decides on the premier and other members of the State Council, and elects the chairman and other members of the Central Military Commission, the president of the Supreme People's Court, and the procurator-general of the Supreme People's Procuratorate. The NPC has the power to recall the above-mentioned personnel.

The NPC is elected for a term of five years. It usually meets once a year. When the NPC is not in session its Standing Committee exercises state power. The NPC Standing Committee is composed of a chairman, several vice-chairmen, a secretary-general and additional members. Members of the NPC Standing Committee may not concurrently hold any position in any of the state administrative, judicial or procuratorial organs. Under normal circumstances, the NPC Standing Committee meets once every two months. Important day-to-day work is handled at executive meetings attended by the chairman, vice-chairmen and secretary-general.

— "China in Brief" (a Chinese government site),
www.china.org.cn/en/china/politicalsystem/nationalCongress.htm

couple of hundred people to meet every couple of months between plenary sessions. This relatively small group can conduct business for the National Peoples Congress, which can be approved the next time the whole group gets together. That's a little *Matrioshka* doll inside the big one. Inside that is the Central Committee's Standing Committee, which functions when its parent organization is not in session. Symbolically, the Standing Committee is the smallest doll inside that Central Committee. And the Standing Committee functions every day.

In the CPC, the National Party Congress is the top representative institution. It represents party members, not the population in general. Its members are chosen by provincial party congresses. The National Party Congress meets every year, but it has over 2,000 delegates. It has the same

functional problems the National Peoples Congress has. So the Party Congress selects a Central Committee of 150-200 people to run the CPC between sessions.

But the Party Central Committee can't meet all that often, and it's too large to really be effective. So the Central Committee chooses a Politburo (political bureau) of a couple dozen people to run the Party's day-to-day business. (These are some of the main residents of the Zhongnanhai compound next to the Forbidden City in Beijing.)

But the Politburo members all have jobs to do as heads of local party operations or running part of the party Secretariat (bureaucracy) overseeing the government. So we get down to the last little *Matrioshka* doll in the Party when the Politburo chooses a Standing Committee of a half-dozen or so, headed by the general secretary.

That merges the legislative structure of the party with the executive structure. And since the Standing Committee of the Politburo includes the president, the prime minister, and their closest associates (remember *guanxi*?), you also ought to recognize the merging of the party legislative structure with the party executive with the government executive. Pretty neat little package, eh?

The Bureaucracies

As the National Peoples Congress met back in March 2003, the new premier reported on a plan to shrink the government bureaucracy and make the government more efficient (*New York Times*, March 7, 2003). These plans, along with promises to stamp out corruption, sounded much like the plans announced every time a new premier takes office or the NPC meets. In 2007, Premier Wen asserted that maintaining economic growth depended on improving efficiency and encouraging innovation (*Xinhua*, 16 March 2007). In 2010, Wen urged greater efforts to improve efficiency through the adoption of the latest technologies (*Xinhua*, 27 February 2010). Adapting the bureaucracy to function in a more open economy is a massive undertaking. The message will be repeated year after year.

The peak of the government bureaucracy is at the State Council. Here, the government ministers and the premier operate to carry out the policy decisions made by the National Peoples Congress (and the Politburo of the CPC). The offices of the government administration are paralleled by the party bureaucracy, headed by the Secretariat.

In Western democracies, civil servants are, ideally, neutral administrators who carry out the policy decisions of the elected political leaders. The elected leaders choose the heads of the bureaucratic departments (ministries) and supervise from the top. In China, the government bureaucrats

are supervised from the top by the government ministers, but they're also supervised from "alongside" by Party cadres who are assigned to their ministries.

In spite of the appearance of a highly centralized bureaucracy, decentralization is also noticeable. Provincial and even more local ministries find ways to adapt national policies to local conditions. This practice has been going on since Imperial times.

More recently, city government and Party officials — especially in the rapidly growing east — have found ways to promote economic change and growth beyond what the central government and Party expected. Shanghai, where former president Jiang Zemin was Party leader until 1989, has been especially successful in pushing the envelope of economic reform and development. Do you think that might have anything to do with *guanxi* connections between national leaders in Beijing and the political elite in Shanghai?

Even the official description of these developments quickly proceeds from describing the "step-by-step" plan for Special Economic Zones to a situation in which "areas adopt different preferential policies" and then to extending "special preferential policies to the Pudong New Zone that are not yet enjoyed by the special economic zones. …"

The centralized, totalitarian model is much too simplistic to describe China. (Is that ambiguity raising its head again?) Be very careful of any simplistic generalizations when you think or write about China.

The PLA

The Peoples Liberation Army deserves special mention. When the Kuomintang attacked Jianxi, the successful Communist region in the late 1920s, the Communists were forced into a retreat that's become known as the Long March. During that year-long running battle, the Party became the Peoples Liberation Army. The civil war and the

---

The Art of *Guanxi*

Guanxi — literally "connections" — is sometimes claimed to be the magic formula for business success in China...

Dr. Shan Ma of Queensland University of Technology's Graduate School of Business argues that because Chinese culture is essentially more people-focused than issue-focused, *guanxi* is a "ubiquitous" feature of doing business in China. People will typically think *guanxi* first and the most important question about a prospective business undertaking may not be about skills, abilities or business issues but rather "Do you have *guanxi* here?"...

Insiders — members of the group — are thus treated differently to outsiders, says Dr. Ma. "Guanxi can give you insider status — or at least bring you closer to the inside," he adds...

Whether or not *guanxi* is a unique aspect of Chinese culture, indelibly imprinted on all behaviour, or simply the legacy of imperfect market and government mechanisms, it is a feature of contemporary life...

from Chin Communications, Melbourne, Australia
www.chincommunications.com.au/news_more.php?id_news=19
accessed 1 March 2010

Japanese invasion that followed made the PLA more and more important. The commanders of the Long March ruled China from 1949 until Deng Xiaoping died. In many ways, the PLA was the Party and the Party was the PLA until well into the Cultural Revolution.

As the Four Modernizations began in the late '70s, the PLA was one of the targets of modernization, but the government didn't have the resources it wanted. Thus the PLA was given a pretty free hand to go into business for itself to raise money for modernization. It ran hotels, resorts, construction companies, and factories that produced pirated copies of recordings, videotapes, and computer software. That last one was a bit embarrassing. Even more anomalous was the PLA business that manufactured and sold TV satellite dishes. This was at a time when the government had "passed a law" making it illegal for individuals to own satellite dishes.

After the PLA's cooperation in putting down the 1989 demonstrations, the government began finding more money for modernization, and PLA eco-nomic adventures were restricted. Still the importance of the PLA is demonstrated by the existence of the Party's Military Affairs Commission and the government's Central Military Commission. Emphasizing the importance of those two bodies is the fact that only the highest-ranking officials are members.

The Judiciary

The Chinese judicial system has one feature that is probably familiar to Americans. There's a Supreme Peoples Court at the top of a hierarchy of Peoples Courts that handle criminal cases. The lower courts have original jurisdiction, while the intermediate and higher courts have only appellate jurisdictions. The courts are responsible to the National Peoples Congress.

Since the beginning of economic reforms, the government has been working on creating a new legal code with a special emphasis on commercial and property law. Lawsuits can now be brought to court. As you might expect, reform is more successful in this area than in criminal law.

There are a variety of criminal law organizations. The public security bureaus (police) include an armed force that's much like a military organization. They are centralized and run by ministries in Beijing. These ministries also operate the prison system.

The key to the system is the Supreme Peoples Procuratorate. Modeled after the Soviet example (which in turn had been modeled on the Napoleonic example), the Procuratorate works closely with the public security bureaus. The ministry is organized nationally with provincial and local branches. Its job is to investigate cases of suspected illegal activity, to prosecute those cases where crime is found, and to guarantee ("defend") the rights of those brought to trial. One result of this process is a conviction rate of over 99% of cases brought to trial. The procurator general also supervises the courts to make sure they are operating correctly.

Local Governments

Sub-national governments are analogous to the national government. There are people's congresses at provincial, city, county, and township levels. They are the twins of local Party congresses. They implement national policies and select delegates for the congresses one step up in the hierarchy. They also select, from *nomenklatura* lists, local adminis-trators. As you might guess from the Pudong New Zone example cited earlier, economic development is one of their main tasks. It requires coordination and cooperation among the local congresses and the local government and Party cadres. When the economic and power prizes are huge, the competition can sometimes overwhelm the cooperation.

At the lowest level of government/Party activity are the neighborhood and village committees. As the roles of the government-owned *danwei* decline, the importance of these committees grows. Rural villages are supposed to have competitive elections for "mayors." In some places they do. In other places, Party cadres are able to prevent elections or rig the voting. There have been many (hundreds? thousands?) of protests about misgovernment at the local level in the past few years. The Party and the government have tried to prevent publicity, but there are indications that villages with honestly elected leaders are less likely to be the scenes of protest.

Party cadres are instrumental in organizing village committees and keeping track of what's going on in the village or neighborhood. These committees organize mediation services, which deal with conflict and give Party leaders insight into what is going on.

Special Economic Zones and Open Coastal Cities

In recent years, the special economic zones have led the country in establishing new systems, upgrading industries and opening wider to the outside world, serving as national models. ...

Since its founding in 1992, the Shanghai Pudong New Zone has made great progress in both absorbing foreign capital and accelerating the economic development. ... The state has extended special preferential policies to the Pudong New Zone that are not yet enjoyed by the special economic zones. ... In 1999, the GDP of the Pudong New Zone came to 80 billion yuan. ... The 5,900 foreign-funded enterprises, with a total investment of nearly US$30 billion, and over 5000 domestic enterprises from all over the country ... have formed six pillar industries.

— "China in Brief" (a Chinese government site),
www.china.org.cn/e-china/openingup/sez.htm

4. CITIZENS, SOCIETY, AND THE STATE

Picture a country where everyone reads the same language, but most people can't understand the speeches made by the "head of state." When Deng Xiaoping was the "paramount leader" (he avoided formal positions of authority), Chinese Central Television (CCTV) had to show subtitles during his televised speeches so most people would know what he was saying. His Sichuan accent was so thick that people in Beijing, Shanghai, and Guang-zhou had a great deal of trouble understanding him.

What you should see in that example is unity and division. Look for that paradox in other places as you remind yourself about your studies of China.

Imagine a country where families in a Confucian structure were responsible for enforcing most laws.

In China, most people (about 57%) live in rural areas. (Just a few years ago, that percentage was much higher.) The incomes of the rural and urban Chinese are dramatically different. The education levels (and the educational opportunities) of rural and urban Chinese are very different. Exposure to new ideas and technologies is affected by residence. Is it any wonder that political attitudes differ greatly? Or is it any wonder that the rural-urban cleavage is the most enduring division in Chinese society? Stories about the unsophisticated rube from the sticks coming to the city abound in Chinese literature.

The power of these coinciding cleavages has sometimes caused the political leaders to pay special attention to the rural population. Land reform was the focus of much effort in the 1950s and '60s. During the Cultural Revolution, intellectuals and students were "sent down" to learn from the peasants while working on farms and in rural villages. One of the first goals of the Four Modernizations campaign was to raise rural incomes. It was successful, but since the early '80s, rural development hasn't kept pace with urban development. Once again at the beginning of 2010, the

> It's an accepted generalization of political science that when **cleavages** (divisions) in society coincide with one another, the boundaries are strengthened. For instance, in the early 19th-century USA, nearly all the slavery supporters lived in the southern part of the country. Nearly all of slavery's opponents lived in the north. The coincidence of the geographic and issue cleavages made the division more powerful than it would have been if slavery and anti-slavery sentiment had been nationwide.

government announced new plans to increase income and reduce taxes for rural residents and to reform the *hukou* (household registration system) [*Xinhua*, 26 and 27 February 2010].

Relaxation of residency restrictions has made it possible for many rural people to move to cities in search of work. However, most of them make the move without official permission. (That's why the government recently announced changes.) Most peasants end up end up (like rural migrants in many Third World countries) living in dire poverty without the support of family. The desperate poverty of rural areas and the promises of the city still motivate people to seek better lives. They make up a large part of the "floating population" (upwards of 100 million unemployed people not connected with any official institution) which is a challenge for the state.

That situation has aggravated another rural-urban difference. Young peasants abandon schools for the chance to get an unskilled job in the city. In the 1990s the number of secondary school students in rural areas declined. It doesn't bode well for official plans for continued growth.

There are important generational cleavages, too.

Traditionally the power elite in China has been much older than in other countries. It's still true today when the young generation of leaders is made up of 60-something men.

Just younger than the current top leadership is the "sent down" generation, about equivalent in age to America's baby boomers. Many of these people lost educational and formative career opportunities during the Cultural Revolution. They also lost their patron-client connections. (Remember *guanxi?*)

The children of the "sent down" generation are a transitional group. They may well, in spite of the example of the Tiananmen demonstrators of 1989, provide the next real power elite.

The urban grandchildren of the "sent down" generation are becoming new materialistic middle and upper classes. Their parents may still want to belong to the CPC, but educated, young urbanites want politics to leave them alone.

The development of these groups of urban materialists is adding to the social class mix. One big question is how a non-political, relatively affluent little group will fit into Chinese society and politics.

Some of these non-political urbanites have joined the Communist Party for practical, not ideological reasons. Others have created or joined groups that look like civil society associations. As long as these groups avoid anything that looks like politics (and the Party and the government are watching), they're allowed to exist. But what is political? It seems that anything the CPC interprets as a challenge to its supremacy is political. Therefore, the independent organizing of the Falun Gong and other religious groups is forbidden.

THE POWER OF TRADITION

At times in imperial China, it was a capital crime to look the emperor in the eye. Anyone approaching the tall throne of the emperor had to kowtow (*koutou*).

Some observers have suggested that one reason the 1989 Tiananmen demonstrations ended so violently was the cheeky behavior of some of the students. The argument suggests that if the protesters had been more deferential to the Party leadership, some more peaceful means of resolving the situation might have been possible.

The 1989 demonstrations were very different from the other mass campaigns in the PRC. They were spontaneous, grassroots social movements. In other ways the demonstrations were not unlike the officially organized mass campaigns common before 1976. Other mass campaigns were efforts to get everyone involved and to politicize daily life. The Great Leap Forward and the Cultural Revolution both began as mass campaigns. So did the effort to rid the country of disease-carrying flies. And before that, the effort to get rid of grain-eating birds. Today, acquiescence to government policy is all that's required.

Education, like health care, was a high priority in the first 30 years of the PRC. Nearly 100% of the children attend elementary schools. Only about half attend high school. Even today, as the emphasis shifts to training skilled workers, politics is part of almost every lesson. The CPC still monitors teachers and students. Most kids belong to the Young Pioneers until they're 15.

Both older and newer forms of political socialization are becoming more obvious. Even though the Internet and e-mail are closely watched and controlled, they expose many people to ideas the CPC isn't fond of. In spite of efforts like that, more and more Chinese are gaining access to information on the Internet [*Wall Street Journal*, 31 December 2009]. In rural areas, traditional spiritual practices and clan loyalties are more visible. A youth culture centered on rock music, video games, television, and fashion is apparent in the cities. And what do urban people think of the successful entrepreneurs who, dressed in Pierre Cardin suits, drive around Shanghai, Beijing, and other cities in their BMWs while talking on cell phones?

Since the institution of the responsibility system, peasants have had more independence in their farming operations. That's given people more ability to figure out what's best for themselves. In the vast humanity of rural China, it's also made them vulnerable to expensive petty tyrannies. Rural cadres and village officials often manage to charge peasants fees that go beyond permissible taxes. Farmers have talked to each other and, in some areas, even organized to resist these administrative fees. News of protests filters out of the villages, even as far as Western media. Protests have taken place. Officials have been attacked. Protesters have been arrested and killed. (See the notes below about local elections.)

In the grand exchange of socialism, Chinese got the "iron rice bowl" (*tiefanwan*). It meant that workers at a *danwei* (literally, a work unit that might be a factory, a mine, a hospital, a government bureau, or a state farm) were provided with not only a salary, but also a lifetime job (sometimes positions that a worker's child could "inherit"), health care, day care, schools, apartments, and pensions. The salaries were low, but more egalitarian than market salaries. The social services came with government controls like ration certificates and permissions to have children. (*Danwei* "social workers" kept track of women's menstrual cycles, made lists of couples eligible to have children, and asked regularly about couples' successes and failures in conceiving children.)

In today's China, people are offered the opportunity to find their own jobs and earn market wages. They give up the benefits of the *danwei*. In fact, many of the *danwei* have gone or are going bankrupt. Deprived of their monopolies, no longer guaranteed markets, and saddled with incredible costs, most can only continue because of subsidies and extravagant lines of credit from government-owned banks.

From the early days of the Communist revolution, elections were encouraged. Communist organizers in villages used elections to unify peasants in the land reform process. The CPC and the government glorify the election of representatives to peoples and party congresses. Since the beginning of the

---

China's 'Iron Rice Bowl' Off the Table

China will phase out the "jobs for life" system for its 30 million public institution employees over the next few years, state media said yesterday [January 7, 2003].

Within five years, the Government will put in place a new system under which the nation's 1.3 million state-owned institutions will draw up employment contracts for their workers. ...

This means the end of lifetime employment for state workers.

— Agence France-Presse, in a story in the *Sydney Morning Herald*, www.smh.com.au/articles/ 2003/01/07/1041566406834.html

Civil service is still seen as a way to get a job and benefits for life. In 2009, over a million people passed the basic qualifications exam and were eligible for about 15,000 government jobs.

— Beijing Calling, "Iron Rice Bowl Dreams." 27 October 2009

---

responsibility system and the Four Modernizations, rural villages have been electing village and township councils — sometimes from among multiple candidates. The National Peoples Congress certified proclamations from 1997 and 1998 that there be more candidates than offices open in these elections. National leaders hoped this would reduce the corruption of local Party and government officials. These elections still don't have the effect they do in Western democracies. In many places CPC cadres are still routinely elected, and in other places clan elders are regularly chosen.

A 2009 report by the Carter Center said that village elections had become nearly universal and that bribery and the lack of civic education were serious problems. Another problem is that Party cadres think democratization is moving too quickly and that peasants are not capable of choosing their own leaders. Nonetheless, the report's authors concluded that the elections did contribute to the legitimacy of the village government.[2]

We can identify political values that have their origins in the past and have been reinforced by socialism.

- **Collective responsibility**. In Imperial times, family leaders took care of all family members; village leaders took care of villagers (landlords' stored surpluses were often distributed freely to peasants during times of crop failure), and regional mandarins built irrigation canals and levees along rivers. In Communist times, the collective and the *danwei* took care of their workers. Currently, peasants and workers are expected to take on the job of supporting themselves. This may contradict collective responsibility, but it reinforces another theme of Chinese political culture.

- **Struggle and harmony.** This is like the yin and yang of Taoist philosophy. Whether it was struggling against the flooding Yangtze, the Beijing dust storms, or the attacking warlords, life was difficult. Striving for harmony against these conditions was preferable to seeking victory — although frequent peasant rebellions were violent attempts to achieve harmony. The communist emphasis on cooperative work fit right in. Hu's mass line of creating a harmonious society fits well with this theme of traditional culture.

- **Deference to moral leaders.** In imperial China, the Confucian ideal was a moral emperor. When an emperor was corrupt, he lost the mandate of heaven. In Maoist terms, the slogan for leaders and cadres was "Serve the people." Even today, the government is anxious to publicize its attempts to prosecute high-level corruption. A 1996 study indicated that at least three-fourths of

the people in China thought that they ought to follow the decisions of "upright leaders."[3]

Print and broadcast media are tightly controlled by a CPC and a government desiring to be the sole sources of information. The central television network broadcasts across the country and regional adjuncts produce some local programming. Rupert Murdoch's STAR Group satellite service began broadcasting Phoenix, a Chinese language channel in 2001. In order to do so, STAR Group agreed to allow the Chinese government control over news content.

The government, the Party, and the PLA publish national and regional newspapers. They feature reprints of important speeches by leaders and news about official events. Some academic institutions and think tanks publish magazines, but they tend to be technical and avoid political topics.

Technology is challenging the state near-monopoly. During the 1989 Tiananmen demonstrations, protesters made use of telephones and fax machines to communicate with each other and with expatriate students in other countries. Today, the Internet offers other opportunities for communication and access to less controlled news. The government makes massive efforts to limit these opportunities. Internet cafes and online discussion groups are monitored and censored. Thousands of people and computers eavesdrop on e-mail traffic. Bloggers and Web page hosts are required to register with the government, which regularly blocks access to undesirable content. Government firewalls sit between Chinese networks and the global Internet. Hackers find ways through firewalls and activists use code words to discuss sensitive topics. But the risks are great. Violators are serving long prison sentences as warnings to others as much as for punishment.

5. POLITICAL AND ECONOMIC CHANGE

Elisabeth Rosenthal, quoted earlier, said that "Slow, stuttering transfers of power, often lasting years, are the rule in Chinese politics." The primary example of that would be the transfer from Deng Xiaoping to Jiang Zemin, Li Peng, and their allies. The transition to President Hu and Premier Wen was much smoother, but it took more than two years for Hu to gain all three positions of supreme leadership.

The successions may be slow and stuttering, but they are peaceful and fairly smooth. Before that was Mao Zedong. When his power was threatened after the failures of the Great Leap Forward, the result was the chaos of the Cultural Revolution where Maoists tried to replace the Party and the government cadres with people loyal only to Mao in new revolutionary institutions.

Economic change in the last 20 years has been deliberate. The disruptions have been severe for many people, but so far have not caused great upheavals (with the exception of 1989). Economic growth, fueled by government spending and foreign investment, has helped to maintain social stability, at least in the eastern cities.[4]

Since Deng Xiaoping took control of the Four Modernizations campaign, political change has been stifled. Many people who might advocate political changes have been co-opted by economic growth and opportunities for material success. The CPC maintains a strong hold on political power and state authority.

Another subject for consideration in this topic is probably the status of Taiwan and the relationship between the two Chinas. People and businesses from Taiwan have become significant investors in the PRC, especially in the provinces just across the Taiwan Strait. There is large-scale trade between the two. Yet, the PRC claims Taiwan as a rebel province. Taiwan wants to maintain its independence and special relationship with the PRC. And there's always the matter of the native Taiwanese independence movement.

Economic change, like political change, is directed by the Party and the government. Economic

change is less amenable to direction from the government than it used to be. But, the government's control of the banking sector gives it the power to prop up failing *danwei* and offer or deny loans to new ventures. Since some sectors of the economy are growing faster than economic activity anywhere else on earth, foreign investors would like to buy pieces of China's banking "industry." In the early 1990s, European and American banks were allowed to buy some shares of Chinese banks. The global economic crisis a few years later caused most of those foreign investors to sell their interests. Remember, banking offers the government an impressive source of power. It's not anxious to share that power — especially with foreign interests. In addition, aligning Chinese accounting and banking protocols with global standards would probably expose massive corruption. And no one in power wants that. Watch for developments in Chinese banking for clues about political change.

6. PUBLIC POLICY

At this point you have read about the major public policy issues. You know that on a national level, policy is made by a self-perpetuating elite in the CPC. You also know that provincial and local officials find ways to adapt or negate those policies when they threaten vested regional or local interests.

In the national context, the elite is very nationalistic. Their goals are long term. China will become, if they have their way, an economic and political superpower. They are learning how to participate in the G8 negotiations. China has joined the WTO. China will change. So will the G8 group and the WTO.

Economic growth is at the top of China's priorities list. What prices are the political elite willing to pay for the growth? Will they abandon millions of surplus workers in the *danwei*? Will they suppress rural discontent or act as they did in the early '80s to improve peasants' standard of living? They've allowed capitalists to join the Communist Party.

Will they share power? Will they share power with markets? As students of Chinese government and politics, we seem to be limited to analyzing results because of the closed decision making system.

As we look at those results, we can see a first-rate education system for a tiny Chinese elite. What of the collapse of rural school systems? What of the inability of peasants and urban migrants to pay school fees? President Hu has talked about subsidizing local schools. Has he done it? In major cities even tourists see beggars on the streets kowtowing to passers-by. Often they bow on the sidewalks in front of "big character" posters explaining their predicaments. Is this a problem the government will deal with? Beggars were arrested and "shipped" out of Beijing during the 2008 Olympics. Will the government continue to deal with the symptoms or address the problem?

Not all the protests in China recently have been about corrupt local officials or unpaid pensions. Some have concerned flagrant and dangerous pollution from factories, old and new. How will the state respond to a restive populace? How will it respond to environmental degradation? Will new policies be developed?

In spite of the promises of the mass line, policy-making appears to be directed by

- concerns about maintaining the power of the current elite
- desires to make China a world power
- needs for an orderly society
- the compliance of a politically-passive citizenry
- hopes for respect from the global community

Can you find examples of government policies or actions to illustrate these?

FOOTNOTES

1 *China Daily* at *www.chinadaily.com.cn*

2 China Program of the Carter Center, "Understanding Chinese Village Elections." February 2009.

3 Hu Fu and Yun-han Chu, "The Transformation of Civic Culture in Mainland China, Taiwan, and Hong Kong," 1996, cited in Almond and Powell, *Comparative Politics Today, A World View*, 2003, p. 444.

4 Outgoing Prime Minister Zhu Rongji is reported to have told the National Peoples Congress in March of 2003 that such government spending must continue in order to maintain a growth rate of at least 7% a year. — "Retiring Premier Says China Must Pump Money Into Economy" by Joseph Kahn, *New York Times*, March 6, 2003.

REVIEW EXERCISE

This little exercise is not meant to be comprehensive. It's meant to get you thinking about some of the basic facts and point out areas you might have to review more thoroughly. My responses follow.

1. It seems that "most similar systems" comparisons between China would involve
   (A) measuring China's and Nigeria's GDPs
   (B) comparing entrepreneurial activity in China with that in Iran
   (C) looking at legislative processes in China and the UK
   (D) finding out how Putin's consolidation of power compares to the efforts by CPC leaders to maintain their power
   (E) examining China's party system alongside of Mexico's party system

2. China's role in global politics has
   (A) been based on spreading of civil liberties and human rights in China
   (B) declined as China concentrated on domestic growth
   (C) grown as its economic power has grown
   (D) declined because China has refused to compromise on the principles of socialism
   (E) grown as its ability to extend its military power has increased

3. One of the major threats to the legitimacy of the Chinese regimes is
   (A) the danger of slowing economic growth
   (B) competition from free enterprise in Taiwan
   (C) non-competitive elections
   (D) lack of civil liberties
   (E) the decrees made by the Central Committee of the national legislature

4. One reason outsiders are skeptical about effective lawmaking by the National People's Congress is that
   (A) most of the delegates serve life-long terms
   (B) thousands of delegates meeting for 10 days a year are hardly able to legislate for a country of over a billion people
   (C) rural delegates outnumber urban delegates and don't understand the issues involved with industrial economies
   (D) only a minority of delegates attend the legislative sessions
   (E) the NPC's Standing Committee of the Central Committee only meets during the annual legislative session

5. A major reason CPC and government executives and legislatures are parallel to one another is that
   (A) the constitution requires it
   (B) government leaders and legislators are better educated and can instruct Party cadres
   (C) the President, the Premier, and NPC delegates are unlikely to be Party members
   (D) more Party and government jobs helps to reduce unemployment
   (E) the structure keeps the CPC intimately involved in governing

6. The PLA
   (A) has remained a strictly military organization since its founding in the 1930s
   (B) has been a compliant tool of political leaders since 1949
   (C) struggled to survive during the Cultural Revolution
   (D) basically withdrew from politics after the Tiananmen protests and attacks of 1989
   (E) remains one of the most important political forces in the PRC

7. The most recent changes in China's legal system
    (A) have evolved from popular demands for stricter law enforcement
    (B) focus on maintaining the economic power of the state owned corporations
    (C) have meant more political control of the judiciary than before
    (D) guarantee greater individual freedoms
    (E) center on the creation of commercial and civil law

8. In its unified state, China's local authorities
    (A) have little or no option about what policy goals to enact
    (B) are constitutionally guaranteed wide local powers
    (C) often find ways to pursue local interests
    (D) regularly hold referenda to determine local policies
    (E) can pretty much ignore the policies made in Beijing

9. Unlike most developing countries, China's people
    (A) benefit from traditionally strong environmental protections
    (B) suffer from high levels of unemployment
    (C) have a standard of living rivaling that of most EU countries
    (D) are nearly half urban
    (E) benefit from nearly universal secondary education

10. Traditional values that have supported authoritarian government in China include all the following EXCEPT
    (A) the need to struggle against adversity
    (B) deference to moral leaders
    (C) the value of harmony in public and private life
    (D) individualism with an emphasis on liberty
    (E) collective responsibility for community well being

    (For responses, see below)

CHAPTER 8 RESPONSES:
1. D, 2. C, 3. A, 4. B, 5. E, 6. D, 7. E, 8. C, 9. D, 10. D

9: Know ... Nigeria

1. INTRODUCTION TO COMPARATIVE POLITICS

The first questions to ask about Nigeria relate to the idea of using it as a case study. In what ways is it typical of Third World countries? In what ways is it not typical? How is it typical of other African countries? Can we usefully compare it to other multi-ethnic countries like Russia or Iran? Are there useful lessons to be learned by comparing it to other resource-rich countries like Iran, Russia or Mexico?

The fact that politics is such a high-stakes game in Nigeria is one of the ways it resembles most Third World countries. The government controls so much of the productive resources, and people see politics as the way to get their share of the "national cake" that is government spending. There's no tradition of accommodation. Politics is a zero-sum game. Can a society that emphasizes communal responsibilities and communal self-sufficiency adapt to accommodation and compromise?

Nigeria is also like most Third World countries because it's divided by ethnic and cultural cleavages. Politics is still a contest between northerners, westerners, and southerners. Sometimes it's a contest between southerners and south-southerners. All those factors (religion, education, geography, wealth, social status, et al) that reinforce those cleavages fit into the political environment as well.

Speaking of environments, another way that Nigeria resembles most Third World countries is the devastation of the natural environment. The amount of arable land in the oil-producing regions has been reduced. Clean water in the Niger Delta is more and more difficult to find. People who

depend on fishing have to find new ways of surviving. The rapidly growing population in the north puts greater and greater pressure on the land. In the state of Plateau, most notably around the city of Jos, herders and farmers fight over available pastures and fields.

Case studies that compare Nigeria with other Third World countries should be instructive in lots of ways. Given the experiments in constitutional engineering in Nigeria, the country would also seem to be a good model for evaluating political science generalizations. For instance, we could ask what we can learn about unitary and federal systems from the Nigerian example. Nigeria is the longest lasting federation in Africa, but the military regimes have been virtually unitary. It would also be a good place to test theories about cleavages, cooperation, and conflict.

It may be a place to evaluate the effectiveness of economic and political liberalization policies. Is transparency a universally good idea in business, politics, and government? Can private enterprise deliver goods and services more efficiently than subsidized parastatals?

If we apply systems theory to Nigeria, it's possible to see a political system overwhelmed by inputs and feedback. That may help explain the ineffectiveness of public policy (poor public services, inadequate food, water, and health care, growing threat of HIV/AIDS, inability to curb corruption). We have to ask whether Nigeria can succeed as a nation-state. Or can republican government work? Are there models from other countries that suggest ways for the political system in Nigeria to work?

2. SOVEREIGNTY, AUTHORITY, AND POWER

Nigeria is a country of nearly 150 million people in West Africa. Its boundaries were created by the competition between French and British imperialists in the 18th and 19th centuries. In 1963, the US State Department published an information sheet on the newly independent Nigeria touting it as a model for the future of African democracy. Today, Nigeria is a country with valuable natural resources, incredible poverty (per capita GDP is about $2,400), and a rapidly growing population. Once able to produce all its own food, Nigeria in 2008 imported $1 billion worth of wheat from the USA[1], $125 million [worth of] sugar[2], and $700 million [worth of] rice from Thailand.[3]

Even though there was no such thing as Nigeria before the 20th century, Nigerian people have rich cultural heritages.

In the north, Islam, trans-Saharan trade, vigorous city states, and several vital cultural/ethnic groups combined in various ways to create a series of civilizations. The modern culmination was a Fulani empire, which ruled a huge area. The political leadership was centered on the Sultan of Sokoto and a Fulani aristocracy. However, before colonial times, people in the north of what is now Nigeria did not see themselves as a single nation.

In present-day Benin (just west of Nigeria) and the southwest of what is now Nigeria, the kingdoms of Oyo, Ife, and Benin were among the political entities that flourished well into the 19th century. The kingdoms were less centralized and less autocratic than the sultanates of the north. There were accepted procedures for unseating rulers. These Yoruba people were no more unified than northerners before the Europeans showed up. Tropical agriculture and trade formed the basis of their economies.

Nigeria's southeast is dominated by the great Niger River delta and dense tropical forests. In this environment lived hundreds of autonomous communities. The societies were often very egalitarian, both materially and politically. (One textbook labels these societies "acephalous," inferring that there were no formal political leaders.[4]) In response to the intrusion of Europeans and contact with Yoruba, Hausa, Fulani, and other groups, many of the people in southeastern Nigeria began to identify themselves as Ibo or Igbo. However, this identification is almost more a negative feature (i.e., "We're not them."). Today, various groups of

A Rich Cultural Heritage

Timbuktu [north and west of the later Fulani Empire] was more than merely a great intellectual nucleus of the West African civilizations … it was one of the most splendid scientific centers of the time period corresponding to the European Medieval and Renaissance eras … it was celebrated as one of the world's most significant seats of learning…

— The Great University of Sankore at Timbuktu, *www.cwo.com/~lucumi/timbuktu.html*

Magnificent terra-cotta objects have been found in Nok, in Nigeria, dating back to a period some time between 500 BC and 500 AD.

… Against this background of creativity and craftsmanship, the Yoruba kingdoms of Benin and Ife sprang up between the 11th and 12th centuries.

— The Story of Africa, *www.bbc.co.uk/worldservice/africa/features/storyofafrica/4chapter7.shtml*

HISTORICAL AND POLITICAL TURNING POINTS

ca. 700	Muslim merchants reach Hausa states
ca. 900	Beginnings of Kanem-Borno empire
ca. 1400	Beginnings of Yoruba and Benin
1485	First Portuguese trading post; beginnings of slave trade
1630	Founding of Lagos
ca. 1800	Fulani takeover of Hausa states
1807	British outlaw slave trade and patrol West African coast
1861	Lagos becomes a British colony
1885	Berlin Conference
1888	Yorubaland becomes a British protectorate
1893	Southeastern area named Niger Coast Protectorate
1903	Northern areas become a protectorate
1914	Creation of the colony of Nigeria
1914-1918	World War I
1920	National Congress of British West Africa founded
1923	Herbert Macauley helps found the Nigerian National Democratic Party
ca. 1935	Nnamdi Azikiwe helps found the Nigerian Youth Movement
1939-1945	World War II

1948	"Nigerianization" of civil service in Nigeria begins
1960	Independence (as a constitutional monarchy)
1963	Nigeria becomes a republic with Azikiwe as president
1966-1979	Military regimes
1967-1970	Biafra declares independence and civil war
1979-1983	Second republic
1983-1999	Military regimes
1991	Abuja created as new capital
1993	Abiola apparently wins presidential election; election annulled; General Sani Abacha seizes power
1995	Ken Saro-Wiwa and other activists hanged; Abiola, Obasanjo and others imprisoned
1998	Abacha dies; Abiola dies
1999	Former General Obasanjo elected president
2003	Obasanjo reelected president
2005	Club of Paris forgives $20 billion of Nigeria's foreign debt
2007	First civilian transition as Yar'Adua elected president
2010	Yar'Adua illness and death crisis

Igbos find themselves in as much conflict and disagreement with each other as with "outsiders."

Near the end of the 15th century, Portuguese and other Western European slave traders appeared on the West African coast. In the north and the southwest, they found organized political entities that were willing to do business with them. Guns and other modern technologies were incentive enough to persuade them to sell their enemies into slavery. No settlers like those who went to the Americas arrived, but merchants and missionaries made their way to Africa. In the 19th century, the imperialists came.

As in India, British trading companies made the initial contacts in Nigeria. Christian missionaries soon followed. When the colonial competitions (especially with France) heated up after 1860, the British government began claiming territory as a run up to the 1885 Berlin Conference.

These European contacts had a variety of effects on the cultures in what is now Nigeria. Bureaucratic regimes were reinforced in the north when they became agents of British colonial rule. In no area did the British show Africans a model of democratic government. They demonstrated authoritarian, law and order administration.

The British also modeled a regime that put politics squarely in charge of an economy based on export of raw materials and cash crops, not on industrialization. The commercial links forged between British merchants and Yoruba traders brought Africans into the global economy of the 18th and 19th centuries, although not as equal partners.

In all areas of the country, British domination strengthened the national identities of Hausa, Fulani, Yoruba, Igbo, and other groups. In the process, the Europeans may have set the stage for undermining future democratic governments by demonstrating that there was one set of rules for those who ran things and another set of rules for those who were "governed."

In the southeast, Roman Catholic missionaries were most successful in establishing congregations and schools. Western education meant that Igbo peoples often went to the front of the line for choosing administrators when it came to establishing a 20th-century country of Nigeria. (By the 1920s, only three percent of Nigeria's elementary schools were in the north of the country.)

Independence movements began in the 1920s — as they did in many colonial areas. By then there were small groups of Western-educated Nigerians, and they believed that World War I had been fought in part for democracy and "self determination of peoples."

Like the colony, the independence movement was divided by geography and culture. The three biggest nationalistic political parties were based respectively on Hausa-Fulani (Northern Peoples Congress), Yoruba (Action Group), and Igbo (National Council of Nigeria and the Cameroons, later called the National Congress of Nigerian Citizens) identities.

> ## A Father of the Nation
>
> Sir Herbert Macauley (1864-1946), politician, nationalist and founder of Nigerian nationalism, was born in Lagos on 14th November 1864, the son of a school principal. He trained as a land surveyor and civil engineer in Plymouth, England.
>
> Upon his graduation and return to Nigeria in 1893, he worked with the colonial government, and later resigned to establish a private practice in Lagos. Subsequently, he began a campaign against colonial rule and discrimination, and in 1922, he founded the Nigeria National Democratic Party, which won all the seats to the Legislative Council. He was later to become the first president of the National Council of Nigeria and Cameroons. …
>
> Sir Herbert Macauley died in Kano on 7th May 1946 in the course of leading the party on a nationwide campaign tour.
>
> — Nigerian Central Bank,
> *www.cenbank.org/macualey.htm*

The independence movement was quite peaceful. After World War II, the British began preparing for Nigerian independence. The colonial administration wrote a constitution that was harshly criticized by Nigerians. A second version was more acceptable, and the first elections were held in 1959. Independence became a reality in 1960.

The first republic began as a constitutional monarchy (Queen Elizabeth II was head of state) with a bicameral parliament, a prime minister, cabinet, a supreme court, and a three-state federal system. Three years later, an elected president replaced the British queen as head of state and a fourth state was created.[5] Government and politics after independence were seen (as they were in colonial times) as jobs for clerks. The Nigerian army attracted the "best and the brightest" of young Nigerian men. A parliamentary system had been created, but people had been taught (socialized) to follow orders.

That may explain why army officers were so impatient with the political leaders' inability to deal with the problems of state building. Regional rivalries and conflicts even made it impossible for the Nigerian government to carry out a census for reapportioning the legislature. (Southerners feared and northerners hoped the census would show that the majority of Nigerians lived in the north.)

The first republic ended in 1966 with riots and attacks on Igbo people in northern cities and attacks on northerners in the south. After appeals for the army's support from Prime Minister Balewa (NPC party) and President Awolowo (NCNC party), a group of Igbo generals led a *coup d'état* that was followed by a countercoup led by generals from Nigeria's "Middle Belt" (the area in the central part of the country in between the territories dominated by the three largest ethnic/cultural groups).

Igbo military and political leaders in the southeastern part of Nigeria then tried to secede and form a new country of Biafra. A two-year civil war ensued. Biafra was not successful in separating itself from Nigeria, and General Yakubu (Jack) Gowon led a military government attempting to recreate Nigeria. He was better at reconciliation and increasing the size of the army than at establishing a civilian government or at economic development.

Another military coup in 1975, the assassination of the military leader in '76, and another coup attempt led to a military government headed by Olusegun Obasanjo. General Obasanjo promised civilian government, and the second republic was created in 1979.

The second republic was based on a presidential/congressional model, not the Westminster model of the first republic. It was also much more centralized and activist (especially in economics) than the first republic. Its leaders had no more success in nation building than did earlier political and military elites. They were more successful at enriching themselves.

More states were created to defuse rivalries between the largest ethnic groups, and a new capital city, Abuja, was created to remove the seat of government from the heart of Yorubaland. The oil boom of the late 1970s brought huge amounts of money and corruption to Nigeria. The crash of oil prices in the early 1980s brought fiscal catastrophe. In 1983, after an outrageously fraudulent second presidential election, a group of Middle Belt generals took over the government.

It took almost ten years of "consultations" and stalling to write a new constitution and carefully create two (and no more than two) political parties. Military leaders got richer and richer during those ten years.

An election in 1993, widely seen as honest, seemed to choose Moshood Abiola, a Yoruba Muslim, as the new president. Factions of the military rulers annulled the election, appointed a civilian president, and then overthrew him. There was widespread disapproval and unrest.

The new military head of state was General Sani iA. According to most observers and many Nigerians, he was different from his predecessors. Corruption, occasional persecutions, and rare political killings might be tolerated, but Abacha relied on those to maintain power and order. When the "winner" of the '93 election publicly tried to claim the office, he was imprisoned. It soon became apparent that General Abacha's goal was to become President Abacha.

"Heart attacks" claimed the lives of Sani Abacha and Moshood Abiola in 1998. A new military leader proclaimed a new republic (the third or the fourth?) and relinquished power in 1999. The winner of the presidential election was none other than Olusegun Obasanjo, the general who had given up power to the second republic 20 years earlier. Obasanjo was reelected in 2003.

Umaru Musa Yar'Adua, Obasanjo's choice as a successor, became the second president of the newest republic in 2007. The election was notable because it was the first time one civilian administration had replaced another and because it was judged by international observers as fraudulent. Nonetheless, most Nigerians accepted the election of the former chemistry teacher, businessman, and governor as a *fait accompli*.

However, questions about the legitimacy of the executive were left wide open when Yar'Adua left the country without notice in late 2009. Public statements issued by his office said he had gone to Saudi Arabia for medical treatment. But there was no official communication from the president. He reportedly returned to Nigeria in February 2010, but was never seen in public again.

The Nigerian Senate and the highest federal court declared Vice President Goodluck Jonathan Acting President in February. It was not clear that either body was acting constitutionally. Acting President Jonathan fired Yar'Auda's cabinet and named his own. Yar'Adua died in May. Acting President Jonathan succeeded him. Establishing personal legitimacy was a major task as was achieving legitimacy for the office of president.

As you study for the exam, be sure to know what's happened since Jonathan became president.

Legitimacy

In all this political tumult, where does political legitimacy in Nigeria come from?

Does it come from

- a history of stable and successful government as in the UK? or
- a long-held sense of national identity and revolution as in China? or
- a protection of individual liberty and representative government as in the USA? or
- an ideology and the improvement of living standards as in China? or
- charismatic leadership? or

- the success of government-led economic development? or
- a history of pragmatic good governance? or
- successful political integration? or
- the operation of the rule of law? or
- honesty in government and governance? or
- government responsiveness to the demands of citizens?

Citizens might be persuaded of a political system's legitimacy by a few or many of these things. But, you ought to quickly recognize that Nigeria seems to lack all of them.

If Nigeria's political system lacks legitimacy, how is it able to continue to function?

Is it because

- so few people have so rarely been involved in governing? or
- because people have made so few demands on government? or
- because people feel powerless to influence the system? or
- because enough people benefit from the system to oppress the rest of the people? or
- because only some people are selectively oppressed?

These are questions you ought to ponder as you review what you know about Nigerian government and politics. These questions seem to invite comparisons with the other countries in this curriculum.

Oil production and subsistence farming dominate Nigeria's economy. In spite of this, the country must import gasoline, kerosene, diesel fuel, and basic foodstuffs. Any attempts at economic growth are likely to require international investment.

But outside help is hard to come by. What outsider wants to invest in a country where corruption

Another Father of the Nation

Olusegun Obasanjo was born in 1937 in the mainly Christian and animist southwest of the country. President Obasanjo is an ethnic Yoruba. He first came to prominence as the soldier who accepted the surrender of Biafran forces in the 1967-70 civil war.

He became head of state in 1976 following a political assassination, and, in 1979, he became the first African military leader to hand over power to a civilian government following national elections. ...

In 1995 he was jailed by the late military dictator, General Sani Abacha, on charges of plotting a coup. He was released in 1998 after Abacha's death.

Despite his earlier protestations that he would not run for the presidency, Mr. Obasanjo changed his mind, saying that he had been persuaded by his friends and supporters.

His People's Democratic Party created a successful coalition of interests. He won power with the backing of many Hausa-speakers from the mainly Muslim north in the face of opposition from many Yoruba. The new president took office amid widespread optimism that a new era had dawned in Nigeria.

— Adapted from Isaacs, Dan,
Profile: Olusegun Obasanjo, 6 February, 2002,
in *BBC News, Africa, news.bbc.co.uk/1/hi/
world/africa/1804940.stm*

is so rampant that visitors who arrive in the Lagos airport are met by groups of men offering (for a fee, of course) to facilitate the visitors' passage through customs? Investment requires Nigerian participation and control by Nigerian partners. The Nigerian partners sometimes offer only their partnership and control, not investment cash or property.

Outside help may be coming. In May 2010, a Chinese company signed an agreement to build

several refineries in Nigeria in exchange for oil drilling rights in Nigerian territory. Oil-poor China may not value the profits or control of refineries in Nigeria as much as it values access to exportable Nigerian oil. Can you update this case?

The IMF has tried to work out structural adjustment plans. President Obasanjo's old organization, Transparency International, nudges Nigeria toward new ways of doing business. But nationalistic Nigerian leaders are reluctant to appear to follow orders from the outside. Oil revenues prevent total collapse.

In 2005 the international community forgave $20 billion of Nigeria's foreign debt. It was probably uncollectible, but forgiveness brought new promises of reform in Nigeria. Nonetheless, in 2007, unions went on strike because the government raised gasoline prices. Do you recognize the connection (or irony) between those two events?

None of these things contribute to political stability or accountability. President Obasanjo sought to project Nigerian influence by sending troops to Liberia, Darfur (Sudan), and Niger. These moves were seen, in part, as a way to demonstrate Nigerian influence They also were intended to unite Nigerians. It's too soon to evaluate the results.

Once again, we come back to very basic questions: Why does Nigerian government work? There are no easy or clear answers. Ambiguity raises its head again.

3. POLITICAL INSTITUTIONS

Federalism: Nigeria has used constitutions written in 1960, 1963, 1979, and 1999. All of them have been long and detailed. While the most recent ones declare that Nigeria is "indivisible," federalism has been an important feature of all the constitutions. Even military regimes have been quasi-federal. (It's hard to include federalism in a military chain of command.) The constitutions go a step beyond US federalism in that they prescribe the forms of state and local governments.

At independence, Nigeria had three states. A fourth was added in 1963, and the number was increased to 12 after the civil war. Today, there are 36 states. President Obasanjo promised in his 2003 reelection campaign to consider creating more states. Why?

Increasing the number of states is seen as a way to defuse ethnic-based political conflict. If there are several states dominated by Hausa-Fulani Muslims, they will compete with each other (as well as with other states) for resources. Similarly, several Yoruba-dominated states will compete with each other. That competition will reduce the domination of the major ethnic groups. In addition, minority groups (like the Tiv and Kaduna) will be better able to compete nationally with the larger groups if they are dominant groups in separate states. This process is mirrored in the creation of more and more local governments (which are mostly administrative units).

The multiplicity of state governments is expensive. Each one has its representative body and its group of government employees. Administrative talent is stretched as thinly as budgets.

The apparent federalism is not what it may seem. Twenty-nine years of military governance did little to empower state or local governments. In addition, nearly all government income goes to the national government — over 80% from oil revenue. The constitution guarantees a percentage of that total revenue to state and local governments, but is silent on how it is to be spent.

The result is a grand competition for funds among the states and local organizations. It's the Nigerian equivalent of American "log rolling" and "pork barrel" legislation. The Nigerian version is called "chop-chop" politics, which focuses power and attention on the national government, not the states.

Executive

Given the effective centralization of authority in Nigeria, you would rightly expect the executive to

A Nigerian Language Lesson

Chop: 1. Food 2. Income 3. Bribe 4. Embezzle money, e.g., "Dat Oga chop belle-full bifor e retire."

— Babawilly's Dictionary of Pidgin English Words and Phrases, *www.ngex.com/personalities/ babawilly/dictionary/pidginc.htm*

"Chop-chop politics" refers to the basic "logrolling" idea. If I help you get your "chop," you'll help me get my "chop."

be crucial to the regime. Nearly 30 years of military rule underlines that.

Military executives have operated in a variety of ways. Each regime has involved a "council" of close advisors, mostly other officers. In the early years of regimes run by Yakubu Gowon and Ibrahim Babangida these councils operated by consensus. The longer they lasted, the smaller and more authoritarian they became. At the other extreme is the harsh, dictatorial rule of Sani Abacha.

These ruling military councils were usually supplemented by a cabinet that was at least partially civilian (key roles in policing, foreign policy, and "justice" were usually held by military officers). The people in these groups functioned like ministers in civilian governments (i.e., administrators). In addition, most military councils organized advisory or consultative groups of traditional leaders. The ruling officers would discuss policy proposals with the *obas* (kings), emirs, and village leaders, usually with an eye to legitimizing those proposals.

The second and later republics substituted a popularly elected president for the prime minister of the first republic. Most people saw the absence of a strong national leader as one of the causes of the conflicts that led to civil war. The presidency is closely modeled on the US example. The president appoints a cabinet, which must be approved by the senate. The president can veto legislation, which can be overridden by the congress.

The realities of politics and government in Nigeria are not always reflected in the constitution and formal structure of the government. The person in the executive office, military or civilian, creates the regime as much as the law. The executive's personality and abilities have shaped the office. The precedents of Obasanjo's presidency may be crucial to the future operation of Nigerian government — especially after the weakened presidencies of Yar'Adua and Jonathan.

Elections

All the Nigerian constitutions have created independent commissions to run elections. The effectiveness and honesty of these commissions has varied widely. Even in the 1999 elections, which are thought by most observers to be the most honest in Nigerian history, varieties of voting fraud were widespread.

Bureaucracy

In the 1960s, Nigeria had a well-educated organization of government employees. The civil service had been built on the British model. But the culture of clientalism and prebendalism overwhelmed the system imposed on Nigeria.

Since independence, the bureaucracy has grown dramatically. Today, government employment accounts for 50% of non-farm jobs. Every new state and local government authority requires its own staff of government administrators and clerks. Governments, civilian and military, have appointed loyal people to protected civil service positions (clientalism). Every policy resulting from "chop-chop" politics requires rewards to those who see that the benefits end up where intended (prebendalism).

Parastatals, the state-owned enterprises, account for much of the government employment. They're great patronage resources. There are over 500 of

these organizations. Nominally independent, their boards of directors are appointed by the government executive. Parastatals are designed to

- create symbols of national pride
- provide basic utilities (water, electricity, public transportation) at subsidized prices
- provide important public services (ports, telephone service, military manufacturing, and most importantly, petroleum marketing) that governments want outside of the private economy
- promote import substitution and industrial development

Legislature

For three-fourths of Nigeria's history, there have been no legislatures. Policy decisions were made and implemented by military councils. In the first two republics, legislatures earned reputations for being ineffectual and corrupt. As in the past, the current legislature is dominated by the executive. President Obasanjo had majority support in both houses. So did Yar'Adua and Jonathan.

The Nigerian legislature is made up of two houses and resembles the US Congress. Each state elects three senators from single-member districts in the state. The federal district of Abuja elects one. The House of Representatives has 360 members. State delegations are based on population. Candidates run in single-member districts.

The Senate must approve all high level presidential appointments and the congress can initiate legislation. The present government's majorities mean that the legislature is a follower, not a leader in the governing process.

Judiciary

At the time of independence, Nigeria had an independent and active judiciary. An active legal community and national bar association supported it. Over time, its powers have been restricted more and more by military regimes.

The 1993-1995 period ended any pretense of judicial importance in Nigeria. Abacha decreed that courts could not review government action, sent cases into military courts, decreased funding, and simply ignored court decisions.

The 1999 constitution created a system that in most aspects should look familiar to Americans. There's a 15-member supreme court appointed by the president and approved by the senate. Beneath that are a court of appeal and federal and state high courts. There is a constitutional court that has powers of judicial review.

Unfamiliar to most Americans would be the *sharia* (Islamic law) courts in northern states and the traditional courts in some Middle Belt and southern states. The *sharia* courts have been the most controversial. Legally, only Muslims come under their jurisdiction and decisions can be appealed to secular courts. But some northerners have publicly advocated replacing all Nigerian courts with *sharia* courts. Non-Muslims see that as a direct threat and part of the ambitions of Muslim northerners to take over Nigeria.

Political Parties

Military government and political parties don't mix well. As you might expect, military rulers have banned parties and banned some politicians from public office. You might not expect military governments to create political parties, but at least one did. In preparation for the 1993 elections, General Babangida decreed the existence of two political parties. General Abacha "may" have had something to do with the formation of the five parties that nominated him for president in 1997.

As noted earlier, the first parties in Nigeria were associated with specific ethnic groups. In the second republic, parties were required to demonstrate nationwide organization and support. A similar requirement was made in 1998 and 1999 when parties were allowed to organize. Nine parties competed in local elections, and the most successful three were allowed to nominate candidates for the 1999 presidential election. The Peoples Democratic Party (PDP) nominated Obasanjo, who won 62% of the vote. The All Peoples Party (APP) and the Alliance for Democracy (AD) jointly nominated Olu Falae.

If you examine the supporters of the parties, it becomes clear that the PDP is the descendent of the Northern Peoples Congress (NPC) of the first republic. The APP is a descendent of the Igbo-dominated NCNC, and the AD a descendent of the Yoruba-dominated Action Group. These parties demonstrate their national character by recruiting and organizing minority ethnic groups outside the territories where their primary supporters are in majorities. Thus the PDP organizes minorities in the south, while the NPC and AD organize minority groups in the north and the Middle Belt.

There's another way in which the realities of Nigerian politics are not described in the constitution. Northerners and southerners in the PDP made a "private," gentlemen's agreement to alternate the presidency. Since Obasanjo was a southerner, the next eight years of presidency were to go to a northerner (Yar'Adua).

The contract broke down when Yar'Adua's death led to Jonathan's presidency. Jonathan was a southerner. PDP leaders from the north announced that they would nominate a northerner to run for president in 2011 so they could reclaim the office that was rightfully theirs after belonging to Obasanjo and southerners for eight years. It's uncertain whether northern politicians will try to reclaim the two years of Jonathan's presidency as well. Do you know how that worked out?

Why this insistence on "owning" the presidency for a full eight years? Think about access to government revenues and opportunities for contracting out public projects.

Interest Groups

Some civic groups have been active in Nigeria since pre-independence times. People are most likely to belong to ethnic-based groups in cities or local associations of farmers in rural areas. These groups often initiate protests when their interests are threatened. Sometimes those protests turn violent. Protests and rebellions in the Niger Delta have often disrupted oil production. In 2009, the government granted amnesty to rebellious groups there in order to restore production and government revenues.

For the past decade, riots have killed hundreds of people in Middle Belt cities like Kaduna and Jos. Growing population, booming tin mining, and desertification of grazing lands to the north bring diverse groups of people into conflict with each other.

The migrants are mostly from the north and are mostly Muslim. They come for mining jobs and pastures for their herds. The "indigenes" are mostly Christian. There are legal and traditional distinctions between migrants and indigenes that make interactions more difficult. Everyone needs jobs and pastoralists need grazing land as much as farmers need land for crops. The competition for jobs and resources is a competition for survival. If you add to that mix, weak leaders and a state with limited capacity, conflicts often escalate.

Obasanjo, Yar'Adua, and Jonathan have sent in federal troops when violence occurs, but they arrive after the fact. Unlike the organized groups of rebels in the Niger Delta, the groups in the Middle Belt are often spontaneous mobs and therefore difficult to negotiate with. So far, no one has come up with constructive ways to approach the basic issues.

Women's market associations have been common in the south for a long time (perhaps even in pre-colonial times). Their concerns are quite local, but vital to the grassroots economy.

Other groups sometimes appear a bit less parochial. The "Kaduna Mafia" is a loosely organized group of military officers and civilians whose support for Babangida helped him maintain power. They may have had a hand in his decision to relinquish power after the election fiasco of 1993. They supported Obasanjo. They probably support Babangida's announced candidacy for the 2011 presidential race.

The National Democratic Coalition (NADECO) is based in southwestern Nigeria. It supported Abiola's campaign for president and his efforts to claim the office after the election was annulled. It has also championed good government.

Unions exist, but they've never been powerful. Ethnic divisions make organizing difficult. After petroleum workers' strikes in 1983 and 1993, the military governments did what they could to di-

---

Some Results of 'Chop-Chop' Politics in Kaduna

A number of notable educational institutions in the country are located in Kaduna State. They are Ahmadu Bello University, Zaria, Kaduna Polytechnic, Kaduna, School of Health Technology, the Federal Fishery Training Institute, Kaduna, College of Advanced Studies, Zaria and College of Education, Kafanchan.

In addition, the state plays host to very strategic military institutions in the country. These are the Nigerian School of Infantry, Zaria, Command and Staff College, Jaji, the College of Aviation Technology, Zaria, and the Nigeria Defence Academy, which now has the status of a University.

...The Defence Industries Corporation of Nigeria and the nation's third petroleum refinery are also located in Kaduna State.

— Embassy of the Federal Republic of Nigeria in Moscow,
www.nigerianembassy-moscow.ru/government/states/kaduna.html

minish the power of unions. Business groups have organized chambers of commerce in most parts of the country, but the economic and industrial dominance of the government means they have little influence nationally.

Professional associations (notably the Nigerian Bar Association, the Nigerian Medical Association, and the Nigerian Union of Journalists) have remained active since independence, but they've been marginalized by military governments for most of that time. Faculty and student groups at universities are active but rarely have any influence beyond their campuses.

Civic groups are less common in the rural and northern parts of the country. People living in these areas (a vast majority of the population) are more likely to be parts of patron-client networks.

Military leaders have ruled Nigeria for most of its existence. It may be surprising then that many officers want to keep the military out of politics. They see their role as professional soldiers, not governors. This is a major cleavage in the officer corps, which is dominated by northerners. Remembering that and the importance of patron-client relationships might help explain the rapid transition from Abacha's dictatorship to the current republic.

Political Elites

Not only are Nigerian elites divided by ethnicity, religion, and geography, they are divided by the routes they take to power (i.e., recruitment).

The military is perhaps the first place to look for a political elite. Although some officers prefer to avoid political involvement, a military commission has been a path to political power in Nigeria. Military governments not only ruled the country, but state and local governments as well.

Northerners have dominated the officer corps and military governments, although Middle Belt generals have often played key roles as heads of state. The officer corps is well educated. Most are

> **A Plea for Legitimate Government**
>
> Politics is business as usual, entailing sinister use of religion and ethnicity to manipulate and divide the people in the quest for short-term political advantages. This elevation of identity politics into the prime strategy of the political elite has worsened the conflict profile of the country and has led to the death of thousands and some of the worst peacetime refugee situations on the continent. ... Thus, Nigeria's corporate survival is being threatened by the actions of those expected to give it meaning.
>
> — Special Press Statement by the Nigeria Labour Congress on Nigeria's 41st Independence Anniversary, *www.nigerdeltacongress.com/ sarticles/special_press_statement_by_the_n.htm*

graduates of one of the military colleges, and many have attended Sandhurst, the British counterpart to the USMA at West Point. While these generals recognize loyalties to "their people" in traditional ways, they are usually very pragmatic in their views of the world.

There are traditional leaders like the *obas* (kings) of Yoruba areas, the emirs of the north, and the village leaders in the southeast. All these positions are more or less hereditary. It is some sense ironic that these leaders resemble other elites in that most are well educated and cosmopolitan. During periods of representative government, many of them hold elective offices.

Nigeria has a relatively large population of well-educated professionals. Universities have been purposely neglected and underfunded since the mid-1980s (because of political activities on campuses), but they still produce skilled graduates. Nearly all higher level civil servants have university degrees, many in public administration. Education has not prevented corruption among these public servants. They are not well paid, paychecks are often months late, and the public and "their people" have high expectations. On a positive note, this civil service has provided a great deal of stability during the political chaos of the past.

Education, relative affluence, and a contemporary outlook on life and the world set these elites apart from the majority of Nigerians. Uneducated, poor, and traditional people feel both contempt and awe for the military, traditional, and educated elites. Those attitudes are returned as contempt for the old-fashioned poor. This gap between elites and the masses is growing.

Patron-client relationships go some way to bridging the gap. The support of a village leader or local emir is often rewarded with access to public goods or services.

Another attempt to bridge the gap is the Nigerian Youth Service Corps (NYSC). University and professional school graduates perform a year of service outside the area of the country where they grew up. Most of the assignments are to rural areas. ("This practice is aimed at maintaining a massive grassroots presence for eventual transformation of the rural areas of the country." [6]) Many of the NYSC participants serve as teachers. Others serve as doctors, pharmacists, engineers, lawyers, accountants, and architects.

The program is more than an AmeriCorps-like service program. It is also meant to promote "intergroup understanding [and give] young Nigerian people opportunities to establish themselves professionally and form friendships and even marry outside their own ethnic areas." [7]

Commercial success is another route to elite status in Nigeria. In the 1993 presidential election, both Moshood Abiola and his opponent, Bashir Tofa, were wealthy businessmen. It helped that were both well known to General Babangida and his inner circle, but their wealth and notoriety of business success helped, too. If Nigeria pursues more economic liberalization, this route to power may become more important.

4. CITIZENS, SOCIETY, AND STATE

People in Nigeria, like those in any other society, belong to a variety of public groups. They most likely affiliate with communal groups centered on ethnicity and culture. These are the home to identity politics. People try to procure public benefits for their own groups. Politicians and other elites manipulate and exploit identity politics to maintain power and position. Religious leaders and international organizations have accused politicians of fomenting religious conflict for political gain. Class differences in Nigeria are overshadowed by communal group differences in part because of this manipulation by elites.

People belong to national groups. These are the places where political integration has been successful and people come together as Nigerians. In this realm of public activity, the country sends peacekeeping troops to other West African nations. Unfortunately in Nigeria, communal identities are much stronger than Nigerian identity.

People also belong to civic groups where they affiliate on the basis of some other commonality. Lawyers belong to the bar association. People belong to country clubs or unions. These civic groups — especially professional associations — were important parts of the independence movement.

Some Lovely Parting Gifts

In Nigeria, former dictator, Gen. Ibrahim Babangida rewarded "nearly 3,000 of his most loyal military chiefs by giving them new Peugeot sedans. Most Nigerians will never be able to afford anything like a new Peugeot 505, which costs the equivalent of $21,000 in Lagos. A senior university professor, for example, earns about $4,000 a year, while a nurse or mechanic is lucky to bring home more than $1,000." (*The New York Times*, Dec. 2, 1993; p. A3)

— The Free Africa Foundation, *www.freeafrica.org/commentaries4.html*

Today, however, these affiliations seem to be the weakest of all in Nigeria.

Cleavages separating ethnic/cultural groups from one another appear to overwhelm other divisions in Nigerian society. A reason for that is the coincidence of ethnic cleavages with religious, geographic, and economic cleavages. Remember, when various divisions between people have the same borders, the separations are likely to be more powerful. Another reason for the strength of these divisions is the value of the prizes of successful identity politics. The national government "earns" oil revenues and funds nearly all public services and sub-national governments.

Anthropologists identify between 250 and 400 ethnic groups in the state of Nigeria. These smaller groups play the identity politics game by banding together and/or allying themselves with one of the "big three" groups.

The primary cleavages (divisions) are geographic, cultural, religious, and ethnic.

The north of Nigeria is a dry savanna (imagine the Great Plains of the US located near the equator). The most northerly regions are on the fringe of the Sahara Desert.

Nearly all the people who are native to this part of the country are Hausa-Fulani or Kanuri. The Hausa-Fulani ethnic/cultural groups were once distinct, but religion, language, and intermarriage now unite them. They make up about 30% of the population of Nigeria.

Nearly all northerners are Muslims. Unlike the Muslims who maintained the great 16th century university in Timbuktu, the people of northern Nigeria are not, in general, well educated. The

---

Communication in a Multilingual Country

pidgin – "A simplified version of some language, often augmented by features from other languages. A pidgin typically arises in colonial situations and is used solely as a trade language." Unlike creoles, pidgins do not have native speakers.

creole – "A language that developed from a pidgin by expanding its vocabulary and acquiring a more complex grammatical structure." It is "the native language of most of its speakers. Therefore its vocabulary and syntactic devices are, like those of any native language, large enough to meet all the communicative needs of its speakers."

— Journal of Pidgin and Creole Languages,
www.ling.ohio-state.edu/research/jpcl/

---

people tend to be conservative and suspicious of modernization — which often means to them anything non-Muslim.

Women have never been freely allowed to vote in the northern states. People and political leaders strive to maintain *sharia*, traditional Muslim law. Highly-publicized cases of women sentenced by *sharia* judges to be stoned for adultery make news in the US. The Nigerian legal system attempts to accommodate *sharia* for Muslims but facilitate appeals to secular courts. National political leaders try to walk the narrow line of advocating a secular state which allows freedom of religious practice.

Most people in the north are subsistence farmers and herders.

The Yoruba who live primarily in the **southwestern** part of Nigeria make up about 21% of the country's population. This is the prime agricultural region of Nigeria, and most people are farmers. Cash crops dominate agriculture economically, but subsistence crops are vital for survival outside the cities. Lagos, the largest city and former national capital, is in this region. The city attracts migrants from all over Nigeria and from neighboring countries.

There are Muslim and Christian Yoruba in about equal numbers. There's evidence from academic studies to indicate that ethnic identity is more important than religious identity to most Yoruba. The level of education among the Yoruba is higher than among the Hausa-Fulani people, and there is greater diversity of economic activity accompanying the diversity of people and opportunities in the cities of the southwest.

The southeast of Nigeria is home to the Igbo people. This group is almost as large as the Yoruba, making up about 18% of the Nigerian population. The Igbo people are the most Christianized of the Nigerian groups. They are also the most educated over all. Remember that, while noting that most Igbo people are farmers.

The Middle Belt of Nigeria runs east to west through the center of the country. There is no dominant ethnic or religious group in this region. The location and cultural characteristics probably help explain why so many of Nigeria's national leaders have come from the area. Agriculture is the main occupation of people here.

Did you notice that farming is the main occupation in all regions of Nigeria? Over half of the people live in rural villages. They are poor and not well educated. Most don't speak English (the language of government, but not necessarily the language of politics). Most of these people have contact with government and politics through local patrons who try to deliver the benefits of government to their supporters (clients).

It's worth keeping in mind as you analyze government and politics in Nigeria that, while these three ethnic/cultural/linguistic groups dominate things, the Hausa-Fulani, the Yoruba, and the Igbo together make up less than 70% of Nigeria's population. Over 200 other groups identify themselves separately and practice the same identity politics as the dominant groups.

Political culture: Nigeria is a complex and heterogeneous place. So is the political culture. It's constructed from British (Western) values and practices on a foundation of many African traditions. Many people recognize themselves as Nigerians in some contexts. But most people "are Nigerians" only after they "are" something else.

Add to those complexities the huge difference between the elite culture and the mass culture.

Nigeria's elite are citizens and politically active. They are urban, well educated, English speakers who are involved in a cash economy.

But the masses — urban and rural — are subjects and not politically active except during some campaigns. They are more likely involved in some kind of patron-client network. They are not well educated (30% of the population is illiterate), do not speak English (except as a **pidgin or a creole derivation**), and most are involved in a subsistence economy even when they earn money.

The elites want representative government, honesty, and civil liberties. The masses are more likely to want results. (Given the expectations people have placed on government, that's a huge demand.)

In colonial times, British administrations controlled nearly all aspects of public life. It shouldn't be surprising then that people expected a newly independent Nigerian government to take charge of things. That kind of expectation continues. It's one of the reasons Nigeria has resisted Structural

Farming and Poverty

Although Nigeria is a country rich in natural resources, more than 70% of the population is below the poverty level.

In 2009, agriculture accounted for 33% of the GDP and employed more than 70% of the population, mainly in subsistence farming and estate [plantation] farming.

— CIA World Factbook, *www.cia.gov/library/publications/the-world-factbook/geos/ni.html*

Adjustment Policies that the IMF has tried to impose.

The large public role in the economy has been made possible in large part because of the oil revenues that flow into the government. The revenues are supposed to fund government services at both state and national levels. This flow of money also makes possible the corruption that is pervasive in Nigeria.

At the lowest levels, security and customs officials at Lagos' Murtala Muhamad International Airport suggest to travelers that gifts will facilitate passengers' progress through the airport. At the highest level, President Obasanjo, as his second term ended, approved the sale of two oil refineries and a contract for the construction of a nationwide chain of health clinics. Beneficiaries of both deals were companies owned by Obasanjo allies. President Yar'Adua cancelled all the deals once he took office. [8] In between are countless other examples. Many people call politicians and bureaucrats "lootocrats." General Sani Abacha's family is reported to have balances in Swiss bank accounts of hundreds of millions of dollars.

Ready for some more ambiguity? This corruption is sometimes part of the traditional culture. The African proverb, "It takes a village to raise a child," became a controversial part of the 1996 US presidential election. What the proverb contends is that everyone is responsible for village children. If someone is fortunate enough to get an education (with the support of the village) and leave for a well-paid job, he is still responsible for the village children (so to speak). If someone gets into a position to control some of the huge resources of government, he is still considered responsible for the village children. In other words, even the head of state has responsibilities to his home village and the other groups that "raised him." Westerners may see nepotism, while Africans see responsible citizenship.

Incorporate this sense of community responsibility with a system of patron-client relationships.

If people are uneducated, illiterate, and far from the seats of power, they rely on more educated and involved people to get things or get things done. In return, they loyally follow the patron. If a patron gets into a position with access to government power, funds, or services, the clients expect more rewards for their loyalty.

Where in that mix is corruption? Where is politics? Are there similar favors done to groups in Western countries? (Why is that Americans don't pay income taxes on money they spend on home mortgage interest? Does everyone agree that the exemption serves a public purpose? Or is it a reward to politically active middle-class supporters of elected politicians?)

Socialization

In any culture, families are the first teachers. In Nigeria, families tend to be large and many of them are polygamous. If community loyalties are strong, they are based on even stronger family loyalties. People who make their livings away from home are expected to support their families even more than their communities. People owe their siblings multiples of what they owe to someone from their village or neighborhood. The political lessons are not just implied, they are explicit.

Between 65% and 75% of children go to primary schools. More kids in the south than in the north attend school. In the north, more boys than girls attend. Education is widely seen as important, but few children get beyond primary school. Secondary and post-secondary education is expensive. Education is in English. Judging from the stated values of the elite, schools are pretty successful in promoting democratic values. Cynicism about political leaders is based in part on the rampant corruption in Nigerian government.

The government has made explicit attempts to shape public attitudes about politics. Everything from public relations campaigns to the creation of political parties has been tried. It's still probable that personal experience is most likely to be the basis of political values. Local officials with educations, English fluency, and power demand deference from citizens and subjects (just like the traditional leaders). They also are likely to have their hands out for bribes. (A student from Nigeria in one of my classes told me that an "A" in her suburban Lagos junior high school cost the equivalent of $50.)

As in other parts of the world, religion in Nigeria is becoming more and more involved in the political culture. Religious experiences are the ways many people learn political values and practices.

In the north, the Fulani domination of Hausa peoples was justified as a reformation of casual Hausa practices of Islam. Similar contemporary influences have made many Muslims more anxious to preserve and expand their influence on secular society.

Christian evangelicals — mostly native but some immigrants from the USA — have increased their efforts to revitalize what they see as casual and more traditional Christian practices in the south and to convert Muslims and others in the north. Like the fundamentalist Muslims, these Christians put an emphasis on influencing secular society.

Media

The media are important vehicles for political socialization in most countries. In Nigeria, they may be more important than in other Third World countries because they've remained relatively free, even during military regimes. Government controls were relaxed under Obasanjo's government, but the authority to control is still in the legal code.

There are about 80 national and local competing newspapers and several major news magazines. But their importance is diminished because they're in English, and a third of the country is illiterate. Some are government-owned, but the privately-owned ones are often critical of the government. The newspapers are all urban, and most are based in the southwestern (Yorubaland) part of the country.

Much of Nigerian television (Nigerian Television Authority or NTA) and radio (Federal Radio Corporation of Nigeria or FRCN) are government-run, at the national and state levels. In 2003, the country launched its first communications satellite to ensure nationwide coverage.

Private radio broadcasters are some of the most competitive in Africa. Nearly everyone listens to radio news, and this is where most people get their political information. There is easy access to BBC and Voice of America (VOA) radio broadcasts. The outside information is popular and valued. Wealthy Nigerians have access to international satellite television news.

In a country where driving across Lagos (in terrible traffic jams called "go slows") used to be faster than making a phone call, even simple business was difficult. In August 2001, two multinational companies bought licenses to establish cell phone networks in Nigeria, and service has improved markedly. There is now adequate cell phone service to create political problems. In 2002, Nigeria attempted to host the Miss World pageant in Abuja. Muslim activists, opposed to things like the swimsuit competition, used text messaging to organize demonstrations which forced the pageant to move to London. There are now over 60 million cell phones in use compared to 1.5 million available landlines. All over the country, entrepreneurs carry cell phones that they rent by the minute to their neighbors. Some have even built platforms high in trees to have line-of-sight access to cell phone towers.

There is limited but growing access to the Internet especially in urban areas. Underfunded universities have had little money for digital technology. Technological development is almost completely in the private arena. Cyber cafes are common in large cities.[9] A new undersea cable reached Nigeria in late 2009, months after the older, primary cable had been damaged. The company that financed the new connection predicted it would meet Nigeria's need for Internet connections for more than a decade.[10]

Electricity is a problem for everyone. Production doesn't meet demand. Rolling blackouts are so common that everyone who can afford a generator has one. (Blackouts are accompanied by the roar of thousands of small gas engines coming to life to power generators.) Businesses need to keep factories and offices open, people need to keep their lights on and their computers and air conditioners running.

City living is a political socialization process, too. Rural people are drawn to cities by the perceived opportunities. Most rural migrants are ill prepared for urban life and what opportunities exist there. They find themselves living in segregated neighborhoods with others of their ethnic/geographic group. They join mutual aid and protection societies in those neighborhoods to learn how to get a job, find housing, and stay out of trouble. In those societies they find themselves at the bottom of a large patron-client network. Without much schooling or English, they find themselves learning first hand what politics are like.

Participation

As the previous paragraph describes, political participation is nearly universal. However, much of the participation is not what Americans would label as efficacious and self-directed.

Voting rates are difficult to estimate. This is a country where taking a census is such a volatile issue that no one knows for sure how many people live where. Because of long periods of military government and electoral fraud, there's no tradition of voting or faith in the system. Elections are possible. The 1993 election was judged open and fair by most observers, but the turnout was estimated at only 46%. That's probably down a great deal from the elections of the 1960s and 1979. The elections of April 2003 drew mixed reviews from foreign observers. Losers loudly rejected the results and went to court to have them overturned. Observers were even more critical of the 2007 elections, and losers once again went to court.

In spite of the flawed process, most people were resigned to the election of Umaru Yar'Adua.

Women were not allowed to vote in northern states until 1979. Even today, they vote much less frequently than men in the north. (Voting lines for men and women must be separate and perpendicular to one another.) Women vote more in the Middle Belt and even more in the south. In Yoruba and most Igbo societies, women played important economic and political roles in pre-colonial times. They still play important public roles in the south today, but they are unlikely to be in elected office or to occupy top bureaucratic positions.

Protest and violence: Grassroots protests have been part of Nigerian political culture since colonial times. Patrons and ambitious political leaders sometimes organize and foment the protests, usually around local issues. The protests occasionally turn violent, especially when urban minorities (in their segregated neighborhoods) can be used as scapegoats.

Quasi-political armed gangs in the delta's oil production areas are involved in nearly continuous low level violence. They regularly attack oil platforms and kidnap foreign workers. Ransoms and "bunkering" (dangerously improvised tapping of oil and gasoline pipelines) fund these gangs. Some of the gangs are connected to local political leaders. The gang leaders usually proclaim their interest in helping local people and cleaning up the environment. But there are few political results of their terrorism.

That's not the same as the violence used by power elites. Military leaders have used violence to obtain and maintain power. Assassination has been a tool used over and over. Political critics and opponents have disappeared. Military force has been used to put down riots and protests. In the context of Third World and African countries, violence in Nigeria is probably less than average, but it's there.

Nigerian Realities

Nigerian economic policies shaped by World Bank and IMF... have so far lead to a dysfunctional electricity privatisation process [and] a heavy and as yet unfulfilled reliance on reform of the gas sector...

It would be simplistic to lay the disaster and inequity of Nigeria's energy and power sector at the feet of the IMF, World Bank and other international donors. However, their influence can not be disconnected from the corruption carried out by the country's elites that has exacerbated poverty and failed to provide power to the nation...

Nigeria is the region's largest oil producer and holds approximately one third of the proven gas reserves of Africa. Yet at least 60 per cent of its population lack access to electricity...

Deregulation of the downstream petroleum market (refining, supply and distribution) has been a key ingredient of World Bank and IMF policy advice since 1999... The process turned into a mockery... The failure to develop refining capacity favours the few elites who benefit from the monopoly that they hold a monopoly over refined oil imports...

— Facilitating whose power? WB and IMF policy influence in Nigeria's energy sector
by the Bretton Woods Project, *www.brettonwoodsproject.org/art-561198*

5. POLITICAL CHANGE

If the question is "How do Nigerian government and politics deal with change?" the answer seems obvious. Ambitious and/or patriotic generals organize enough support to take over the government. There have been at least seven military coups. Most have not created distressingly authoritarian regimes. (That's a normative statement. But in African or Third World contexts it's quite supportable.) Most of the military regimes have not made great improvements except in the area of law and order.

The tradition of military takeovers has been the "default position" for Nigerian government and politics. Elected leaders have been less willing to compromise or take risks to resolve big issues, knowing that a group of generals would come along to rescue Nigeria. The 2007 and 2010 transitions might change that pattern.

But change happens in other ways, too.

Constitutional Engineering

DeGaulle and the authors of France's fifth constitution assumed that creating the right institutions and procedures could solve the problems of republican government in France. Nigerians have had similar hopes for their country.

Federalism was grafted on to the Westminster model in the first constitution. The second constitution was modeled on the US example in hopes that new institutions and procedures would provoke political behavior more appropriate for republican government.

General Babangida went to great lengths to design a political system that would be successful. (Some of those lengths were probably designed to keep him in power.) He even decreed the existence of only two political parties ("one a little to the left and one a little to the right of center" [11]). Even General Abacha went through some motions of designing a republican government.

The job of creating functioning government in Nigeria is much greater than it was in France.

After all, France had more than 150 years of national political experience after its revolution before the 1958 constitution was approved. (It also had national hero Charles deGaulle.) Nigeria had less than 40 years of national political experience before its 1999 constitution.

The idea of engineering solutions to Nigeria's difficulties extends to the present day. In 1996, the Abacha government created the Vision 2010 Committee. Its job was to set goals for Nigeria's 50th anniversary and create a blueprint for reaching those goals. The report called for large-scale privatization, more efficient government, and industrial development.

In February 2005, President Obasanjo created a National Conference for Constitutional Reform. His political opponents — especially those from the southeast — kept reminding him and the public that the constitution had never been publicly ratified or approved. In 1999, the 1993 constitution was proclaimed by military rulers to be the basis for a new regime. No public debate. No ratification.

The conference collapsed in July 2005, when delegates were unable to reach agreements about the sharing of oil revenues. Two years later, the issue resurfaced. The Citizen's Forum for Constitutional Reform (CFCR), a coalition of over two hundred Nigerian NGOs, held a one-day meeting in Abuja to consider constitutional revisions. Pressure for change, especially from southerners, continues. [12]

The way Nigeria has dealt with the IMF may be helpful in assessing how Nigerian government and politics deal with change.

Nigeria's first economic policies, like those of most new post-colonial countries, centered on import substitution and industrial development. Growing oil revenues in the 1970s supported these plans.

The oil crisis put Nigeria in the position of paying a quarter of its oil revenues in interest on international debt. General Buhari's government began negotiations with the IMF for debt restructuring and relief. It broke off talks because of the Structural Adjustment Policies (SAP) the IMF demanded. General Babangida's government renewed the discussions but also rejected the IMF demands. However, Nigeria got some help from the IMF because it began implementing a Nigerian plan that promised most of the results the IMF plan aimed at. The Nigerian plan avoided the politically difficult issues of reducing subsidies for gasoline and reducing government spending. Nigeria could win IMF cooperation without complying with the IMF's proposals because it receives relatively little IMF aid (about 20% of the Third World average).

This kind of adversarial negotiations between the IMF and Nigeria continues. The Club de Paris is an informal group of more than 20 countries that have provided loans to other countries. In June 2005, the club agreed to forgive about two-thirds of Nigeria's foreign debt because "of the economic reform program implemented by the Nigerian authorities... and their willingness... to finance an exit treatment from the Paris Club."[13] This arrangement avoids Nigerian capitulation to IMF restructuring conditions while promising real economic change.

6. PUBLIC POLICY

The making of public policy in Nigeria is a matter of elite politics. And there are plenty of elites who compete to make policy.

There are the traditional elites, who these days often seek elective office to enhance and legitimize their power. Many national legislators and state governors are described by the press as "chiefs." This is a title applied to local leaders by the British in colonial times, but it has stuck. Business elites are also visible in the shaping of policy. So are military, religious, and professional elites.

It often seems that government policy reflects the desires of the elites rather than the needs of the country. At least that's one explanation for such a low standard of living and vast underemployment in a country where economic growth is universally declared to be a primary goal. It also explains the massive pollution in oil-producing areas. One of the things that Nigeria's elites require is a steady flow of government revenue to maintain themselves. Since nearly all government revenue comes from oil, maintaining oil production is a top priority.

Another explanation for Nigeria's economic problems and problematic policies is Nigeria's poverty. In spite of incredible oil wealth, the needs of Nigeria and its people are overwhelming. The educational system is inadequate. The country can't feed itself. HIV/AIDS is a growing problem. Polio is a threat. Many people don't have access to clean water.

Of course, prebendalism and corruption have to be considered as factors that influence or distort policymaking.

The great ethnic cleavages, reinforced by religious, educational, geographic, and standard of living factors also play a role in making (or not making) policy. Polio wouldn't be a threat if some Islamic leaders didn't see vaccination as an anti-Muslim threat from the Christian West.

Global factors have to be considered. High oil prices give governments more choices. Demands from groups like the Club of Paris and the IMF limit choices.

The political culture is part of the policymaking environment too. Elite values of democracy and basic civil liberties might be contagious. But there is a powerful sentiment favoring authoritarian stability over chaos and economic decline.

What's going on now in Nigeria? Will a new president make a difference? What policies are being made? Who is making them? Is there negotiation in the process? Look for evidence to support your answers to questions like these.

FOOTNOTES

1 Office of the United States Trade Representative, "Nigeria," *www.ustr.gov/countries-regions/africa/west-africa/nigeria*

2 International Trade Center, *www.intracen.org*, 23 July 2010

3 Africa News Network, "African Agriculture," *africanagricultureblog.com/2010/02/Nigeria-spends-700-million-to-import.html*

4 Kesselman, Mark, Joel Krieger, and William A. Joseph, *Introduction to Comparative Politics*, 2004

5 Scholars and observers disagree about whether the creation of the Midwest state was an attempt to defuse three-sided political conflict or an attempt to dilute Yoruba political power.

6 Momoh, H.B., *National Youth Service, A Global Perspective, www.utas.edu.au/docs/ahugo/NCYS/first/1-Nigeria.html*

7 Enemuo, Francis C., *Innovations in Civic Participation, www.icicp.org/CountryProfiles/FF2000Nigeria.htm*

8 "Nigeria blocks huge clinic deal," BBC World News, 7 August 2007 at *news.bbc.co.uk/2/hi/africa/6934794.stm*, accessed 18 August 2007

9 Media information in part from *Country Profile: Nigeria*, BBC News, *news.bbc.co.uk/1/hi/world/africa/country_profiles/1064557.stm*

10 Rebekah Heacock, "New Submarine Cable Lands in Lagos," Global Vloices Online, *globalvoicesonline.org/2009/09/07/nigeria-new-submarine-internet-cable-lands-in-lagos/*

11 McCormick, John, *Comparative Politics in Transition, 2001, p. 409.*

12 "CSOs Insist On Constitution Review," *This Day, Lagos*, July 24, 2007

13 "Paris Club News," *www.clubdeparis.org/news*, September 3, 2005

REVIEW EXERCISE

This little exercise is not meant to be comprehensive. It's meant to get you thinking about some of the basic facts and point out areas you might have to review more thoroughly. My responses follow.

1. Nigeria is like other developing countries in all the following ways EXCEPT
   (A) environmental concerns are less important than economic development
   (B) the rapidly growing population creates challenges for the government and the economy
   (C) its economy is dependent upon a single cash crop
   (D) most of the economy is controlled by the government
   (E) a primary feature of domestic politics is the competition between ethnic groups for economic and political advantage

2. A primary heritage of British imperialism in Nigeria is
   (A) a Westminster-style regime
   (B) a thriving industrial sector of the economy
   (C) an aristocracy
   (D) the use of English as a common language
   (E) the subordination of the military to civilian governments

3. There is political pressure to create more states in Nigeria because
   (A) unitary government has proven to be unsuccessful in Nigeria
   (B) so many ethnic communities want a state to claim as their own
   (C) the needs of people in various regions are so different from others' needs
   (D) real political power is exercised by state governors
   (E) Hausa political leaders see that as the best way to extend *sharia* (Islamic law) to more parts of the country

4. A primary reason the president is the focus of politics in Nigeria is that
   (A) oil revenues flow through that office to the states
   (B) military leaders offered models of executive governance
   (C) the constitution requires such a high degree of transparency in the operation of the presidency
   (D) nation-wide campaigns expose presidential candidates to more people
   (E) Nigeria's presidents have been models of honesty and competence

5. In Nigeria, parastatals are supposed to
   (A) substitute for underdeveloped private businesses
   (B) encourage creation of domestic industries
   (C) provide subsidized basic services
   (D) ensure that functions vital to the country are carried out
   (E) do all the things listed in the above choices

6. The primary political parties in Nigeria today
   (A) represent political ideologies
   (B) have close connections to other West African parties
   (C) are primarily catch-all parties
   (D) are descendants of regional and ethnic parties at the time of independence
   (E) function as pragmatic, compromise-seeking groups

7. One of the main reasons for the weakness of civil society in Nigeria is the
   - (A) ways that religious leaders discourage involvement in non-religious groups
   - (B) depth of the divisions between regional ethnic groups
   - (C) near absence of an educated elite outside of the military
   - (D) rapid urbanization
   - (E) association of most groups with military governments

8. The geographic cleavages in Nigeria are reinforced by cleavages of
   - (A) wealth
   - (B) education
   - (C) religion
   - (D) language
   - (E) all of those factors

9. A major difference between elite and mass political culture in Nigeria is that
   - (A) the majority of people depend upon the cash economy
   - (B) elites only get involved in politics during electoral campaigns
   - (C) while elites have personal contacts, most people rely on mass media for news and analysis
   - (D) the elite values civil liberties while the masses value economic stability
   - (E) only the elite depend on patron-client networks

10. Corruption can be seen as inherent in Nigerian culture because
    - (A) political integration has been so thorough
    - (B) there is a strong sense of communal responsibility
    - (C) oil revenues are usually seen as "free money" since they come from natural resources
    - (D) individualism is a powerful force
    - (E) British influences are so powerful

(For responses, see below)

10: Know ... Mexico

1. INTRODUCTION TO COMPARATIVE POLITICS

We have to ask how Mexico fits into the various classification systems used by political scientists. Is it a Third World country? Is it most like the industrializing successes, the "Asian Tigers?" Or is it on the cusp of structural adjustment and most like Russia?

We're still not sure what will replace the one-party rule of the PRI. Will it be a functioning three-party system of coalition politics? Will it be a competitive two-party system? Will the PRI make a comeback? Or will it be another version of a single-party democratic centralism? Or will narco-terrorism push the system in a non-democratic direction?

Will the decline of the PRI's dominance offer opportunities for state parties and governments to exercise more independence? Will negotiation and compromise become part of Mexico's political culture?

Among developing nations, Mexico is unusual. What has made it so successful at stable government, industrial development, and political change? Why did those successes come under such pressures in the 1990s? How will it face the pressures of the 21st century?

Should our study of Mexico focus on the transition to a multi-party democracy? Or on the internal changes which have promoted reform? Or on the economic pressures for change? Or on the battles for power?

2. SOVEREIGNTY, AUTHORITY, AND POWER

Mexico is a country of more than 110 million people with a rich and ancient cultural heritage. The Mayan and Olmec civilizations have their origins more than 3,000 years ago. Mexico borders on the Pacific Ocean and the Caribbean Sea just south of the United States. It's almost three times the size of Texas, but it was once much larger. The country has valuable mineral resources. In spite of the fact that the per capita GDP is about $13,500, perhaps 35% of the people live below the Mexican poverty line. Mexico has the least equal distribution of wealth among the six countries in the AP Comparative Government and Politics curriculum that we know of.

Spaniards who were intent on sending as much wealth as possible back to Spain, spreading

A Measure of Income Distribution

The GINI Index is a measure of the distribution of income in a country. The higher the index, the more unequal the distribution. Mexico may be most unequal among the countries in this curriculum, but it is about average for Central American countries.

Country	GINI Index
Denmark	29
Canada	32
Nicaragua	43
USA	45
Mexico	48
Costa Rica	48
El Salvador	52
Honduras	54
Guatemala	55

— *CIA World Factbook*, 2010

Catholic Christianity, and creating landed estates for Spanish nobles colonized Mexico in the 16th century. The colonial administration was run by Spaniards who made sure that the newly created landed aristocracy had estates and medieval rights to peasants' labor. They also made sure that the Spanish church was one of the largest landholders and that all profits and taxes (less some corruption) were sent to Spain.

The contemporary Mexican regime rests on a long, violent evolutionary struggle — although most Mexicans would prefer to describe the struggle as revolutionary.

First was the long, bloody revolution against Spanish rule (1810 to 1821).

Then came a long, difficult stage of nation building from 1821 to the founding of the Partido Revolucionaro Institucional (PRI) in 1921. Mexico lost half its territory to the USA in this period. The political struggles were between

- descendants of Spanish immigrants who owned huge land grants from the Spanish crown, Catholic Church elites, and conservatives who opposed democracy and economic reform
- *Mestizo* (people of Spanish and Indian ancestry) middle and upper classes who were more likely to favor democracy, protectionist trade policies, and secular government
- champions (some of them parish priests) of native people who were mostly poverty-stricken farm workers and unskilled laborers.

There was a diversity of political perspectives during this nation-building period. Conservative, pro-clerical monarchists competed with radical, anti-clerical socialists. Almost every idea between those extremes was part of the debate. Populist authoritarians like Porfirio Diaz most often prevailed.

Historical Context

This nation-building period coincided with political tumult and controversy all over the world. There was political unrest in Europe in 1848 and 1871. The Opium Wars "opened" China, brought change, and paved the way for the Boxer Rebellion. The Victorian period in England came and went. In the USA, we fought a civil war over slavery and states rights. Bismarck and Kaiser Wilhelm created Germany. And World War I. The USA became a world power. The Russian Revolution began. And, when Trotsky found himself unwelcome in Russia, he escaped to Mexico City.

— Adapted from
"The People and History of Mexico,"
www.mexconnect.com/

It was the "populist republicans" of the "Sonoran Dynasty" who founded the PRI. These anti-clerical, capitalist advocates of import substitution from northern Mexico finally created a modern country. Their success was probably guaranteed when President Lázaro Cárdenas (1934-40) added land reform and nationalization of key segments of the economy to the PRI agenda. That brought many farmers and union workers into the catch-all party as members of organized groups.

The PRI policies and actions

- reduced the power of landowners
- reduced the power of the Catholic Church at a national level
- limited the power of foreign investors
- made accommodation and bargaining the way to get things done
- and created an activist, centralized government.

The results also magnified the power and authority of the PRI leaders and created the basis for the patron-client system in Mexico.

President Cardenas also established precedents for the operation of the regime, most of which persist to this day. They include

- single six-year terms for presidents after which the retiring president leaves politics quietly
- the naming of the new president by the outgoing president
- making the president central to a powerful, centralized political system
- a huge patronage machine centered on the president
- government-organized unions
- subsidies to favored businesses
- import substitution as a key to economic development
- public works projects to favored communities

(Do you know which of these are no longer current? You should.)

Things began to change with the economic boom of the 1960s. New groups, left out of the old corporatist coalition, began to organize. Student protests of 1968 (and their bloody suppression) were visible examples.

Other changes came with the economic slowdown of the 1970s. The oil price boom and collapse trapped the Mexican economy in a no-win situation in the '80s. Political change began to accompany economic change, as economic liberalization became "the flavor of the decade." That put a real crimp on government-funded patronage, for one.

The assassination of President Salinas' choice for successor (Luis Colosio), the rebellion in Chiapas, and the economic crisis of the '90s were all signs of even bigger changes. Salinas' constitutional and electoral reforms were attempts to modernize the system and maintain support for the PRI. The climax was the PRI's loss of the presidency to Vicente Fox and Partido de Acción Nacional (PAN). Mexicans and other observers watched Fox's presidency carefully. In the end, the legislative opposition to Fox's proposed reforms made them impossible.

HISTORICAL AND POLITICAL TURNING POINTS

before 1500 ...... Olmec, Mayan, Toltec, Aztec and other civilizations	1978-1982 .... Oil crises
1519 .... Arrival of Cortés and Spaniards	1982 .... Debt crisis
1810-1821 .... War for independence	1985 .... Earthquake in Mexico City
1836 .... Independence of Texas	1988 .... Carlos Salinas elected president
1846-1848 .... War with USA; loss of California and New Mexico	1994 .... NAFTA becomes effective and the Zapatista Rebellion in Chiapas on January 1; presidential candidate Colosio assassinated; economic crisis
1876-1911 .... Diaz regime (Porfiriato)	
1910-1921 .... Revolution	
1917 .... Constitution	1996 .... Electoral reforms
1927-1929 .... Crister Rebellion	1997 .... PRI first loses majority in Chamber of Deputies
1929 .... PRI's predecessor founded	
1934-1940 .... Cárdenas government	2000 .... PRI presidential candidate beaten for first time by Vicente Fox
1938 .... Oil industry nationalized (Pemex)	
1939 .... PAN founded	2006 .... PAN candidate Calderón elected president
1953 .... Women get the right to vote	
1968 .... Massacre of Tlaltelolco	

Fox was succeeded by PAN's Felipe Calderón. He defeated Mexico City Mayor López Obrador in a very close election. Obrador and his supporters claimed that the election was fraudulent and that Calderón had stolen the victory. For months, huge crowds of PRD supporters demonstrated in Mexico City. The results of these protests, in the short term, were negligible.

What is the current state of opposition politics in Mexico? Drug cartels are a major challenge to the sovereignty, legitimacy, and efficacy of Mexico's regime and its current government.

Calderón declared war on the cartels and sent the army into areas of northern Mexico where the police were unable to maintain law and order. The army was marginally effective in some areas, but the level of cartel violence grew as rival gangs fought each other for control of territories near major US cities.

The balance of political power in Mexico depends upon the course of this war. The resurgence of PRI popularity in the 2009 elections resulted, in part, from what looked like Calderón's failures to wrest control of northern Mexico and the border areas from the drug gangs.

3. POLITICAL INSTITUTIONS

Mexico is a federal republic with a very strong central government (another legacy of Spanish rule). The 1917 constitution created a structure with three branches, a system of checks and balances (which should sound familiar to students in the US), and guarantees of civil and social rights.

The system was controlled until 2000 by a single

'Just Across the US Border...'

"We know what manufacturers want…" says Alma Colleli, Executive Director of San Benito Economic Development Corporation. "We are ideally located to offer the competitive advantages and global logistics companies are demanding. We have the low wage, skilled workforce in Mexican maquiladoras (assembly plants) across the border. The region also has the infrastructure and multi-modal transportation and distribution systems required to compete in the global market… favorable taxes, incentives and low cost of doing business in a business-friendly area that offers great quality of life."

— United Business Media PRNewswire, "Manufacturing Jobs Alive and Well Here, Says Rio South Texas Economic Council," *www.prnewswire.com/news-releases/manufacturing-jobs-alive-and-well-here-says-rio-south-texas-economic-council-89593467.html, 31 March 2010*

Juárez Violence Puts Factories on Defensive

U.S. companies flocked to the border city of Juárez because it was one of Mexico's most business-friendly cities. Now, an entire industry is adjusting to doing business in Mexico's deadliest town.

Just across the U.S. border from El Paso, Texas, Juárez has turned into a murderous battleground as two rival drug cartels vie for a lucrative entry route into the U.S. A dozen homicides a night isn't uncommon…

Until two years ago, Juárez was a thriving manufacturing hub. The 1994 North American Free Trade Agreement paved the way for the rise of so-called maquiladoras, assembly lines where everything from laptops to motorcycles are built with cheap local labor and shipped back across the border tariff-free…

— Nicholas Casey, *Wall Street Journal*, 26 March 2010, *online.wsj.com/article/SB10001424052748704094104575144180091658768.html*

authoritarian party, in which the president of the country was central. Some political scientists have described it as democratic centralism guided by pragmatism rather than ideology.

The Executive

From 1929 until Vicente Fox's election, the president was the head of the PRI. The president is elected to one six-year term (*sexenio*). PRI presidents chose candidates for other offices and selected their successors (in a practice called *dedazo*) after bargaining within the party elite. *Dedazo* was replaced in 1999 by a primary election, and PRI candidates for the 2000 and 2006 presidential elections were chosen that way.

The president also appoints a huge number of officials, many of whom have appointment powers themselves. Thus the president sits at the apex of a gigantic patronage hierarchy. What evidence do you see for changes resulting from the PRI loss of this office?

The president is in charge of foreign policy, can initiate legislation, create government agencies, and issue decrees and regulations with the force of law.

Between 1929 and 1997, the president had a supportive majority in the legislature and had **all** his proposed legislation approved. The president's cabinet is traditionally made up of close friends and supporters. When the PRI held the office, leaders of the PRI's corporatist groups also served in the cabinet. Cabinet ministers head their own patronage-based political machines. Fox's and Calderón's cabinets were less close-knit groups than PRI cabinets.

Because the president is limited to one six-year term, there tends to be a very large turnover at the very top of the executive branch. New presidents want their own supporters (*camarillas*) in positions of high authority.

Mexican Political Parties

Partido Accion Nacional
www.pan.org.mx

Partido de la Revolucionario Institucional
www.pri.org.mx/

Partido de la Revolución Democrática
www.prd.org.mx/

Patronato de Apoyo Social
www.pas.org.mx/

Partido del Trabajo
www.pt.org.mx/

Partido Verde Ecologista
www.partidoverde.org.mx/pvem

The Legislature

The bicameral congress is made up of a 128-member Senate and a 500-member Chamber of Deputies. Ninety-six senators are elected directly and 32 are chosen in proportion with their parties' popularities. Three hundred of the deputies are elected from single-member districts. Two hundred are elected proportionally from party lists.

Like the president, who is limited to one six-year term, legislators (and nearly all other elected officials) are not allowed to serve consecutive terms.

The legislature has been marginalized in Mexican politics by

- 60 years of PRI domination
- presidential choice of candidates (as head of the PRI)
- presidential authority to make decrees
- reliance on the executive for information (i.e., no legislative staff)

With the development of coalition politics within the legislature since 1997 and the election of Vicente Fox in 2000, the legislature is asserting more of its formal authority. The PRI and PRD have outnumbered PAN representatives in the Chamber of Deputies since 2000. The majority stalled nearly all of the PAN reform proposals. In opposition for the first time, the legislature became more active than ever before.

The mid-term elections of July 2003 saw PAN lose nearly a quarter of legislative seats to PRD and PRI candidates. Within two weeks, journalists were talking about Fox not only as a "lame duck" president, but as a "dead duck" one as well.[1]

As Calderón was elected in 2006, PAN increased its representation in the Chamber of Deputies from 148 to 206 seats. However, three years later, PAN lost 59 seats, and the PRI and its allies won a near majority of 241 seats in the Chamber of Deputies. This suggests to most observers that the PRI is on track to take back the presidency in 2012. Do you know how valid that prediction was?

Elections

The PRI's monopoly on power was legitimized by its electoral victories. The party controlled the Comisión Federal de Elecciones (Federal Elections Commission or CFE), which validated vote counts. CFE election results were widely seen as fraudulent. Nonetheless, nearly every victory was probably authentic. Most observers and many, if not most, Mexicans believe the climax of electoral fraud took place during the 1988 "election" of President Carlos Salinas de Gortari.

One of the 1990s' reforms was the creation of an independent Instituto Electoral Federal (Federal Electoral Institute or IEF). The IEF gained a reputation for running honest elections that was tarnished a bit by the 2006 presidential election. Watch for further developments.

Since 1997, PRI success at the ballot box has declined, more people are voting, and the PAN candidate has become president. Voter turnout fell, however, in the July 2003 legislative elections to 41%. In 2006, turnout was just over 59%, a little lower than in 2000.

The Judiciary

Mexico's legal system has operated on Roman and Napoleonic traditions. That means, for instance, there is much more reliance on written law than on precedent and there is more reliance on investigation by judges and law enforcement than on adversarial process.

There is a hierarchy of state and federal courts topped by a federal supreme court. As in the USA, the upper level courts are primarily appellate courts. The supreme court can declare laws and government actions unconstitutional by a vote of eight or more of the eleven judges. The courts have only very rarely made rulings that were unfriendly to the president.

Individual constitutional rights are broad, and individuals can ask the courts for injunction-like protection from government actions (*amparos*). This is important because of the power of regulatory agencies in Mexico.

In July 2008, President Calderón signed a constitutional amendment creating an adversarial system for criminal law. By 2016, all criminal courts will operate under this new system. The transition has begun in several states, but it will be a gradual change. Everyone from cops on the beat to judges will need to learn new ways of operating.

The Bureaucracy

Most of the half million federal bureaucrats work in Mexico City. There are over a million more federal government employees in schools and another million in state industries. More than half a million people work for state and local governments.

For lower-level civil servants, there's job security to compensate for low wages. Mid-level jobs and above are patronage positions. There are opportunities for advancement — especially at the transition from one *sexenio* to another. Civil servants work for their patrons (bosses) more than for the state. When a minister gets a new portfolio (i.e., a new ministry to administer), his staff (his *camarilla*) moves with him to the new ministry.

The Military

The Mexican army has a tradition of being non-political. Like the Chinese army of the 1980s, it's been given opportunities to engage in businesses. The army has been used occasionally to maintain domestic law and order and most recently to fight the drug cartels. There have been cases of corruption — especially involving the drug trade — reaching into the military leadership, but they are less common than among the police.

Local Governments

There are 31 states (*estado*) and a federal district for the capital city (*Distrito Federal*). State and local governments depend on the national government for nearly all their funding. This is one of the things that makes them subordinate. The other important factor is that the personnel, both elected and employed, depend on patrons for their jobs. Loyalty, it should be remembered, does not guarantee competence. Nor does it rule out competence.

The disruption of the PRI monopoly on power has interrupted some of these patron-client networks. The electoral and political reforms at the top of the system have the least effect on local government and politics.

Elites

In spite of the PAN and PRD successes in electoral politics, the political elite is increasingly integrated in Mexico. PRI leaders rise through particular *camarillas*. These are based on geographic, "old school," and family connections. The "old school"

connections are made not only through the National University of Mexico (Universidad Nacional Autónoma de México or UNAM), but frequently through prestigious graduate schools in the USA like Stanford and Harvard.

Almost all the people at the very top are natives and residents of Mexico City (*capitalinos*). They are well educated, many with graduate degrees in economics and political science (*técnicos*), not in law like many of the US elite. PAN leaders are more likely than PRI or PRD leaders to have gained success in business before entering politics.

Below the leading elite, people are more likely to be *politicos*, that is, people who have achieved a level of power through political experience.

The older, more experienced *politicos* are often referred to as *los dinosaurios* because of their age and resistance to political reform.

4. CITIZENS, SOCIETY, AND THE STATE

The cleavages that divide the Mexican populace are

- racial: 60% of the population is *Mestizo* and 30% is Amerindian

- geographic: 75% of Mexicans are urban dwellers (Mexico City's population is 18 million); the northern part of the country is more prosperous than the center or the south (except for Mexico City) — the farther south you go, the greater the poverty of the people

- social class: 1) rural farmers, nearly all Indians, are the poorest and most exploited; 2) the poor urban, unskilled workers; 3) the growing working class; 4) a middle class that grew rapidly after World War II; 5) an upper-middle class that holds much of the political power; and 6) a tiny rural, landowning class that holds much of the rest of the political power.

The racial and class cleavages have been institutionalized to a degree by the corporatist structure of the PRI (see the next section about parties).

The north-south division is reflected in the strength of PAN in the north and PRD around Mexico City. The Zapatista rebellion in Chiapas may also be a reflection of that split, although it also illustrates the racial and class divisions. (Remember, when cleavages coincide, as they do in Chiapas, they are the most divisive.)

For an urban society, Mexico is still symbolically connected to its rural and Indian origins. Political integration has been quite successful. Nearly all citizens see themselves as Mexicans; there's a common language, and a common religious faith. If the Aztecs and the Mayas are powerful symbols of Mexican culture, revolution is the symbol of Mexican politics. The heroes of the revolution are still heroes. Social justice, a primary theme of revolution, is still held up as a national value — although that is changing in present-day Mexico.

Mexican nationalism and the country's relationship to the USA are other prominent parts of the political culture. The dictator Porfirio Diaz once lamented, "Poor Mexico. So far from God and so close to the United States." That's only one aspect of the relationship. Other aspects include the *maquiladoras* near the Mexican-US border, the relative prosperity of northern Mexico, and the migrants — legal and illegal — who leave for the USA and send millions of dollars of postal money orders home from there.

Some political scientists call Mexican politics "informal." To them it means that who you know and who knows you are more important than the formal structures and procedures of government and politics. The patron-client relationships (*camarillas*) are, from the top of the system to the bottom, the critical features. Even peasants in remote villages know how the system works and how to take advantage of it (although the benefits they receive are pretty minimal). At the

grassroots level, this participation is often more cynical than enthusiastic. And everyone knows who has the power above them. The status and power of strong leaders is important in Mexican culture beyond politics as well.

This is "clientalism." Hand in hand with this clientalism is corporatism. With its origins in church-dominated medieval Europe, corporatism starts from an assumption of community, not individual rights. People, it is assumed, are members of groups which make up society. What's necessary is that groups be represented in the process of making decisions in the best interests of the whole society. If that decision-making process is guided by a wise and moral leader, things will work out for the best.

Do you see how corporatism is connected to clientalism?

Machine politics based on clientalism and corporatism can easily slide into corruption. Leaders of corporatist groups or *camarillas* can be co-opted by offers of position or material rewards. Patrons can help maintain clients' loyalty by offering rewards for votes. Clients can repay their patrons with votes or manipulated ballot tallies. The PRI used all these to maintain power. Electoral reforms of the 1980s and '90s did as much to bring PRI's monopoly on power to an end as did changes in public opinion.

The nature and rewards of machine politics may explain why surveys show that people think the system is legitimate, but they're very critical of the people running the regime. It may also be why people credited the government with bringing economic prosperity in the 1950s and '60s **and** blamed the government for the economic problems of the '80s and '90s.

Parties

The Partido Revolucionaro Institucional (Institutional Revolutionary Party or PRI) is still the only nationally organized party. It was in control of government at all levels from its founding in 1929 until 1997.

It's organized through a huge hierarchy of personalized patron-client relationships (*camarillas*) and through corporatist representation of large groups of workers, farmers, small-scale entrepreneurs, public employees, and civic groups. (There was once a group to represent the military, as well.) The main groups, all created by PRI leaders, are

- Confederación de Trabajadores de México (CTM or National Confederation of Labor)
- Confederación Nacional Campesina (CNC or National Confederation of Peasants)
- Confederación Nacional de Organizaciones Populares (CNOP or Popular Citizens Movement)

The PRI built these corporatist groups into its structure. The party's monopoly on power made corporatism an integral part of governing Mexico. Historically, the PRI has used combinations of threats, violence, rewards, government-funded campaigns, and voting fraud to maintain its power.

The end of the PRI monopoly has begun to break up the corporatist structure of Mexican politics as well. As PAN and the Partido de la Revolución (PRD) appeal to segments of the PRI's corporatist groups, the diversity of Mexican politics begins to resemble the diversity of Mexican society.

As a party, the PRI solicits votes not only through policy promises, but also through patronage jobs, economic development projects, access to public services, and material gifts to voters.

In the 1990s, PRI reforms began making the party more democratic. Whether those reforms will be sustained is open to question. Some of the leadership, the *técnicos*, educated in economics and government (often in the USA) favor the changes, but others, the *politicos* (or *los dinosaurios*) do not want to lose the power they hold at the center of a crucial institution.

PRI supporters are more likely rural, less educated, and older than supporters of other parties.

The Partido de Acción Nacional (National Action Party or PAN) is almost as old as the PRI, but it was a party exclusively in opposition until 2000. Like PRI, its roots are in the north of the country, but it has resisted centralization and supports a more market-driven economy. It has also opposed the anti-clericalism of the PRI.

The success of Fox, Calderón, and PAN probably came about because of this center-right party's persistence, efforts to make alliances with other centrist groups, Mexican economic crises, scandals involving PRI elites, and PRI-instigated electoral reforms.

PAN supporters are more likely urban, middle class or upper-middle class northerners than supporters of other parties. It has long had the reputation of being the party of the wealthy.

The Partido de la Revolución (Democratic Revolutionary Party or PRD) began as a coalition of leftist socialist parties and a reformist wing of the PRI. Originally its biggest asset was its leader, Cuauhtémoc Cárdenas, son of the popular former president. Mexico City's popular mayor, Andres Manual López Obrador, a protégé of the younger Cárdenas, was the PRD presidential candidate in the 2006 elections. The party has been competitive in legislative elections; Obrador's loss to Calderón was not clearly the result of a fair election.

So far PRD is a pragmatic opposition party. PRD supporters tend to be younger, more likely working class, more politically active, and better educated than supporters of other parties. They're also more likely to be urban or from small towns.

Interest Groups

Until recently, most interest groups have been co-opted by the PRI. Even the student leaders of the 1968 anti-government demonstrations were recruited by the PRI. Some powerful groups like entrepreneurs and the Catholic Church remained outside the PRI. They made their preferences known through personal relationships with the president and his cabinet.

Lobbying and negotiations within the PRI were the only effective ways to influence policy. The representation of corporatist groups created fairly formal channels for accommodation. The patron-client relationships offer alternative ways to influence policy. This process tends to keep issues small and localized.

These days, there are more and more local civic groups. Sports clubs are common in cities and villages. Neighborhood and village improvement societies are encouraged and often reap benefits of patron-client politics. Environmental groups have grown in number and size because NAFTA encouraged links with US environmental groups. These developments have complicated the system. The groups are gaining the reputation of more effectively representing the interests of their members than the formalized, corporatist groups of the PRI.

Because politics and governing are changing and these groups are outside of the traditional PRI structure, their influence is small. But the end of the PRI monopoly on power may offer interest groups more chances to influence policy.

Political Socialization

The national government controls formal socialization. (That means the PRI controlled it until very recently.) There is a prescribed curriculum for all schools, public and private. The education ministry provides textbooks to all schools. The Mexican revolution, revolutionary values, and the achievements of government are emphasized. More and more middle class and upper-middle class students are going to Catholic and private schools where government supervision of curriculum is less strict (especially under the PAN presidents). It's likely that anti-socialist and pro-clerical lessons get taught in those schools.

Personal political experience is the other great teacher. Nearly everyone has experience with government and party *politicos*. More people, even peasants, are active in civic groups. Most of these experiences are limited to local politics, but some are beginning to disrupt or challenge the *camarilla* organizations.

People have tended to participate by supporting parties and voting or by seeking to influence policies that affect them directly. Voting is required, and attending rallies is expected and rewarded.

Violence is also part of the political culture. It's there from the very top, where political assassinations take place, to the bottom, where peasants rise up to alleviate injustice. The political reaction

A New Era?

The deportment of PRI governments traditionally has been dictated by the party's upper echelon, the old guard, commonly known as *los dinosaurios*. These now discredited veterans are being battered by the country's press for being out of touch with Mexican society and realities. Their tactics worked well in a nation that had been narrowly ruled by an autocratic system since its 'modern day' rebirth in the 16th century, when Hernan Cortéz eliminated the Aztec empire. In the past two decades, however, the forces of global capitalism and increased trade relationships with free-market democracies have enlightened and invigorated Mexican political culture, which previously had been an archetype of passivity.

— Marsden, Graham, "Dinosaurs, Foxes and Democracy," published by the Council on Hemispheric Relations, *www.coha.org/WRH_issues/wrh_20_10_dinos.htm*

to rising rates of violent crime, kidnapping, and political corruption has been swift and sometimes effective (for instance, PAN lost the governorship of Chihuahua in 1998 after credible allegations of corruption against the party's governor). However, in Oaxaca, the PRI governor with a reputation for dishonesty is still in power. In a comparative context, violence is less common in Mexico than in many other industrializing countries. But it still seems to be the last resort of frustrated political ambition.

Machismo is almost a cliché when discussing Latin American cultures. In Mexico, it's used to explain the prevalence of political centralization and violence. Women didn't get to vote in Mexico until 1953. There are few women in politics. But things are changing. The participation of women in politics is rising. More middle-class women are attending university. More working class women have jobs outside the home. And women's groups are among the most active of the new civic groups that have been formed in the last 20 years. Finca, Compartamos, Accion International, and 32 other micro-credit banks have made more than a million small loans to help establish small businesses in Mexico in the past decade. Almost all of the loans have been made to women.[2]

Mexico's mass media have traditionally been publicity agents for the PRI and PRI presidents. All of them depended upon government press releases for political news. The government held a monopoly on newsprint. Favored newspapers and magazines were allowed to buy on credit, and sometimes bills were never sent. Unfavored publications had to pay up front IF there was paper available. Journalists and editors received "*chayotes*" (cash gifts) from public officials.

When in the 1970s, the newspaper *Excélsior* started publishing articles critical of the government, public money financed a hostile takeover that ousted the editor and key writers.

Broadcast media is been controlled by two large corporations, Televisa and TV Azteca, which bring in 93% of all broadcast advertising revenue. TV Azteca, a former parastatal, was privatized in the early '90s. As a government-owned network, it was loyal to the PRI-dominated system. Today these two networks are owned by PRI loyalists. There is a bit of competition from Rupert Murdoch's SKY satellite system and his Direct TV, but the costs of subscribing restrict the distribution and influence of both.

5. POLITICAL AND ECONOMIC CHANGE

Compared to other industrializing and Latin American countries, Mexico has institutionalized and maintained civilian political authority for a long time. Factors which facilitated this success include

- the emphasis on the importance of revolution
- the term limits on presidents and the high turnovers at the top every six years
- the value placed on pragmatic bargaining to resolve political conflicts within the PRI
- the authoritarian channeling of political conflicts within the PRI for so long

PRI dominance has encouraged competition among elites and "behind the scenes" negotiations. It also offered many prizes to those who played by the PRI rules.

Current changes have many causes:

- urbanization and the growth of the middle class
- economic crises — especially related to the Mexican government's deficit spending
- globalization as NAFTA and international economic support has brought more transparency to Mexican politics and economics
- privatization, which has the potential to create more independent elites and more routes to power

- communications technology, which means growing access to information and allows more Mexicans to see more clearly global standards and practices and allows local discontent to become global (see "Ejército Zapatista de Liberación Nacional" at *www. ezln.org.mx* or "Zapatistas in Cyberspace" at *www.eco.utexas.edu/faculty/Cleaver/zapsincyber.html*)

These things all played roles in ending the PRI monopoly on the presidency in 2000. They have played roles in the popularity of López Obrador. Look at Calderón's record for evidence of further changes.

6. PUBLIC POLICY

Policy is made at the very top of the Mexican regime. The president's closest advisors are the most enthusiastic supporters. Within the PRI, union and peasant groups' representatives may resist presidential policymaking because they have identifiable power bases.

There is bureaucratic resistance to some presidential policies. Fox and Calderón have seen this in action because they have not been able to replace all the PRI appointees in government. Sometimes this resistance comes from policy disagreements. Other times it stems from corruption or simple incompetence.

Fox and Calderón also saw resistance in the legislature. This never happened to PRI presidents. Public opinion of the PAN presidents went down because they were unable to chart new policy courses. The election results of 2003 and 2009 underlined the governments' powerlessness and loss of popularity.

Economic policy is central for whomever makes policy. Growth is vital. Restructuring is important. Responding to global competition is important. Deficit spending is probably dangerous, although oil revenues may help avoid that pitfall.

Social welfare issues may be discussed more than in the past.

As you look at what is going on in Mexican policy making, what is being discussed? Whose proposals are becoming policy? Whose popularity is up? Whose is down? Has drug cartel violence in the north subsided or grown? Is there any progress toward resolving the insurgency in Chiapas? Are there visible problems elsewhere in Mexico? You should have clues about all those things.

FOOTNOTES

1   *The Economist*, July 10, 2003

2   *New York Times*, March 19, 2003

REVIEW EXERCISE

This little exercise is not meant to be comprehensive. It's meant to get you thinking about some of the basic facts and point out areas you might have to review more thoroughly. My responses follow.

1. While Mexico resembles other Third World countries in some ways, it is most UNLIKE many other Third World countries because
    (A) of the absence of large-scale ethnic competition and conflict
    (B) its *rentier* economy is so dependent upon oil production
    (C) the political party system has replaced patron-client networks
    (D) it has had nearly 200 years of independence
    (E) large numbers of people are subsistence farmers

2. In order to build a modern state in Mexico in the early 20ᵗʰ century, PRI politicians had to contend with the power of all the following EXCEPT
    (A) foreign investors
    (B) Indian farmers
    (C) monarchists
    (D) hacienda landowners
    (E) the religious hierarchy

3. In the Mexican regime, the executive (head of government)
    (A) is limited to a single term in office
    (B) has few patronage opportunities
    (C) can do little to direct the country's foreign policy
    (D) is free to choose a successor
    (E) oversees elections

4. The legislative electoral system in Mexico
    (A) guarantees that legislators are chosen by majorities in their districts
    (B) ensures that all viable interest groups are represented
    (C) guarantees that more than one party will be represented in the legislature
    (D) allows parties to choose legislators after the voting
    (E) marginalizes radical parties

5. The change to an adversarial criminal law system in Mexico means that
    (A) judges will evaluate evidence produced by prosecutors and convict accused criminals
    (B) prosecutors will have more power to put people behind bars
    (C) police investigations will determine sentences
    (D) jury trials will be nearly eliminated
    (E) accused criminals will now have an active role in their own defense

6. A primary reason that Mexican states have little power is that
    (A) population is uniformly spread across the country and not concentrated in urban areas
    (B) state officials are appointed, not elected
    (C) the constitution gives them little authority
    (D) nearly all state government revenue comes from the national government
    (E) it's inexpensive to bribe state officials

7. Corporatism in the PRI
    (A) allowed the party to operate many large businesses
    (B) ensured that private businesses controlled policy making
    (C) meant that social-economic groups were represented in the party
    (D) guaranteed private ownership of public utilities
    (E) is reflected in the exclusion of organized religious interest groups

8. Which of the following definitions is *incorrect?*
    (A) *dinosaurios* – experienced political activists who often resist reforms
    (B) *camarillas* – female politicians holding important posts in political parties
    (C) *politicos* – activists and party officials
    (D) *técnicos* – well-educated political officials and party leaders
    (E) *capitalinos* – residents of Mexico City

9. A major reason for the decline in the power of the PRI has been
   (A) a refusal of party leaders to consider political reforms
   (B) economic, social, and educational changes in Mexican society
   (C) rapid growth of privatized industry
   (D) the growth of evangelical Protestant religious movements
   (E) increases in oil revenues that PRI leaders controlled

10. Pragmatism has long been a feature of Mexican political culture. In Mexico, this has meant that
   (A) promises made by political candidates are rarely kept
   (B) PRI platforms have not changed much in the past 50 years
   (C) Obrador's leadership of the PRD is based on doctrinaire socialism
   (D) political compromise is not a highly respected behavior
   (E) ideological parties have not been notably successful

(For responses, see below)

11: Know ... Iran

1. INTRODUCTION TO COMPARATIVE POLITICS

When I began learning about Iran, I kept noticing the extraordinary things. It's a theocracy. It's a theocratic republic. It's a Shiite theocratic republic. It's in a part of the world dominated by Arabs, but it's not an Arab nation. Most everyone speaks Farsi, not Arabic. Iran (Persia) has a grand history going back thousands of years. Most of its neighbors seem to be post-colonial constructs.

But, political science is all about making generalizations. Unique examples don't fit into that paradigm. So you have to recognize how Iran is like other countries. You have to see what institutions and political processes in Iran do the things that are done in other political systems. You have to be able to understand how the characteristics of Iran make it like other nation-states.

Where do we start? How about beginning with Persian authoritarianism? Add to that the image Shiites have of themselves as a persecuted minority. Mix them with a bit of early 20th century

democratic thought and you'll have a long-term historical context.

Iranian experiences during the Cold War, the Islamic Revolution, the war with Iraq, and economic stagnation and unemployment provide a short-term context. Most Iranians are too young to remember the first three. But, you need to recognize how those things affect today's regime and politics.

Similarly, import substitution funded by oil revenue, influential market sectors, and concentrated land ownership provide a context for economic policymaking. Iranian political and economic isolation must also be taken into account.

Politically, there is a Persian ideal of authoritarian leadership that is just. How does that fit within a theocracy based on *sharia*? There is also a powerful theme of the need to represent the people. It goes back to the constitutional reforms of the early 20th century and the state-centered economic reforms of Mossadeq that has been reinforced by global democratization. It was recognized in Khomeini's political philosophy as the need to represent the will of the people. The constitution recognizes representative government in an elected president and legislature, the Majlis. But, how do those representative politics coexist with unaccountable theocratic leaders who hold ultimate power?

Don't get distracted by Iranian religious, ethnic, or linguistic specialness. Neither mass society nor the elite is unified. Policymaking doesn't happen

HISTORICAL TURNING POINTS

559 BCE	Empire of Cyrus the Great
332 BCE	Conquest by Alexander and Greeks
250 BCE	Parthian Dynasty
226 CE	Sassanian Dynasty
638	Arab/Islamic conquest
1219	Mongol invasion
1501	Safavid Dynasty establishes Shiism as state religion
1796	Qajar Dynasty

POLITICAL TURNING POINTS

1905	Constitutional revolution
1908	Oil discovered
1925	Reza Khan overthrows Qajar Dynasty
1941	Muhammad Reza Shah Pahlavi becomes shah
1950s	Mossadeq nationalizes oil industry; US coup restores shah
1960s-70s	White Revolution/Khomeini in exile
1979	Islamic Revolution
1980-88	War with Iraq
1989	Khomeini dies - Khamenei succeeds him as Supreme Leader

after a power struggle in the Assembly of Religious Experts

1997	Reformist Khatami elected president
2000	Reformist candidates win control of Majlis
2004	Conservatives regain control of Majlis
2005	Conservative Ahmadinejad elected president
2009	Ahmadinejad reelected; major opposition demonstrations; Revolutionary Guard emerges as a primary political force

through some quiet automatic consensus. When Mahmoud Ahmadinejad was elected in 2005, the next major political event was the rejection of several of his cabinet choices by a conservative Majlis. You'll have to look beyond the obvious for political cleavages. Why, for instance, do most of the Grand Ayatollahs in Iran disagree with Khomeini's doctrine of the Guardianship of the Jurist?

In spite of oil wealth, Iran — like Nigeria — fits the model of a Third World country. Most people are poor. A huge proportion of the population is dependent on government or government-sanctioned charities. There is ethnic conflict, especially in the north. But there are conflicts within the dominant ethnic and religious groups. Merchants, peasants, entrepreneurs, religious charitable foundations, and military interests jockey to influence policymaking. And, as a *rentier* economy, Iran

is dependent on the global markets, even if it is somewhat isolated.

2. SOVEREIGNTY, AUTHORITY, AND POWER

The Iranian regime may be unique in claiming to be a constitutional theocratic republic. Khomeini's political philosophy — *ve-layat-e faqih* (Guardianship of the Jurist) — rejects democracy but embraces representing the will of the people. To Westerners, it sounds like an oxymoron or a hypocritical rationalization. But the constitution does include important democratic and theocratic elements. Politics determines which elements are more important.

You should be able to recognize, if not list, which government officials are elected and which ones unelected. You should also be able to list the primary powers of each and the limitations on their powers.

Elected and Unelected Leaders in Iran

Elected

President

Majlis

Assembly of Religious Experts

Unelected Supreme Leader

Expediency Council

Guardian Council

Judiciary

Cabinet

Directors of Bonyads

Revolutionary Guard Officers

Wealth and Power to be Reckoned With

...The Islamic Republic is a strange dictatorship. As it ... relies on the bullies of Hezbollah and the equally thuggish Revolutionary Guards. The powers that be claim to derive legitimacy from Allah but remain on top with gangster-like methods of intimidation, violence and murder.

Who controls today's Iran? ... The real power is a handful of clerics and their associates who call the shots behind the curtain and have gotten very rich in the process.

Ironically, the man most adept at manipulating this hidden power structure is one of Iran's best-known characters — Ali Akbar Hashemi Rafsanjani, who has been named an ayatollah... He was the speaker of parliament and Khomeini's right-hand man in the 1980s, president of Iran from 1989 to 1997 and is now chairman of the powerful Expediency Council and the Assembly of Experts...

He played it smart, aligning himself in the 1960s with factions led by Ayatollah Khomeini, then becoming the go-to guy after the revolution. A hard-liner ideologically, Rafsanjani nonetheless has a pragmatic streak. He convinced Khomeini to end the Iran-Iraq war... In the 1990s he restarted Iran's nuclear program. He is also the father of Iran's "privatization" program. During his presidency the stock market was revived, some government companies were sold to insiders, foreign trade was liberalized and the oil sector was opened up to private companies. Most of the good properties and contracts, say dissident members of Iran's Chamber of Commerce, ended up in the hands of mullahs, their associates and, not least, Rafsanjani's own family, who rose from modest origins as small-scale pistachio farmers...

The 1979 revolution transformed the Rafsanjani clan into commercial pashas. One brother headed the country's largest copper mine; another took control of the state-owned TV network; a brother-in-law became governor of Kerman province, while a cousin runs an outfit that dominates Iran's $400 million pistachio export business; a nephew and one of Rafsanjani's sons took key positions in the Ministry of Oil; another son heads the Tehran Metro construction project (an estimated $700 million spent so far). Today, operating through various foundations and front companies, the family is also believed to control one of Iran's biggest oil engineering companies, a plant assembling Daewoo automobiles, and Iran's best private airline (though the Rafsanjanis insist they do not own these assets).

...The gossip on the street ... has the Rafsanjanis stashing billions of dollars in bank accounts in Switzerland and Luxembourg; controlling huge swaths of waterfront in Iran's free economic zones on the Persian Gulf; and owning whole vacation resorts on the idyllic beaches of Dubai, Goa and Thailand...

— Klebnikov, Paul, "Millionaire Mullahs," Forbes.com, 07.21.03,
www.forbes.com/free_forbes/2003/0721/056.html

The regime, like all Persian and Iranian regimes, is highly centralized. But there are many institutions and people holding power and authority.

For example: The religious charitable foundations (*bonyads*), whose directors are appointed by the Supreme Leader, were created from the factories, mines, and estates seized from the elite of the last shah's regime. Their revenues may be half the size of government revenue (which comes mostly from oil). The largest *bonyad* employs nearly half a million people. It is exempt from taxes. *Bonyads* do not have to publish balance sheets. They are great opportunities for patronage and corruption.

In the 1980s, the military was seen as opposing the Islamic Revolution. Its officer corps was purged several times. Khomeini's Revolutionary Guards were eventually integrated into the army and put in charge. Nonetheless, professional military officers were essential during the war with Iraq. To keep track of what's going on in the Revolutionary Guards and the military, the Supreme Leader appoints clerics as chaplains to each military unit. It's difficult to know if the chaplains' prime duty is provide spiritual services or to report back to the Supreme Leader about the loyalty of the armed forces. Today, Revolutionary Guard leaders are just as likely to be monitoring the loyalty of religious and political leaders.

The Iranian Revolutionary Guard Corps (IRGC) was founded in 1979 as a politically reliable military force. It's power grew during the war with Iraq. During Ahmadinejad's first term, IRGC members and veterans made up a majority of appointed officials and two-thirds of the cabinet. They also gained control of many parastatals, bonyads, and commercial services (like banking and engineering). There is also good evidence that the IRGC is involved in the lucrative black market economy.

After the disputed 2009 election, the IRGC and its adjunct the Basij Resistance Force (or Basij) were the primary law and order forces that put down protests. The IRGC is intimately involved in Iran's nuclear program as well.

Merchants, known as *bazaaris*, are powerful economic and political actors. As a group, they seem to be pragmatic — forming temporary alliances to meet their needs and protect their business interests. Some of their interests are not legal — smuggling and the black market are profitable enterprises.

There's an educated middle class. Its influence is greater than its small size would indicate. Declining voting rates in the 2004 and 2005 elections were seen as signs of withdrawal from politics,

---

Religious Economy

Book a nice hotel room, eat a meal or buy a soft drink — chances are the money flows to one of Iran's "foundations" and on to the country's powerful, hard-line clerics. The impressive holdings of the foundations, or *bonyads*, cover nearly every aspect of life from soybean farms to luxury hotels. Outside Iran, the *bonyads'* wealth include cargo ships and a New York office building...

No serious restructuring of the anemic economy is possible without breaking the *bonyads'* stranglehold. But that means confronting an ultra-powerful establishment, which some experts say includes confidants and key allies of supreme leader Ayatollah Ali Khamenei. A growing number of critics accuse the *bonyads* of acting as autonomous conglomerates outside any normal controls or scrutiny.

Some of the *bonyads'* funds still go to social programs like clinics or to families who lost relatives in the 1980-88 war with Iraq. But the groups increasingly look more like hard-edged businesses with strategic plans and rich portfolios.

The full extent of the *bonyad* wealth is difficult to ascertain, since they are neither audited nor obliged to fully disclose their ventures. But the *bonyads'* own material gives a hint of their reach. About 70 different farm-related companies are operated by *bonyad* groups... Tourism holdings include more than 24 hotels... The *bonyads* run global shipping lines from offices in London and Athens, Greece, and there is the Bonyad Eastern Railway at home... Iran's best-selling soft drink, Zam Zam (formerly Pepsi), is a *bonyad* brand.

The *bonyad* boards are rooted in Iran's political culture. Many directors were leaders of the revolution and enjoyed close ties with its leader, Ayatollah Ruhollah Khomeini...

— Alexander's Gas and Oil Connections: News & Trends: Middle East,
www.gasandoil.com/goc/news/ntm00633.htm

The Basij

They may wear a uniform or ordinary street clothes. Their numbers are unclear. They rush the streets with brute strength.

They are the Basij, Iran's volunteer paramilitary group that for more than a week has cracked down on the thousands of protesters in the bloody aftermath of the Islamic republic's disputed presidential election...

While the Basij – the word means "mobilization" in the Farsi language – is often described by outsiders as shadowy and mysterious, Iranians have had run-ins with the militia for three decades.

The Basij was established in 1979... as a popular auxiliary arm of the Islamic Revolutionary Guard, a military unit under the direct control of Iran's supreme leader, to defend the principles of the movement.

The group, at least at first, was made up of men either too old or young to serve in the Revolutionary Guard. Until now, they were perhaps best known for the "human wave" attacks during the Iran-Iraq war that reportedly cleared out minefields for the professional military...

After the Iran-Iraq war, the Basij returned to its role as an internal security force to enforce Islamic morality...

While experts say there is a hardline ideological core to Basij, its members, who often come from lower-class backgrounds, are attracted to the perks that the Basij (and its superior agency, the Revolutionary Guard) has to offer: a little cash, a seat at a university, and a bit of authority...

Samira Simone, "Feared Basij militia has deep history in Iranian conflict," 22 June 2009, CNN.com/world
www.cnn.com/2009/WORLD/meast/06/22/Iran.basij.militia.profile/index.html

but middle class voters turned out in great numbers in 2009 and led the protests that followed the flawed elections. Most of these people work for the government or the *bonyads*. They are suspected of secularism and holding sympathies for Western values. The suspicions are based, in part, on the large numbers of technically illegal satellite dishes visible in middle class neighborhoods. These suspicions sideline them in an Islamic theocracy.

Separated in many ways from that elite are the urban and rural masses of poverty-stricken Iranians. Their power comes from their support of religious leaders and their numbers. President Ahmadinejad's election is testimony to both of those sources of power. These people make up the rank and file of the vigilante *Basij*. They are supported by the *bonyads* that dole out welfare and jobs.

Diversity is recognized, even in the constitution. But authorities exert pressure for conformity.

That's often seen as demands that local schools teach in Farsi rather than local languages (which are constitutionally protected).

Another form of diversity is the growing cleavage between the elites and the masses. Rafsanjani's loss in the 2005 election signaled that gap. The demonstrations and riots after the 2009 election confirmed it. The rapidly growing population of poor young people, rural and urban, learns politics from the imams, the *bonyads*, and the IRGC. The Islamic Revolution is ancient history. No one is sure what lessons these young people will take away from their life experiences.

Political authority comes from representation, Islamic truth, adherence to *sharia*, and Khomeini's ideology. Power comes from the government, the *bonyads*, and violence or threats of violence. The purges of the 1980s reminded outside observers of the Stalinist purges. (Assassinations of opposi-

Distribution of Powers

SUPREME LEADER

is the "vital link" between branches of government

determines the "interests of aIslam"

can dismiss the president

is the commander-in-chief of the military and can appoint and dismiss officers

nominates and can remove judges and prosecutors

appoints half the members of the Guardian Council

appoints the Minister of Justice

appoints Imam Jum'ehs at principal city mosques

appoints the director of national radio and television

appoints directors of *bonyads*

directs a staff of over 600

PRESIDENT

administers government

presents annual budget to Majlis

supervises economic matters

proposes legislation to Majlis

is chair of the National Security Council

appoints vice president(s) and cabinet (except Justice Minister)

appoints local governors and mayors

appoints directors of parastatals

MAJLIS

"represents the nation"

enacts ordinary laws (not *sharia*)

investigates and supervises affairs of state

approves or removes cabinet members

appoints half the members of the Guardian Council from a list presented by the chief judge

can approve budgets, foreign loans, treaties

GUARDIAN COUNCIL

approves or vetoes Majlis legislation

approves candidates for all elective offices

ASSEMBLY OF RELIGIOUS EXPERTS

elects and can dismiss the Supreme Leader

EXPEDIENCY COUNCIL

resolves conflicts between Majlis and Guardian Council

meets in secret

initiates legislation

tion figures outside of Iran resembled the killing of Trotsky in Mexico.) The purges reminded some Iranians of SAVAK (the shah's secret police). The *Basij* remind outsiders of Mao's Red Guards. They remind Iranians not to stray far from strict interpretation of Islamic law and the ruling clerics' teachings.

Iran's economy is plagued by unemployment, inflation, poverty, government subsidies, and a rapidly growing population. The rapid population growth means there is a huge group of young people — mostly uneducated, unskilled, and unemployed. The economy is characterized by government direction and dependence on oil revenues. Both the *bazaaris* and the *bonyads* demand protection from competition for their economic activities and have power to get most of the protection they want. Economic isolation since the 1980s has meant Iran has been dependent upon itself. There are voices arguing for liberalization, but they're weak and hardly heard.

3. POLITICAL INSTITUTIONS

Sorting out the structure of Iranian government is not as simple as listing executive positions and institutions in one column, legislative institutions in another, and judicial features in a third. It's time to appreciate ambiguity again.

This descriptive process isn't that simple for more familiar Western systems either, but we know the exceptions and the rationales for them. (For instance, how do we classify a British quango like the Prescription Pricing Authority?)

In the Iranian regime, the president and the cabinet are obviously parts of the executive branch. Local officials and heads of parastatals, appointed by the president, are also part of the executive.

But, what about the Supreme Leader? He is to "determine the interests of Islam." He can dismiss the president. He is commander-in-chief of the armed forces. He nominates and can remove judges and prosecutors. He appoints half of the Guardian Council, imams at principal mosques, the Minister of Justice, the director of national radio and television, and the heads of the *bonyads*. These powers are executive powers, but the policy implications are much broader.

Is the Expediency Council that can meet secretly and legislate as well as mediate between other branches of government an executive or a legislative body? And where does the Assembly of Religious Experts fit in?

The judges, from village imam to the highest appellate court act judicially. But in a system based on the "guardianship of the jurist" is the Supreme Leader also part of the judiciary?

You should be asking similar questions about the Revolutionary Guard, the *Basij*, the directors of the *bonyads*, and the military chaplains who report, not to superior officers, but to the Supreme Leader.

I think your best bet here is to identify **powers** or **actions** as executive, legislative, or judicial, rather than classifying positions or institutions. Thus when the Supreme Leader appoints the Expediency Council, he's acting as an executive. When he overrules a judge by removing him, he's acting both as an executive and as a judge.

So, you need to learn what powers each position or institution has and what functions are performed.

What else should you know about the structure of the state?

The Majlis is a unicameral legislature. Members are elected every four years by majorities in single member districts. The Majlis considers budgets and bills proposed by the president and the cabinet. It can vote no confidence in members of the cabinet. The bills passed by the Majlis and approved by the Guardian Council are statute law, not *sharia*.

The president is rather like a corporate president who works under a Chief Executive Officer (CEO). He is elected every four years by a majority of a popular vote. He can serve no more than two consecutive terms.

The judges are all clerics. The judicial system is hierarchical, so decisions can be appealed.

The bureaucratic ministries are dominated by clerics and their technocrat relatives. The Culture and Islamic Guidance Ministry oversees the media and issues licenses to newspapers, magazines, and journals. It also has a hand in regulating the content of the Internet.

The Intelligence ministry operates domestically and internationally. Through connections to local imams, it may indirectly control the *Basij*, also known as *Hezbollahis*, who take to the streets sporadically to stifle dissent and to strictly enforce Islamic rules about women's dress, public displays of affection, consumption of alcohol, and proper piety. Most government ministries are heavily involved in economic activities.

Elections

Majlis elections are held every four years. The most recent was in 2008. Presidential elections are also held every four years, most recently in 2009. Candidates must be approved by the Guardian Council. The primary factors in the Council's evaluation are a candidate's loyalty to the "guardianship of the jurist" and the ability of the candidate to win. Up to a third of legislative candidates is regularly disqualified (often including some incumbents), and most presidential candidates have not been allowed on the ballot.

Elections are non-partisan and winners must receive a majority of votes cast, which sometimes requires second-round run-offs. The voting age is 18.

Government media clearly favor some candidates, ignore others, and actively oppose others. Mosques serve as polling sites where imams and Revolutionary Guards oversee voting. Gangs of *basijis* —moving around on motorcycles — ensure that opposition groups don't operate openly near polling stations. All those features of Iranian elections help explain Ahmadinejad's unexpected success in 2009. He was declared the winner before all the votes were counted.

Parties

Political parties were legalized in 1998, but the Iranian party system is still in its infancy. Many powerful people and groups prefer to work through informal channels. Parties and coalitions are often formed just prior to elections around prominent candidates. Most of the parties disappear after the voting. The persistence of the Green Path Movement, organized by unsuccessful presidential candidate Mir-Hosein Musavi, was an exception.

The *bonyads* or Islamic charitable foundations are important political and economic actors. These charities were given property confiscated from the Pahlavi elite. They now have assets of over $100 billion. The largest, with assets of over $20 billion, is the Foundation of the Oppressed. It operates Iran's two biggest newspapers, over 100 construction companies, more than 250 factories and mines, and nearly 500 agricultural enterprises. The directors of the foundations are appointed by the Supreme Leader. The *bonyads* are tax exempt. The distribution of "profits" and the jobs they offer provide a social welfare system and a huge unregulated economic sector. With dependent constituencies and rewards to offer, the foundation directors are politically powerful.

Clerical and secular politicians are divided by personal and organizational loyalties, but they're also divided over familiar issues. Should the government be the primary economic power or should markets have more influence? How extensive should the welfare system be? Should Iran make changes to encourage foreign investment or continue to pursue import substitution? Of course, the answers to these questions also affect the nature of the "guardianship of the jurist." And that's in question, too, but not on the surface of anyone's discussion (except among exile groups). Directors and beneficiaries of *bonyads* as well as *bazaaris* oppose opening the economy to global markets.

An extension of all these questions is the development of nuclear power — civilian or military. The construction of nuclear-powered electricity generators would free Iran to sell more oil. That would bring in more money for internal investment or social welfare. The development of nuclear weapons would make Iran a formidable global power, make some hard policy choices easier and others more difficult. Keep track of developments in this area as examples to use when taking the AP exam.

4. CITIZENS, SOCIETY, AND STATE

The premise of an Islamic theocratic republic seems to be that religious men ultimately know what is best for people and have to limit populism. This means that the definition of citizen common in Western political cultures won't apply in Iran. And it means that political participation will differ.

There are elections and people vote. Representatives are chosen. But the candidates are evaluated and must be approved by a tiny unrepresentative group that is responsible only to the Supreme Leader. The percentage of people voting declined from 2000 to 2009.

There are ephemeral political parties and there are groups that sometimes act politically. None of the parties or other groups can be identified as catch-all parties.

The Revolutionary Guards and the *Basij* are some of the most politically active groups. They not only help administer elections and recruit voters, they use violence and intimidation to prevent any effective opposition to the regime and its rulers. Thus, the large scale protests following the 2009 elections were stopped by gangs of roving vigilantes who killed and beat up protesters. Some observers suggest that this kind of intimidation was responsible for middle class withdrawal from politics in 2005. It's too soon to know what effect the 2009 repression will have on participation. Many older people remember the political executions of over 25,000 people in the first decade of the Islamic Republic. Most people are too young to remember and aren't taught about that in schools.

One thing to remember is that if the opponents of the regime are intimidated and fragmented, supporters are fragmented as well. The off-again, on-again campaigns to strictly enforce proper behavior and dress illustrate these divisions. The major issues dividing the regime elite are over economic issues and the role played by the government in economic and social welfare activities.

There are some quiet social movements among the educated middle class and factory workers.

Women campaign for more equal legal rights and job opportunities. Police broke up small, quiet protests during the last two presidential campaigns. The fact that more than half of university students and nearly half of Iran's physicians are women probably means that there's more activism to come from women. But the educated, middle-class women are a tiny group.

Industrial workers had socialist and communist unions in their past, but today there are no independent unions. Wages, benefits, and job security are determined by employers — many of whom are *bonyads*. So worker activism tends to take place on a small scale and out of the public eye (partly because reporting on it is not allowed).

The government licenses all publications and can revoke those licenses at any time. During Khatami's presidency, more licenses were issued and fewer revoked than earlier. Under Ahmadinejad's first term, government controls tightened somewhat. After the 2009 election, newspapers that were sympathetic to the losers and the protesters were quickly shut down. Western news reports claimed that dozens of journalists were in prison months after the election. Radio and television is even more strictly controlled by the government. Generally, only middle class households can afford access to outside media via satellite television, and the government has made efforts to interfere with satellite transmissions from abroad.

Before 2005, the Internet offered some information and a forum for discussion. Blogs of all persuasions could be found. However within a month of Ahmadinejad taking office, an Internet censorship committee and elements of the judiciary began ordering ISPs to deny access to political sites. In 2010, the government announced plans to create an isolated Iranian computer network whose only connections to the global Internet would be through government servers. While people find ways to work around government barriers, access is not easy.

President of the People

Mahmoud Ahmadinejad was born near Tehran, in 1956. The son of a blacksmith, he was one of seven children in a middle class family. He holds a PhD in traffic and transport from Tehran's University of Science and Technology, where he was a lecturer. He was appointed mayor of Tehran in 2003.

In 1980, Ahmadinejad was part of the student gatherings with the Ayatollah Khomeini...

He joined the Revolutionary Guards voluntarily after the revolution, and he is also reported to have served in covert operations during the 1980-88 Iran-Iraq war... It is alleged that he directed assassinations in the Middle East and Europe...

With the war behind him, Ahmadinejad went into politics. He was appointed governor first of Maku and later governor of the newly created province of Ardabil...

As the Mayor of Tehran, Ahmadinejad... curtailed many of the reforms put in place by the moderates who had run the city before him. He shut down fast-food restaurants, required male city employees to have beards and long sleeves, and instituted separate elevators for men and women in the municipal offices.

He is a self-described principlist; that is, acting politically based on Islamic and revolutionary principles...

He has a reputation for living a simple life and campaigned against corruption and has said, "We did not have a revolution in order to have democracy,"

— BBC World News, Al Jazeera, the Peoples Daily (PRC), BabNet (Tunisia), and GlobalSecurity.org

Since the Islamic Revolution demanded a near-total reordering of politics and society, civil society was destroyed in the decade after 1979. The military and the educational system were purged of anyone suspected of questioning the clerical regime of Khomeini. Most of independent **civil society** that remains exists in the privacy of middle-class neighborhoods. Between 1997 and 2005, there was some revival in the economic sphere (business associations), in artistic circles (especially literature and film), and around the publication of non-political journals. That revival was forced underground by Ahmadinejad's government.

Political cleavages in Iran appear in surprising places. The clerics who run things are not the highest ranking Shiite clerics. The Grand Ayatollahs and most of the Ayatollahs still argue for the traditional Shiite practice of staying out of politics and governance. The clerics in power follow Khomeini's revolutionary ideology. Both groups can unite in opposition to secularists.

The major religious cleavage, though, is between the dominant Shiites and the 10% of Iranians who are Sunni Muslims. The "invisibility" of the Sunnis is illustrated by the fact that there are no Sunni mosques in Tehran.

There are ethnic minorities on the borders of the country. The Azeris in the north are Shiite, but not Persian. About 24% of Iranians are Azeris. In unlikely nightmares, the Persian clerics who rule in Iran fear Azeri demands to secede and unite with Azerbaijan. The fact that Supreme Leader Khamenei is an Azeri is an indication of how integrated the Azeri and Persian elites are.

The social class cleavages are the biggest ones in Iran. They tend to coincide with geographic cleavages. The north side of Tehran, in the cool and beautiful foothills, is middle- and upper-class "territory." The south side of Tehran, in the flat outwash plains, is home to the poor and the recent migrants from the countryside. And the peasants in the rural villages are separate from all the urban groups. The middle classes are more highly educated, more cosmopolitan, and more secular. The lower classes are likely to be devout followers of the local imam, poorly educated, and under or unemployed. The uniting of the urban and rural poor to elect Ahmadinejad might be a sign of things to come.

5. POLITICAL AND ECONOMIC CHANGE

Iran has a history of authoritarianism and change brought about by conquest and force. In many ways, 21st century Iran continues those traditions. There are, however, a couple of signs that change in the future might come about through more reasoned and peaceful processes.

In ancient times, emperors conquered and were conquered. In modern times, coups led by one elite overthrew governments by other elites. The Pahlavi Dynasty came to power that way. The first Pahlavi shah was forced out by international pressure from the Russians and the British. The second shah stayed in power with the help of a coup planned, directed, and funded by the US and British intelligence agencies in the 1950s.

One of those persecuted and forced into exile by the Pahlavi regime went to Iraq and then to France. In exile, he developed a revolutionary ideology and gathered disciples. When he returned to Iran, Khomeini was the charismatic religious and political leader of a revolution.

The Islamic Revolution can be a case study in revolutionary change.

It was a reaction to the Pahlavi authoritarianism and to the White Revolution. The White Revolution was aimed at modernizing Iran's economy as Díaz's authoritarian modernizations had done in Mexico. As in Mexico, only a tiny elite had opportunities to grow rich. The White Revolution widened economic, religious, and cultural cleavages in Iran.

Like the Russian Revolution, the Islamic Revolution was directed from the top by an ideology-driven small leadership. In its early stages it brought together a wide range of opposition to the Pahlavi regime. As in Russia and France, the first post-revolutionary government was a moderate one that fell to radicals. The success of the radicals who followed Khomeini's ideology led to a "terror" not unlike the original in France and a "reshaping" of society similar to Mao's Great Proletarian Cultural Revolution.

Notice how many political comparisons there are in the preceding paragraphs? That should be hint to pay attention to similarities — if not generalizations — that you see in your study of the countries in the AP curriculum.

Since 1979, Iran has seemed to pursue parallel contradictory paths. One is theocratic and the other is democratic. All the cards have been stacked in favor of the autocrats. There have been elections, which have been reasonably fair and open. They haven't had a great effect on policies. The election of a "reformist" president in 1997 did not bring about much reform. In fact, it probably encouraged the authoritarians to solidify their own power. Elections from 2004 to 2009 are evidence of that. Democratization may be a global trend, but it hasn't penetrated the political actions of the regime's elite in Iran. The apparent withdrawal from politics by the educated middle classes and their children since 2000 and the failed attempts at reform in 2009 imply that future change may not come democratically. The huge population of young people in Iran, most religious and not well educated, reinforces that notion.

Pay attention to political changes and their causes during Ahmadinejad's presidency. Be aware, too, that neither scholars nor journalists may get accurate views of the situation. Scholars have not been able to do much more than visit Iran and talk to middle-class academic colleagues. Reporters are limited by government policy and their inability to get in touch with people outside of the middle class.

Ahmadinejad's election in 2005 took outsiders by surprise. They had talked to their educated, middle-class contacts and thought Rafsanjani, reputation for corruption and all, would win the election. Ahmadinejad, the network of *bonyads*, the organizing of the *Basij*, the preaching of local imams, and the supervision of the Revolutionary Guards overcame the accepted wisdom and the expensive media campaign run by Rafsanjani.

In the early 20th century, economic change came because of global forces. The discovery in Iran of a source of oil that the British could control and be assured of led the British navy to switch from coal-powered ships to oil-powered ships. The British oil industry in Iran did bring income into the country, but it also brought dependency.

In the early 21st century, economic change might also come because of global pressures. However, there are global and domestic pressures working against change as well. Economic sanctions, promoted by the US, isolate the Iranian economy and force it to continue the practice of import substitution. The directors of the *bonyads*, powerful clerics, and solders would lose constituencies, income, wealth, and patronage if their inefficient operations were exposed to global competition. Similarly, the *bazaaris* don't want to see Wal-Marts in Tehran (like the ones in Mexico and China), because they couldn't compete (and the black market might be affected).

So, in spite of a weak *rentier* economy, poverty, inflation, unemployment (the need to create 800,000 jobs a year), economic change will come slowly. The elites have a stake in maintaining the status quo. And, after all, it was Khomeini who said economics was for donkeys.

There are signs of change you should pay attention to. The rulers might be amenable to pragmatic change. In the early days of the revolution and during the war with Iraq, patriotic, religious, and policy virtues included having large families to strengthen the country. By 1989, with the end of the war, even the clerical hard liners recognized the emergency of the rapidly growing population. Government policy and actions rapidly began reflecting the new patriotic and religious line of ensuring smaller, healthier families.

The other sign of change you should pay attention to is the Iranian effort to flex its nationalistic "muscles" through its nuclear potential. The leaders may be trying to use the nuclear industry as a bargaining chip against international sanctions. Maybe the Shiite leaders want to wrest Islamic leadership from the Sunnis in Saudi Arabia, Pakistan, Egypt, and Turkey. President Ahmadinejad's offer to give nuclear technology to other Muslim states is one that deserves serious attention.

Pay attention and know what's going on so you can do an excellent job of answering questions about change in Iran.

6. PUBLIC POLICY

People in the US and US media, when they think about Iran, focus on the relationship between the two countries. Whether the American president is identifying Iran as part of the "axis of evil" or an Iranian leader reiterates Khomeini's "great Satan" line, attention is drawn to the conflict. The actions by Iran's government to foment Shiite Islamic revolution and spread nuclear technology are policies that outsiders have to pay attention to.

Lost in that focus are the ongoing policy debates taking place in Iranian politics. Even the powerful clerics are divided on economic policy. Should Iran try to attract more foreign investment? Should economic policy aim to make markets more powerful? Or should the state remain in control of economic activity and development? Should the country use its assets to provide a welfare state? The reformers, the conservatives, and the populists push to influence policy.

There are also debates within the political elite about the role of representative government. The clerics at the top of the government and the *bonyads* have power and vested interests in holding on to that power. But there is a democratic tradition more than 100 years old. Global democratization may not have much immediate effect on impoverished peasants or slum dwellers, but even Khomeini's doctrine emphasizes rule in the interests of the people. The regime is young and pliable. Built on faith, the charisma of Khomeini, and the violence of the *Basij* and the Revolutionary Guard, it looks powerful. The Pahlavi regime, based on Persian traditions, economic growth, and the violence of the army and SAVAK, looked as powerful in the mid-1970s.

One of the problems in analyzing the policy process in Iran is the large number of places within the system that policy can originate. The Supreme Leader, the Guardian Council, the Expediency Council, the Majlis, the president, and populist leaders of the poor can all propose policy directions that need to be taken seriously. Rarely do they agree. Similarly, there are as many places where policy choices can be eliminated.

Policy gets made, then, in an opaque process of personalized politics behind the scenes. As you read about policy decisions made in Iran, especially after Ahmadinejad's re-election, hypothesize (or read others' hypotheses) about where the proposals came from and who had to concur. That may provide clues about the policymaking process and the direction of decision making in the future.

The previous section (5. Political and Economic Change) deals with these topics in more detail. You might want to re-read it within the context of the process of making policy.

Review Exercise

This little exercise is not meant to be comprehensive. It's meant to get you thinking about some of the basic facts and point out areas you might have to review more thoroughly. My responses follow.

1. Iran is similar to most less-developed countries in all the following ways EXCEPT
   (A) poverty is endemic
   (B) political participation emphasizes group participation rather than individual participation
   (C) government subsidies make necessities more affordable
   (D) its free-market system dominates the economy
   (E) ethnic conflict exists between major groups

2. Which institution in the Iranian regime is elected?
   (A) the Judiciary
   (B) Guardian Council
   (C) Assembly of Religious Experts
   (D) local government officials
   (E) the Supreme Leader

3. The origin of the wealth of the *bonyads* was
   (A) aid received from foreign NGOs
   (B) property seized by the Iranian Republic
   (C) oil revenues
   (D) *zakat*, the obligatory charity donations that Muslims make
   (E) the sale of ancient Persian artifacts to Western museums and collectors

4. The Iranian Revolutionary Guard Corps has grown in power since its founding primarily because
   (A) its officers have avoided political action
   (B) it was an armed force that was reliably loyal to the leaders of the Iranian Islamic republic
   (C) of military aid from China and Russia
   (D) of its reputation as a peace keeping force
   (E) citizens elect the officer corps from local constituencies

5. A significant limitation on the representational nature of the Iranian legislature is that
   (A) legislators must swear to support proposals from the Supreme Leader
   (B) seats are reserved for most minority religious groups
   (C) members of the Majlis must be clerics
   (D) only the president's party can nominate candidates
   (E) all candidates have to be approved by the Guardian Council

6. The Iranian regime gains legitimacy through all the following methods EXCEPT
   (A) free and open debate of major issues
   (B) nationalistic policies and pronouncements
   (C) an elected national legislature
   (D) adherence to *sharia*
   (E) upholding Ayatollah Khomeini's Guardianship of the Jurist

7. A certain amount of separation of powers in the Iranian regime is illustrated by the
   (A) requirement that the Expediency Council approve all legislation
   (B) Assembly of Experts' power to name and dismiss the Supreme Leader
   (C) Grand Ayatollahs' veto over the selection of the Supreme Leader
   (D) power of the Majlis to dismiss the president
   (E) president's ability to appoint the Guardian Council

8. A characteristic of Iranian elections is the
   (A) proportional system used to determine winners
   (B) active involvement of two parties
   (C) election every two years of a third of the national legislature
   (D) requirement that a majority is needed to win
   (E) very small constituencies that elect legislators

9. Privately-owned media in Iran
   (A) must compete with government-owned media
   (B) are forbidden from reporting on religious matters
   (C) operate freely in the knowledge that they cannot dispute the regime or government policies
   (D) enjoy freedom of the press
   (E) are only allowed to publish or broadcast in non-election years

10. Political and economic change in Iran has
   (A) always involved pressure from foreign countries
   (B) usually led to greater prosperity for the country
   (C) usually come through force and violence
   (D) often occurred because of religious conflict
   (E) resulted from ethnic competition for valuable resources

(For responses, see below)

12: INTERNATIONAL ORGANIZATIONS

International organizations are mentioned only in passing in the AP curriculum, but you should have some familiarity with the most successful of the transnational organizations. This chapter has some detail on the European Union and brief sketches of the World Bank, the International Monetary Fund, and the United Nations.

I've emphasized the EU because Britain is an important member, because the EU's role as a political organization is growing, and it's the one most often asked about on the AP exam. If the details help you to make sense out of things, use them. You should know, in general, the **extent** of the EU's operations, the **representative aspects** of its structure, and the **democratic values** embodied in its operations and institutions and **examples** of those things.

The World Bank and the IMF are described here because they have great importance for Russia, China, Mexico, and Nigeria. The UN is primarily involved in international relations, but issues it deals with often have ramifications for domestic policy making in the countries described in the AP curriculum

The European Union

1. INTRODUCTION TO COMPARATIVE POLITICS

Studying the EU provides some wonderful case study examples. Comparing the formation of the Russian Federation or the Nigerian republic with the creation of the EU could be a valuable exercise. Studying the ways in which the architects and leaders of the EU bridged the multiple cleavages dividing people in so many different nation-states might provide valuable lessons for other state-building projects. Using EU institutions as topics for systems analysis can also be fruitful, though very complex. (How do you separate the political system from its environments in this instance?)

2. SOCIETY, AUTHORITY, AND POWER

The European Union has its origins in the post-World War II recovery period. Its main thrust has been economic cooperation, but from the very beginning political developments have paralleled the economic ones. The **"three pillars"** identified by the early organizers were

1) trade and economic cooperation
2) law enforcement and human rights and
3) foreign policy and European security.

The EU's claims to legitimacy rest on its creators' efforts to see that citizens as well as member states are represented in EU operations. In addition, hopes for achieving legitimacy hinge on efforts to promote trade, economic growth, economic stability, and protect human rights.

Since 1948, the number of countries and the issues involved have grown dramatically. More growth in both areas is likely.

Political culture is both novel and an amalgam of national political cultures of member states. Most EU citizens share some basic liberal democratic values and practices. Individual freedoms, the rule of law, competitive elections, and an independent civil society are the primary ingredients. A specific EU political culture is being created as people participate and institutions evolve.

3. POLITICAL INSTITUTIONS

If you recall Madison's accounting of the really big debating issues at the USA's Constitutional Convention, you should be familiar with some of the big issues the EU must deal with. Big nations and small nations; richer nations and poorer nations; populist, statist, and corporatist demands for representation. French political scientists and politicians were leaders of the EU organizing efforts. So, it shouldn't be surprising to find attempts to resolve the issues through institutional structures.

Here's how the EU administrators describe their organization on "Europa," the EU's web site (*europa.eu*):

> The European Union (EU) is not a federation like the United States. Nor is it simply an organisation for co-operation between governments, like the United Nations. It is, in fact, unique. The countries that make up the EU (its 'member states') remain independent sovereign nations but they pool their sovereignty in order to gain a strength and world influence none of them could have on their own.
>
> Pooling sovereignty means, in practice, that the member states delegate some of their

decision-making powers to shared institutions they have created, so that decisions on specific matters of joint interest can be made democratically at European level.

The EU's decision-making process in general and the co-decision procedure in particular involve three main institutions:

- the European Parliament (EP), which represents the EU's citizens and is directly elected by them;
- the Council of the European Union, which represents the individual member states; and
- the European Commission, which seeks to uphold the interests of the Union as a whole

This "institutional triangle" produces the policies and laws that apply throughout the EU. In principle, it is the Commission that proposes new laws, but it is the Parliament and Council that adopt them. The Commission and the member states then implement them, and the Commission ensures that the laws are properly taken on board.

Two other institutions have a vital part to play:

- the Court of Justice, which upholds the rule of European law, and
- the Court of Auditors, which checks the financing of the Union's activities.

The powers and responsibilities of these institutions are laid down in the Treaties, which are the foundation of everything the EU does. They also lay down the rules and procedures that the EU institutions must follow. The Treaties are agreed by the presidents and/or prime ministers of all the EU countries, and ratified by their parliaments:

- The Treaty of Pairs (1951)
- The Treaties of Rome (1957)
- The Merger Treaty (1967)
- The Single European Act (1987)
- The Treaty of Maastricht (1992)
- Amsterdam Treaty (1999)
- Treaty of Nice (2003)
- The Treaty of Lisbon (2009)

Principal objectives of the Union are:

- Establish European citizenship;
- Ensure freedom, security, and justice;
- Promote economic and social progress;
- Assert Europe's role in the world.

The **European Parliament** is the only directly-elected body of the European Union. The 736 Members of the European Parliament are there to represent you, the citizen. They are elected once every five years by voters right across the 27 Member States of the European Union on behalf of its 500 million citizens.

Parliament plays an active role in drafting legislation which has an impact on the daily lives of its citizens and has joint power with the Council over the annual budget of the European Union.

The main functions of the parliament are

1) to legislate the directives, regulations, and decisions which make up the body of European law,

2) to adopt the budget proposed by the Council and the European Commission and

3) to supervise the European Commission, after approving the appointments of commission members.

The balance of power in the European Parliament (EP) between Europe's right and left is quite even.

If the EP represents the citizens, t**he Council of the European Union** represents the nation-states. Ministers from the member governments meet at the council's Brussels headquarters to constitute the council. But the same ministers do not meet every time the council meets. The prime ministers meet regularly to discuss broad issues of policy and governance. Other ministers meet on a schedule to discuss more specialized topics. When the Common Agricultural Policy is the topic, ministers whose portfolios[1] include farm policy will meet. When foreign ministers meet, EU foreign policy will be discussed.

Out of these discussions and drafts from the commission (see below) come bills which are proposed to the EP for enactment and policies concerning foreign relations and security.

As you ought to expect, voting is a complex process in such an institution. The council uses a "qualified majority" voting system to propose directives, regulations, and policies. Members' votes are weighted by countries' populations.

The purpose of qualified majority voting is to help resolve that old "big, powerful states vs. smaller, weaker states" issue. The five largest countries cannot band together and pass things over the objections of the others. Nor can the smallest countries pass things over the objections of the largest. Widespread agreement is necessary for approval. This not only improves the likelihood of achieving legitimacy with EU citizens, it makes more likely the cooperative negotiations necessary for productive decisions.

The **European Commission** is the EU's executive branch. The member countries' governments appoint the members of the commission The appointments have to be approved by the EP. To ensure their independence from their own countries, commissioners are employed by the EU and cannot be recalled by the governments that appointed them.

There are 17 major departments in the commission's directorate and 18 specialized offices.

The European Commission is a powerful institution. The EU description noted earlier says it is the "driving force" of the EU. It's also quite undemocratic. It's a huge bureaucracy. How could it be democratic? You should expect to see contests for power between the appointed commission and the elected EP and between the commission and the council.

The **European Court of Justice** meets in Luxembourg. It is a court of first instance (it has original jurisdiction) in cases involving EU directives and regulations.

The **Court of Auditors** is the independent accounting "firm" of the EU. It's there to ensure confidence in the honesty of the EU's fiscal activities.

Other important institutions:

The European Economic and Social Committee is intended to represent the corporatist interests in the EU. In the USA, we'd say it represents organized civil society. Employers' groups, trade unions, farmers' groups, and consumer groups are represented. Its role is advisory. Advice is given to the EP, the council, and the commission.

The Committee of the Regions exists to represent local authorities and minority cultural groups, which might otherwise be overwhelmed by democracy.

The European Ombudsman is an office that responds to individual citizens' complaints about EU operation. It's designed to give a voice to grievances found to be legitimate by the officials in the ombudsman's office.

The European Investment Bank finances projects to create "balanced development." That means it funds projects for economic growth in the poorer regions of the EU.

The European Central Bank is one of the "power institutions" in the EU. From its headquarters in Frankfurt, Germany, it makes monetary policy (sets interest rates), regulates foreign exchange, and issues currency for members of the Monetary Union. Its Governing Council (the heads of the member countries' national banks and six executives of the ECB) is totally independent in the exercise of its policies. Its stated goals are economic growth and price stability (meaning less than 2% a year inflation).

The European Coal and Steel Community and even the Common Market may have begun as cooperative trade organizations. But it should be obvious that the EU is much more. And it's much more than a simple administrative organization. It is directly and indirectly representative and in some ways functions as a more activist government that the US government does.

4. CITIZENS, SOCIETY AND THE STATE

Since we're dealing with an international organization, it is important to note national divisions as well as regional ones. Nonetheless, regional economic cleavages have been more politically relevant than national ones. As the EU admits countries from Eastern and Southeastern Europe, other divisions might become more important than they are now. Some disagreements over human rights have emerged, but they have been minor.

One cleavage, which is likely to become more important as Eastern European nations join the EU, is the division between more agriculturally dependent and less agriculturally dependent economies. The Common Agricultural Policy has long been the most expensive EU program and one of the primary controversies in the EU. This has been true in spite of the fact that in the current

New 'Old Guard' Too 'Clubby'?

The most public (and notorious) example of the supervision of the European Commission by the European Parliament took place in 1999.

On March 16, 1999, Radio Free Europe/Radio Liberty reported :

"In an unprecedented move, the 20-member commission, including its president, Jacques Santer, stepped down overnight. The move followed within hours the publication of an independent report which harshly criticized the commission for failure to control mismanagement, fraud, and cronyism.

"The affair is the climax of a struggle between the powerful, unelected commission and the European Parliament, an elected body which is seeking to strengthen democratic accountability in the EU. In January, the parliament threatened to topple the commission in a censure motion unless the allegations were properly investigated by an independent panel. The report of that panel, as now issued, criticizes by name only some of the commissioners, but it also accuses the entire commission of general irresponsibility. It thus badly damaged the credibility of the whole body of commissioners."

www.rferl.org/nca/features/1999/03/F.RU.990316150102.html

The World Socialist web site reported:

"The resignation of all 20 members of the European Commission has plunged the European Union into the worse crisis of its 42-year history. It came after ... a report into allegations of fraud, corruption and mismanagement.

"The investigation was ordered after the Commission narrowly avoided a no-confidence motion in the European Parliament in January. This centred on allegations directed against Commission President Jacques Santer, Research Commissioner and former French Socialist Prime Minister Edith Cresson, Commission Vice President Manuel Marin of Spain, Commissioner Monika Wulf-Mathies, a former German trade union leader now in charge of EU regional policy and Portuguese Commissioner Joao de Deus Pinheiro. The findings of the independent investigation, contained in a 140-page report, were savage. They denounced the Commission for losing political control and allowing a culture of ignorance and incompetence. ... "

www.wsws.org/articles/1999/mar1999/ec-m17.shtml

member nations of the EU, with the exception of Greece, agriculture has contributed less than the world average (6%) to the economies. The differences have been small. Farming in Germany and Luxembourg produces less than 1% of the GDP. In Spain and Ireland, that figure is around 4%.

However, all the new and candidate members, with the exceptions of Malta and Slovakia, are above average in their reliance on agriculture. Some, like Romania (15%), Macedonia (11.9%), Turkey (9.34%) , and Bulgaria (7.5%) are far

above the world average. The enlarged gap is likely to make the Common Agricultural Policy an even more contentious issue.

The economic divisions between the wealthier and poorer member states have caused the most difficulty. The divisions caused by the differences between highly industrialized member states (like Germany) and less industrialized members (like Romania) have also been apparent. You can find evidence of attempts to address these issues if you look at the political framework of the EU.

Relative Wealth in the EU

An important cleavage dividing some EU members from others is relative wealth. Some countries are considerably better off than others. Here is the GDP per capita for EU member states (with the world average and the USA added in to provide context):

$ 9,000	Macedonia
$10,500	World Average
$11,200	Turkey
$11,500	Romania
$12,600	Bulgaria
$14,500	Latvia
$15,400	Lithuania
$17,600	Croatia
$17,900	Poland
$18,600	Hungary
$18,700	Estonia
$ 21,200	Cyprus
$21,200	Slovakia
$21,800	Portugal
$23,800	Malta
$25,100	Czech Republic
$27,900	Slovenia
$30,300	Italy
$32,100	Greece
$32,600	EU
$32,800	France
$33,700	Spain
$34,100	Germany
$34,900	Finland
$35,200	United Kingdom
$36,000	Denmark
$36,600	Belgium
$36,800	Sweden
$39,200	Netherlands
$39,400	Austria
$42,200	Ireland
$46,400	USA
$78,000	Luxembourg

— CIA World Factbook, *www.cia.gov/library/ publications/the-world-factbook/rankorder/ 2004rank.html*, 26 April 2010

The chart showing GDP per capita illustrates some of the economic disparities among member states. These factors may cause some political problems as the EU decides what programs to fund and who pays the costs. So far, the wealthier countries have been willing to "share the wealth." However, economics is tricky, and slow growth, high unemployment, and EU restrictions on deficit financing are creating difficult situations. The fear of Euro advocates is that excessive deficit spending (like that in Greece in 2009 and 2010) will depress the value of the Euro on world money markets. The addition of poorer countries to the EU and to the monetary union may make this issue more urgent. Those poor countries might perceive deficit spending as even more important to economic stimulus than do the industrial powerhouses of France and Germany.

Given the EU's short history, it's hard to identify political culture for the entity.

Voting for the European Parliament is proportional within each country. European parties have made successful efforts to link up across national borders, and there are now several substantial European parties. However, participation in European Parliamentary elections is lower than in other elections.

A reason for this relatively low voter turnout may well be the perception that the EU is only distantly relevant to most people's lives. It's also likely that the newness of European-wide elections means that people have not gotten into the habit of participating yet. More experience, more visible actions by the EU, and more lessons in school may play roles in increasing participation.

A notable distinction is that about one-third of the members of the elected European Parliament are women. That percentage is higher than in most of the member countries.

5. POLITICAL CHANGE

Political change in the EU has been slow, deliberative, rational, realistic, and democratic. Or you could say it's been rapid, visionary, romantic, and arbitrary. Here comes ambiguity again. Change in the EU has been all those things. Can you identify examples of those adjectives?

One more thing: change has been cooperative. The treaties among the member countries have been negotiated between equally sovereign nation-states. The national referenda on topics like monetary union have been democratic.

The visionary realists who cooperated in creating the EU probably deserve a lot of honor. The first half of the 20th century in Europe was characterized by so much bloodshed, horror, and conflict that the results of EU-building are stunning. The wars of the second half of the 20th century, while terrible, have not come close to matching the horrors of earlier years. (That's my bit of editorializing.)

6. PUBLIC POLICY

As you know by now, policy making in the EU is a complex and slow process. The route from the Commission or a council of ministers to adoption by the EP is tortuous. With new members, policy making might slow down even more. But, policy is made.

The economic and fiscal policies that made monetary union possible are based not only on politics, but also on sophisticated economic expertise. A question that only time will answer is how quickly the policy can adjust to rapid changes, like the rise in oil prices that began in 2005 or the recession of 2008-2010. You should watch for policy decisions from the EU in this area.

Other global or transnational policies have also been adopted. Environmental standards, regulations for travel and migration, and basic standards for human rights are examples. Other issues, like social welfare and economic development, are still seen as primarily national issues and EU policy has been slower to develop. Pay attention to EU policy making. It will make news, but the reporting is likely to be more thorough in British and European media. Look for it.

The World Bank

The World Bank (WB) describes itself this way at the World Bank Group web site (*web.worldbank.org*):

> Since inception in 1944, the World Bank has expanded from a single institution to a closely associated group of five development institutions.
>
> Our mission evolved from the International Bank for Reconstruction and Development (IBRD) as facilitator of post-war reconstruction and development to the present day mandate of worldwide poverty alleviation in close coordination with our affiliate, the International Development Association, and other members of the World Bank Group, the International Finance Corporation (IFC), the Multilateral Guarantee Agency (MIGA) and the International Centre for the Settlement of Investment Disputes (ICSID).
>
> Reconstruction remains an important part of our work. However, the global challenges in the world compel us to focus on:
>
> - poverty reduction and the sustainable growth in the poorest countries, especially in Africa;
> - solutions to the special challenges of post-conflict countries and fragile states;
> - development solutions with customized services as well as financing for middle-income countries; regional and global issues that cross national borders— climate change, infectious diseases, and trade;

- greater development and opportunity in the Arab world;

- pulling together the best global knowledge to support development.

At today's World Bank, poverty reduction through an inclusive and sustainable globalization remains the overarching goal of our work.

The International Monetary Fund (IMF)

On its web site (*www.imf.org*) the IMF describes itself as follows:

The International Monetary Fund (IMF) is an organization of 186 countries, working to foster global monetary cooperation, secure financial stability, facilitate international trade, promote high employment and sustainable economic growth, and reduce poverty around the world.

The IMF was conceived in July 1944, when representatives of 45 countries meeting in the town of Bretton Woods, New Hampshire, in the northeastern United States, agreed on a framework for international economic co-

operation, to be established after the Second World War. They believed that such a framework was necessary to avoid a repetition of the disastrous economic policies that had contributed to the Great Depression.

The IMF came into formal existence in December 1945, when its first 29 member countries signed its Articles of Agreements. It began operations on March 1, 1947.

The IMF is helping many emerging market countries tackle the problems brought on by the devastating global economic crisis. Its lending to low-income countries has also been stepped up, as these countries start to feel the effects of the crisis. And it is providing policy advice to advanced countries, for instance on how to address problems in their financing and banking sectors, and how to design effective stimulus packages."

The United Nations

The United Nations makes the news more often than the World Bank and the IMF, and policy debates about the US role in the UN are part of the American political landscape. You probably know more about the UN than the other two. Its web site (*www.un.org/en*)

The UN grew out of the military alliances during World War II that fought against Germany, Italy, and Japan. The permanent members of the Security Council with veto powers were those allies. The difficulty of political change in the UN is illustrated by facts like

- the continued representation of China by the Kuomintang government of Taiwan for over 20 years after the Communist revolution in China and

- the inclusion of Germany and Japan among the G8 nations, but their exclusion from permanent seats on the Security Council

The ability of the UN to adapt to change has been apparent in the

- admission of over 100 new nations since its formation

- successful peacekeeping missions it has engaged in all over the world

- adaptations it made when the Soviet Union broke up

- elimination of smallpox and the active campaigns against HIV-AIDS

DEMOGRAPHIC DATA FROM THE CIA WORLD FACTBOOK 2010

POPULATION OF NATIONS

(smallest to largest)

UK	61,000,000
Iran	66,000,000
Mexico	111,000,000
Russia	140,000,000
Nigeria	149,000,000
USA	307,000,000
China	1,338,000,000

POPULATION DENSITIES

(lowest to highest)

	people per kilometers^2
Russia	8
USA	31
Iran	40
Mexico	57
China	139
Nigeria	161
UK	251

POPULATION AGE STRUCTURE

(lowest to highest percentage)

	people under the age of 15
Russia	15%
UK	17%
USA	20%
China	20%
Iran	22%
Mexico	29%
Nigeria	42%

SIZE OF NATIONS

(smallest to largest land areas)

	kilometers^2
UK	245,000
Nigeria	924,000
Iran	1,648,000
Mexico	1,964,000
China	9,597,000
USA	9,826,000
Russia	17,098,000

LITERACY RATES

(lowest to highest percentages)

	Total	Men	Women
Nigeria	68%	76%	61%
Iran	77%	84%	70%
China	91%	95%	87%
Mexico	91%	92%	90%
USA	99%	99%	99%
Russia	99%	100%	99%
UK	99%	99%	99%

GDP

(smallest to largest; purchasing power parity)

Nigeria	$353 billion
Iran	$876 billion
Mexico	$1,173 billion
Russia	$2,103 billion
UK	$2,165 billion
China	$8,767 billion
USA	$14,250 billion

GDP PER CAPITA

(smallest to largest; purchasing power parity)

Nigeria	$2,400
China	$6,500
Iran	$12,900
Mexico	$13,200
Russia	$15,200
UK	$35,400
USA	$46,400

GINI INDEX

(lowest to highest; higher numbers indicate greater inequalities of income)

UK	34.0
China	41.5
Russia	42.3
Nigeria	43.7
Iran	44.5
USA	45.0
Mexico	48.2

describes the organization in this way:

> The United Nations is an international organization founded in 1945 after the Second World War by 51 countries committed to maintaining international peace and security, developing friendly relations among nations and promoting social progress, better living standards and human rights.
>
> Due to its unique international character, and the powers vested in its founding Charter, the Organization can take action on a wide range of issues, and provide a forum for its 192 Member States to express their views, through the General Assembly, the Security Council, the Economic and Social Council and other bodies and committees.
>
> The work of the United Nations reaches every corner of the globe. Although best known for peacekeeping, peacebuilding, conflict prevention and humanitarian assistance, there are many other ways the United Nations and its System (specialized agencies, funds and programmes) affect our lives and make the world a better place.
>
> The Organization works on a broad range of fundamental issues, from sustainable development, environment and refugees protection, disaster relief, counter terrorism, disarmament and non-proliferation, to promoting democracy, human rights, governance, economic and social development and international health, clearing landmines, expanding food production, and more, in order to achieve its goals and coordinate efforts for a safer world for this and future generations."

Other International Organizations

Other organizations that may be relevant to your study of comparative government and politics include:

THE GROUP OF 8 (G8)

The University of Toronto G8 Information Centre (*www.g8.utoronto.ca*)

THE PARIS CLUB

The Paris Club web site (*www.clubdeparis.org/en*)

THE ORGANIZATION FOR SECURITY AND CO-OPERATION IN EUROPE (OSCE)

The OSCE web site (*www.osce.org*)

THE INTERNATIONAL ATOMIC ENERGY AGENCY (IAEA)

The IAEA Web site (*www.iaea.org*)

ORGANIZATION OF PETROLEUM EXPORTING COUNTRIES (OPEC)

OPEC web site (*www.opec.org*)

COUNCIL OF EUROPE (COE)

The Council of Europe web site (*www.coe.int*)

SHANGHAI COOPERATION ORGANIZATION (SCO)

The SCO web site (*www.sectsco.org/EN*)

Review Exercise

This little exercise is not meant to be comprehensive. It's meant to get you thinking about some of the basic facts and point out areas you might have to review more thoroughly. My responses follow.

1. The EU can be a comparative case study if you are interested in
    (A) compromises that make federalism functional
    (B) evaluating the efficacy of voting systems
    (C) institutions that can bridge political cleavages
    (D) state building
    (E) all of the above

2. The original goals of European cooperation centered on
    (A) protecting human rights
    (B) economic development
    (C) building a military system for the physical protection of the continent
    (D) fighting international crime
    (E) political unity

3. Basic elements of an EU political culture include all the following EXCEPT
    (A) protecting individual freedoms
    (B) ensuring rule of law
    (C) promoting an independent civil society
    (D) encouraging religious uniformity
    (E) guaranteeing competitive elections

4. The main institutions of the EU include all the following EXCEPT the
    (A) European Military Commission
    (B) European Parliament
    (C) Council of the European Union
    (D) European Court of Justice
    (E) European Commission

5. The citizens of the EU are represented in the
    (A) European Parliament
    (B) Council of the European Union
    (C) European Commission
    (D) European Court of Justice
    (E) European Bank

6. Member nations of the EU are represented in the
    (A) European Parliament
    (B) Council of the European Union
    (C) European Commission
    (D) European Court of Auditors
    (E) European Bank

7. Qualified majority voting is designed to
    (A) ensure that voters know what they're voting about
    (B) reduce the power of temporary coalitions
    (C) make majorities nearly impossible
    (D) prevent large, rich countries from dominating the EU
    (E) facilitate rapid decision making

8. The European Commission
    (A) meets on a regular schedule about various policy topics
    (B) is staffed by technocrats loaned to the EU by member governments
    (C) takes policy positions advocated by the Court of Auditors
    (D) has the power to propose legislation
    (E) elects members of the European Council

9. One of the major cleavages among EU member nations is based on
    (A) the use of adversarial and inquisitorial criminal justice systems
    (B) how industrialized members' economies are
    (C) length of democratic experience
    (D) levels of energy use
    (E) membership or non-membership in NATO

10. EU elections differ from those in most member states because
    (A) more women are elected to the European Parliament
    (B) only a few members of the European Parliament are elected at any one time
    (C) they are held at unusual intervals
    (D) representation is based on population
    (E) in order to vote, people must go to the country where they are citizens

(For responses, see below)

Testing Yourself

As described in Chapter 3 and in the official Advanced Placement literature, the AP Comparative Government and Politics exam has two sections. The first thing you get to do is to answer as many of the 55 multiple-choice questions as you can or wish to in 45 minutes. Next, you are allowed 100 minutes to respond to the free response section.

If you think it's a good idea for you, read through the questions and **underline all the verbs**. Then when you plan and write your response, make sure you fulfill all the tasks asked of you.

need to review, and, perhaps, to learn some new things.

When you're ready, go ahead and "take" the sample multiple-choice test. After that, when you're ready, rehearse for the free-response questions.

Beginning on the next page is a sample multiple-choice section of the exam. It's followed by a sample free-response section. A key and annotations about each of the questions follow. I think the collection of questions is pretty realistic.

It's time to do some of that rehearsal that is vital to your success. Use this sample test as a way to get that practice, to get hints about what you

Make these rehearsals as realistic as possible. For the multiple-choice section, give yourself 45 uninterrupted minutes. Answer as many questions as you can and wish to. When you're finished, score your result using the key on Page 182 . The annotations that follow the key provide additional information and insights on ways to improve your test-taking skills. For the free-response section, allow yourself an amount of time appropriate to the questions you're practicing on. Study the FRQ commentary that begins on Page 202 to assess your work.

A Practice Version of the Multiple-Choice Section of the AP Exam for Comparative Politics

Directions

Each of the questions or incomplete statements below is followed by five suggested answers or completions. Select the one that is best in each case and then fill in the corresponding oval on the answer sheet on Page 212.

1. In Iran, one basic political conflict arises from
    (A)   Westernized groups seeking national glory and traditional groups advocating greater engagement with the global economy
    (B)   the cleavages separating Azeri and Aryan ethnic groups
    (C)   the need of the Islamic elite to accommodate religious minorities to stay in power
    (D)   competing democratic and religious ideals
    (E)   competition between *bazaaris* and the charitable Islamic foundations (*bonyads*)

2. Colonial influences on the political culture of Mexico include all the following EXCEPT
    (A)   the large scale state involvement in the economy
    (B)   the loss of half its territory to the USA
    (C)   the executive domination of the other parts of the regime
    (D)   the system of unequal alliances between patrons and clients
    (E)   the relative absence of Indians among the political elite

3. Which of the following factors help explain the ongoing conflict in the Caucasus (SW Russia)?
    I.   Large numbers of people are Muslims.
    II.   Most people there are Russians.
    III.   The area has rich oil and gas resources.
    IV.   Industrial development there has led to high standards of living.
    V.   Rival ethnic groups compete for political power.

    (A)   I and II only
    (B)   II, III, and IV only
    (C)   All five factors, I, II, III, IV, and V help explain the conflict
    (D)   I, III, and V only
    (E)   III, IV, and V only

4. Participation in the European Union is a political controversy in the UK in large part because
    (A)   the efficiencies promoted by the Common Agricultural Policy threaten British farming techniques
    (B)   the sovereignty of the British Parliament is threatened by EU treaties and courts
    (C)   trade with Japan, China, and the USA is more important to the British economy than trade with the EU
    (D)   the EU's common defense policies conflict with the UK's membership in NATO
    (E)   the British political elite see the United Nations (and the UK's Security Council veto power) as more important to British interests than the EU

5. Experience with public policy making in the USSR and the Russian Federation has probably taught Russians
   - (A)   the value of individual responsibility
   - (B)   the value of publicly advocating policy positions
   - (C)   that political leaders cultivate close relationships with grassroots organizations
   - (D)   that the state, rather than being made up of the people, holds power over people
   - (E)   the importance of involvement in civic groups

6. Which of the following organizations is the most powerful seat of political power in the Peoples Republic of China?
   - (A)   National Peoples Congress
   - (B)   National Party Congress
   - (C)   State Council Standing Committee
   - (D)   Politburo of the Central Committee of the National Party Congress
   - (E)   Politburo Standing Committee of the National Party Congress

7. A development in the functioning of the National Peoples Congress of the PRC during the last decade is
   - (A)   the growing proportion of peasants among the delegates
   - (B)   a reduction in the percentage of Communist Party members among the delegates
   - (C)   the growing power of the standing committee determined to shape government policy
   - (D)   an increase in demands by delegates for more detailed reports from government officials
   - (E)   the extension of meeting times to accommodate the extensive debates over economic liberalization reforms

8. The Soviet *nomenklatura* system will continue to be an obstacle for reform in the Russian state for some time to come because
   - (A)   private industries discriminate freely against the beneficiaries of the old system
   - (B)   people who rose up through the *nomenklatura* ranks are still in positions of authority
   - (C)   the skills and knowledge required for success in the *nomenklatura* system are irrelevant to today's market economy and republican government
   - (D)   foreign investors rarely have the knowledge to enable them to understand the "insider" politics involved in doing business in Russia
   - (E)   representative government requires a degree of transparency impossible without the record keeping of the *nomenklatura* system

9. Political conflict in the Peoples Republic of China has historically been confined to the Chinese Communist Party
   - (A)   because of the decentralized organization of the party
   - (B)   because disagreement from outside the party has been harshly suppressed
   - (C)   through the nearly continuous use of mass campaigns to recruit new members
   - (D)   because competitive elections were held only within the party
   - (E)   by allowing open debate on policy positions at all levels of the Communist Party Congresses

10. In the United Kingdom, the monarch serves primarily as
    - (A)   a mediator between competing political forces
    - (B)   a symbol of national unity and political legitimacy
    - (C)   the final authority on matters of public policy
    - (D)   an administrator of government programs
    - (E)   a reminder of Great Britain's former power and wealth

11. It is not unusual for outside observers to be skeptical about the constitutional nature of Nigeria's regime because
    (A)   the current basic law was written so recently
    (B)   the legislature in the fourth republic has never passed a national budget
    (C)   so few people vote in national elections
    (D)   in spite of federalism described in the constitution, powers of state governments are only vaguely defined
    (E)   pragmatic compromises on major issues usually emerge before the legislature begins consideration of them

12. Unitary states, like the UK and Iran,
    (A)   function more successfully in countries with less ethnic or cultural diversity than in those countries with greater diversity
    (B)   are based on sovereignty of individual units of sub-national government
    (C)   rely on written constitutions to protect of individual liberties
    (D)   are more common in Europe than in Asia
    (E)   are unusual among the world's regimes

13. A major reason for the uncertain progress Russia has made in establishing a new regime since 1991 is
    (A)   frequent turnover in the office of president
    (B)   a long tradition of decentralized political authority
    (C)   the success of economic liberalization in raising living standards
    (D)   intense competition between monarchist and democratic political parties
    (E)   democratic centralism practiced for more than 70 years by the Communist Party in the USSR

14. Presidential power in Mexico is limited by
    (A)   an elite group of permanent expert bureaucrats in important ministries
    (B)   a tradition of powerful legislative leadership
    (C)   limits on presidential appointment powers
    (D)   the growing influence of parastatal corporations
    (E)   the expectation that presidents will retire from politics at the end of their terms in office

15. Since nearly all Mexicans are Roman Catholic
    (A)   the government is relieved of the task of operating schools
    (B)   the clerical elite play a large role in policy making
    (C)   moral and ethical issues rarely become public policy issues
    (D)   the impact on government of social class and ethnic cleavages is greatly reduced
    (E)   observers are often surprised that the role of the church is a political issue in Mexico

16. The principle of non-reelection in Mexico
    (A)   makes legislators dependent upon civil servants for expertise
    (B)   gives a president greater power in the last years of a *sexenio*
    (C)   inspires elected officials to fulfill campaign promises quickly
    (D)   limits the influence of any single camarilla
    (E)   motivates politicians to run for office in geographically dispersed districts in successive elections

17. One of the keys to successful parliamentary government is
    (A)   democratic centralism
    (B)   deferential shadow cabinets
    (C)   collective responsibility
    (D)   non-assertive prime ministers
    (E)   legislative independence

18. A major difficulty in establishing a regime in Nigeria has been the
    (A)   competition between advocates of federalism and advocates of a unitary system
    (B)   diversity of pre-colonial and colonial political experiences in the nations that make up Nigeria
    (C)   volatility of voter preferences over the past 50 years
    (D)   domination of minorities by the Hausa-Fulani majority
    (E)   unwillingness of citizens to publicly debate political issues

19. The political consensus in the United Kingdom during the 1950s and 1960s meant that government activity included
    (A)   operating airlines and railroads
    (B)   dictating wage settlements to labor unions
    (C)   setting strict limits on eligibility for welfare and unemployment payments
    (D)   creating institutions of higher education for training public administrators
    (E)   taxation policies that encouraged businesses to hire more workers

20. Which of the following is the most important source of legitimacy for Nigeria's fourth republic (beginning in 1999)?
    (A)   honesty in government
    (B)   a history of stable government
    (C)   the promotion of a sense of national unity
    (D)   maintenance of an acceptable level of law and order
    (E)   the success of government-sponsored economic development

21. Which Iranian institution below is correctly paired with its authority?
    (A)   Expediency Council   approves candidates for elective office
    (B)   Supreme Leader   appoints local officials
    (C)   President   can veto Majlis legislation
    (D)   Supreme Leader   appoints the Minister of Justice
    (E)   Majlis   elects the Supreme Leader

22. Nation-states must adjust to all the following trends of globalization EXCEPT
    (A)   international markets for investment funds
    (B)   the increasing wealth and power of corporations not exclusively associated with a country
    (C)   the potential of global warming caused by human activity
    (D)   the growing acceptance of the concept of "crimes against humanity"
    (E)   the narrowing of the economic gap between rich and poor nations

23. Before 2000, the political route to the presidency in Mexico centered on
    (A)   inherited wealth
    (B)   a reputation for honesty and fairness
    (C)   individual recruitment of grassroots support
    (D)   loyalty to the PRI organization and the President
    (E)   repeated electoral victory by wide margins in a legislative constituency

24. A hopeful sign for the development of a republican regime in Russia is the
    (A)   electoral failures of the party that was formed from the remnants of the USSR's Communist Party
    (B)   the popularity of United Russia's youth group, NASHI
    (C)   popular rejection of the concept of a government-directed economy
    (D)   liberal political values held by young, urban, and well-educated Russians
    (E)   growing concentration of power in the office of president

25. The Four Modernizations campaign in China was a response to
    (A)   declining rates of industrial production
    (B)   rapid development of new communications technology
    (C)   the emphasis on political and social goals of Mao's leadership
    (D)   increasing disparities between rich and poor in China
    (E)   failures of social service programs like education and health care

26. Which of the following countries is NOT correctly paired with a major unresolved issue in its political environment?
    (A)   China   balancing urban and rural economic development
    (B)   Iran   large scale unemployment
    (C)   Nigeria   maintaining a stable political party alignment
    (D)   Russia   mitigating conflicts caused by identity politics
    (E)   United Kingdom   eliminating political corruption

27. Among the measures taken by Putin's government in Russia to resolve outstanding issues of federalism was the
    (A)   withdrawal of Russian troops from Chechnya
    (B)   legislation allowing the president to appoint regional governors
    (C)   abolition of sub-national units of government below the level of republic
    (D)   claim that the United States threatened Russian sovereignty through the expansion of NATO
    (E)   invitation to UN mediators who were to help resolve conflicts surrounding the desires of many republics to secede

28. Interest groups in the Peoples Republic of China differ from interest groups in industrialized democracies in that
    (A)   the groups in China are headed by members of the political elite
    (B)   interest groups in China often result from grassroots organizing
    (C)   interest groups in China lobby Communist Party, not government officials
    (D)   the Chinese groups aim to influence policy making, not resolve administrative and bureaucratic problems
    (E)   Chinese interest groups represent the interests of the Communist Party to the affinity groups (e.g., industrial workers, peasants, and women)

29. Observers have raised questions about the democratic nature of Iranian elections because of the participation of
    (A)   political parties
    (B)   non-Muslims
    (C)   women
    (D)   the Revolutionary Guard
    (E)   Iranians in exile

30. Some people in Nigeria have advocated re-writing the Fourth Republic's constitution because that 1999 document
    (A)   gave control of elections to an independent, non-partisan commission
    (B)   was imposed on the country by a non-democratic, military government
    (C)   created too many states
    (D)   gave governors too much control over government spending for public services
    (E)   did not recognize the Muslim majority of Nigeria's population

Refer to the following chart in answering Questions 31 and 32:

**Percentage of Elected Women in Legislatures
(Sizes of legislatures have changed over time.)
(Source: The Inter-Parliamentary Union)**

	1997	2000	2005
Iran	4.0	3.4	4.1
Mexico	13.9	15.9	23.7
Nigeria	na	3.3	5.8
Russia	7.5	5.7	8.8
Peoples Republic of China	21.0	21.8	20.2
United Kingdom	7.8	17.0	18.7
World Average	11.7	13.8	15.9

31. From these statistics, we can infer that
    (A) more women were elected to legislatures in 2005 than in 1997
    (B) it is not possible to identify trends in the election of women legislators over the time period described
    (C) nations usually described as Third World countries elected fewer women than other countries
    (D) all the nations for which data is displayed elected more and more women over the time span described
    (E) over the time period described, women came to play a larger role in electoral politics

32. These statistics most support the investigation of which of the following hypotheses?
    (A) A common norm of political culture accounts for the small percentage of women elected in Iran and Nigeria.
    (B) Ideologically driven electoral rules are important for electing larger percentages of women legislators.
    (C) The higher the levels of educational achievement, the larger the percentage of women legislators elected.
    (D) Long national experience with elections leads to the success of greater percentages of women candidates.
    (E) Lower income countries are less likely to elect women legislators than higher income countries.

33. In the Iranian regime, executive power is exercised by the
    (A) Supreme Leader
    (B) President
    (C) Supreme Leader and the President
    (D) Supreme Leader, the President, and the Majlis
    (E) President, the Majlis, and the Assembly of Religious Experts

34. The universal health care system provided by the UK's National Health Service
    (A) provides an example of political and social unity to citizens
    (B) helps maintain the political cleavage between upper and lower classes in the UK
    (C) is a controversial program which politicians regularly propose to eliminate
    (D) was initiated by PM Tony Blair's government in the 1990s
    (E) is not a source of political controversy

35. Which of the following were goals of increasing the number of states in Nigeria in the years after independence?
    I.   devolving political power to local authorities
    II.   dividing the largest ethnic groups into competing political entities
    III. giving more nations political bases
    IV.   encouraging cooperation and alliance-making

    (A) I and II only
    (B) I, II, and III only
    (C) II and III only
    (D) II, III, and IV only
    (E) I, II, III, and IV

36. In the Iranian regime, which of the following is NOT able to be a check on the power of another national-level actor in the regime?
    (A) Guardian Council
    (B) Supreme Leader
    (C) President
    (D) Expediency Council
    (E) Majlis

37. The legitimacy of Mexico's constitution is based partly on articles that
    (A) give outgoing presidents the power to name their successors
    (B) give official recognition to the power of members of the clergy
    (C) prohibit foreign ownership of natural resources
    (D) create a limited numbers of political parties
    (E) preserve property rights of all landowners

38. The concept of democratic centralism as practiced in the Peoples Republic of China is best illustrated by the
    (A) duty of party cadres to create "correct ideas" out of the "scattered and unsystematic ideas" of the masses
    (B) rank of the Chinese Communist Party as the largest political party in the world
    (C) opening membership in the Communist Party to entrepreneurs
    (D) factionalism that is the focus of intra-party competition
    (E) recognition of eight non-communist parties in the constitutionally described "system of multiparty cooperation and political consultation"

39. Local governments in Mexico have had limited powers because
    (A) mayors and governors in wealthier areas had access to more tax revenues than local officials in the poorer parts of the country
    (B) parties other than the PRI have long been successful in asserting power in local governments
    (C) traditionally, PRI presidents selected successful candidates
    (D) there is competition between local officials in adjacent states
    (E) recall petitions can remove governors and mayors from office

---

Refer to the following excerpts in answering Question 40:

Building quango spends £1.4m without laying a brick

A controversial quango set up to help build schools and hospitals have spent £1.4million — without a brick being laid.

The Scottish Futures Trust (SFT), a not-for-profit organisation launched two years ago to fund major building plans, have spent £1million on wages and £400,000 on consultants…

> Aitken, Mark, " Building quango spends £1.4m without laying a brick Sunday Mail, 25 April 2010.
> *www.dailyrecord.co.uk/news/scottish-news/2010/04/25/building-quango-*
> *spands-1-4-m-without-laying-a-brick-86908-22210736/* (5 May 2010)

Lib Dems reject Tory plans for NHS board

The Liberal Democrats would not support Conservative plans to create an independent board to run the National Health Service, Norman Lamb, the party's health spokesman, said on Thursday…

The idea of an independent board was "crazy" and "a nonsense", Mr Lamb said… "To have an independent, non-elected quango responsible for £100bn of public money is simply incredible…"

> Timmins, Nicholas, "Lib Dems reject Tory plans for NHS board." Financial Times, 29 April 2010.
> *www.ft.com/cms/s/o/6a44b34c-53bd-11df-abao-00144feab49a.htm* (30 April 2010)

40. Judging from these two news reports, quangos are controversial in the UK because
    (A) they are efficient vehicles for implementing public policy
    (B) they are supported by Conservative Party leaders and opposed by the leaders of the other major parties
    (C) public opinion favors a reduction of the role of government in the economy
    (D) there is too little public accountability for quangos
    (E) citizens believe that government agencies waste money

41. Which of the following are constitutional elements of Nigeria's fourth republic?
    I.   a powerful presidency
    II. a House of Representatives elected from single member districts
    III. a prime minister responsible to the House of Representatives
    IV. parallel secular and sharia appellate courts
    V.   presidential veto power over bills passed by the National Assembly

    (A) I and II only
    (B) I, II, and IV only
    (C) II, III, and IV only
    (D) II, III, and V only
    (E) IV and V only

Refer to the following passage in answering Questions 42 through 44:

In what experts say is nothing short of a revolution [because of 2008 constitutional amendments] Mexico is gradually abandoning its centuries-old Napoleonic system of closed-door, written inquisitions — largely a legacy of Spanish colonial rule — that had long been criticized as rife with corruption, opaque decisions, abuse of defendants and red tape that bogged down cases for years.

Instead, for the first time, defendants will be presumed innocent until proved guilty, instead of the other way around, as they are now. The police will use more forensics and meticulous fact-gathering. Plea bargains, mediation and probation, never tried before in Mexico, will become standard [by 2016].

And, in what many consider one of the biggest leaps, courtroom doors will be thrown open to the public for oral trials before a trio of judges where victims and the accused can confront one another and evidence will be laid out in the open...

The effort to make the Mexican system more open and transparent is intended to bolster public confidence in criminal justice and root out the effects of organized crime, which many legal experts and others believe manipulates the system in its favor...

"The system is in crisis," said Carlos F. Natarén, a law professor at National Autonomous University in Mexico City. "It doesn't leave any of the parties satisfied. There is no efficiency in combating crime, and it's an area where we systemically find violation of rights."

Archibold, Randal C., "Mexican Prosecutors Train in U.S. for Changes in Their Legal System,"
New York Times, 24 April 2009. *www.nytimes.com/2009/04/25/us/25prosecute.html* (28 April 2010)

---

42. The excerpt quoted above suggests all the following EXCEPT
    (A)   many Mexicans lack faith in the old criminal justice system
    (B)   presumption of guilt made it easier to convict criminals in the old system
    (C)   adversarial processes will increase the efficiencies of the criminal justice system
    (D)   public trials will be less likely to be influenced by corruption
    (E)   transparency will reduce defendants' ability to manipulate the system to their advantage

43. A basic concept of comparative politics discussed in this news article is that
    (A)   revolutionary changes take a long time to become effective
    (B)   legal systems serve the interests of power elites more than others
    (C)   inquisitorial justice systems are inherently unfair
    (D)   citizens' faith in their legal system is a major factor in establishing a regime's legitimacy
    (E)   scientific standards of evidence gathering are crucial requirements in inquisitorial justice systems

44. Which of the following best explains a similarity between Mexico's Napoleonic system and the system in the country named below?
    (A)   Nigeria's system is similar because of colonial influences
    (B)   The UK's system is similar because of European influences on its criminal code
    (C)   China's system is similar because of the authoritarian traditions of pre- and post-revolutionary regimes
    (D)   Russia's system is similar because of that political cultures' long-standing respect for individual rights
    (E)   Iran's system is similar because open trials are required by *sharia*

45. One of the more important assets the Russian regime has in the effort to establish a rule of law is the
    (A) apparent acceptance of the ideas of judicial independence and due process since Gorbachev's first proposals
    (B) reputation of the Soviet procuracy for adhering to legal rules and transparent procedures
    (C) high numbers of lawyers among the political elite
    (D) high esteem in which judges have traditionally been held
    (E) the willingness of the executive and legislative branches to abide by the decisions of the Constitutional Court since 1991

46. The legitimacy of the Iranian regime is based, in part, on all of the following EXCEPT
    (A) nationalism
    (B) parliamentary elections
    (C) general acceptance of Islamic law
    (D) open competition among a wide range of political ideas
    (E) government facilitation of private social welfare systems

47. Hu Jintao described the goal of China's 11th 5-Year Plan as "building a harmonious society." Which of the following elements of that task was NOT part of earlier party plans?
    (A) narrowing income gaps between people
    (B) promoting honest, friendly relationships among all people
    (C) great improvements in morals and education
    (D) gradual improvement of the legal system
    (E) ordered market competition

48. One of the primary difficulties in studying comparative politics is that
    (A) cultural and physical environments limit the choices that political leaders make
    (B) competition between short-term and long-term goals frequently obscures the political decision-making processes in non-industrial countries
    (C) governments determine the outcomes of policy decisions
    (D) people in various cultures value different things and prioritize their values in different ways
    (E) public policy is formulated in representative institutions

49. The Westminster model of representative government differs from the presidential model primarily in its
    (A) legislative sovereignty
    (B) federal structure
    (C) publicly funded election campaigns
    (D) use of proportional election procedures
    (E) expectation that the head of government will initiate public policy proposals

50. Among the political beliefs held by most Nigerians is the idea that
    (A) all people are created equal
    (B) everyone should be politically aware and active
    (C) traditional and elected leaders deserve citizens' loyalty
    (D) individual action is the key to political success
    (E) democracy is normally preferable to other kinds of government

51. Which of the following complicated the assumption of office by Nigerian President Goodluck Jonathan in early 2010?
    I.   the location of the homes of Jonathan and President Yar'Adua
    II.   Jonathan's residence in New York City prior to his becoming president
    III.   the isolation of Yar'Adua in hospitals in Saudi Arabia and Nigeria
    IV.   the fact that Yar'Adua and Jonathan represented different parties

    (A)   I only
    (B)   I and III only
    (C)   II, III, and IV only
    (D)   II and III only
    (E)   II and IV only

52. Which of the following most adequately expresses a defensible thesis about political change in the United Kingdom?
    (A)   Membership in the European Union has created the environment favorable to constitutional change in the UK.
    (B)   Centuries of conflict with European powers (especially France) encouraged experimentation with a variety of forms of political institutions.
    (C)   Voters have regularly supported pragmatic policy changes and rejected ideologically motivated policy changes.
    (D)   economic growth like that in the 1990s, has often motivated large expansions of social welfare programs.
    (E)   Economic changes in the UK, especially outside the greater London area, have resulted in public demands for more centralized economic development policies.

53. China's military organization, the Peoples Liberation Army (PLA), is linked to the Communist Party in all the following ways EXCEPT
    (A)   the assignment of political officers to all military units
    (B)   the election of the chair of the Central Military Commission, the PLA's commander-in-chief, by the National Peoples Congress
    (C)   membership of PLA representatives on the Party Central Committee
    (D)   Party General Secretary Hu Jintao's continuing role as chair of the Military Affairs Commission
    (E)   by PLA generals serving on the Party Politburo

54. Among the international challenges facing President Medvedev when he took office was
    (A)   Russia's declining economic growth rate
    (B)   Russian oil pipelines running through nationalistic former Soviet republics
    (C)   the presence of so many former KGB and FSB officers in top government positions
    (D)   the obsolescence of much of Russian industry
    (E)   the rising costs of social welfare programs

55. China's Communist Party exercises direct control over which of the following means of political socialization?
    (A)   contents of the mass line
    (B)   Party and non-party newspapers
    (C)   curriculum in technical universities
    (D)   news reports on radio, television, and the Internet
    (E)   advertising by joint venture companies

Practicing for the Free-Response Section of the AP Exam for Comparative Politics

If the multiple-choice half of the exam primarily tests your factual knowledge, the free-response half primarily tests your understanding of concepts, generalizations, patterns, and your analytical skills. As you think about this, remember the six topics in the outline:

> **Comparative Politics (theory)**
> **Sovereignty, Authority, and Power**
> **Political Institutions**
> **Citizens, Society, and State**
> **Political and Economic Change**
> **Public Policy**

Your written communication skills are also being tested, but only to the extent that you use those skills to demonstrate your grasp of this branch of political science. Your penmanship, grammar, and spelling won't be graded, but your message will be. If your handwriting is so obscure that an exam reader can't tell if you intended to write "possible" or "impossible," you won't get any benefit of the doubt. And you won't be asked about your intent. Similarly, if errors in your grammar or spelling result in a sentence that contradicts what was in your mind, the written words are all that will be evaluated.

In the past few years, most FRQs have been multi-part questions. In 2010, the FRQs averaged over four verbs each. In other words, students were asked, on average, to respond to four tasks for each question. Try not to neglect any of those tasks, but don't give up on any one because you can't think of a way to respond to others.

As described in Chapter 3, there are eight items in the free-response half of the test. The first five are "Short-Answer Concept" items. Take about six minutes for each one. (These five questions make up 1/4 of your free-response score.)

The sixth item is a "Conceptual Analysis." This is an expanded version of a "Short-Answer Concept"

question. Take about 30 minutes to respond. With that much time, you should plan what you're going to write before you write. (This item is another 1/4 of your free-response score.)

The last two items are "Country Context" questions. While examples will contribute to your responses to previous items, examples are what these items are all about. Take about 20 minutes for each of these, and, once again, plan your responses. (These two questions make up 1/2 of your free-response score.)

You don't have to answer these items in this order. Just make sure you label each response correctly so the exam reader knows what you're responding to.

RESPONDING TO THE QUESTIONS

As you work on this review, remember what the AP description says about the free-response questions.

1. These questions are designed to allow you, the test taker, to use your "powers of analysis to build logical structures with supporting arguments and interconnected elements."

2. And they will allow you to present uncommon yet correct responses.

In practical terms, that means there are several correct factual responses and you have to use your analytical and persuasive abilities to earn all the possible points.

If you can't recall factual information to address a question, you've defined your next job in reviewing. Go back to your textbook and your notes and find information that is relevant. Then put your analytical abilities to work and figure out how to identify, describe, and explain the necessary "things."

Whatever rehearsal you do ought to define what kind of studying and preparation you should be doing next.

IMAGINING QUESTIONS

This can be one of those academic games. It can also be a useful way to review what you know.

There are six topics in the course outline. Any and all of these topics for any of the six countries might be subjects for free-response questions. If it helps you, sit down with the outline (see Chapter 2 or the outline on the AP Comparative Government and Politics web site) and imagine what might be asked about each topic. Are you prepared to answer those questions?

A further word about game playing — As you can see there are 36 very general areas from which the free-response questions can come (six topics about six countries). Some of the areas like those in Topic 3 are incredibly broad. Trying to predict what questions might be asked and preparing only for some possible topics is going to be a losing strategy. Save your energy for analysis and study that's useful to you.

LOOKING AT SOMEONE ELSE'S FREE-RESPONSE QUESTIONS

If you tried to imagine what kinds of free-response questions might be asked, you've seen the breadth of possibilities. You may have seen the sample questions in the AP course description (*www.collegeboard.com/student/testing/ap/ sub_compgov.html*). Your teacher may have shown you some of the questions from past exams. (If not, ask to see some.) As you look at past test questions, remember the free-response questions shown for the exams before 2006 will be similar *only* to the "Country Context" questions on the exams after 2005.

Additional sample FRQs can be found at my "Studying Comparative" blog (*studyingcomparative.blogspot.com/*). Each spring, I post realistic samples of all kinds of FRQs.

CREATING RUBRICS

The grading guidelines used when evaluating the responses that students write are called rubrics. The rubric for each question describes how many points are possible and what examples and information are appropriate for earning those points. You can find examples of these rubrics along with the free-response questions asked on earlier exams at the AP Central Web site (*www.collegeboard. com/student/testing/ap/sub_compgov.html*).

As you look at the questions, you should be able to figure out what examples would earn points for each question. (You remember, don't you, that the weighted score for each one is the same even thought the raw scores differ?) To reemphasize my point from Chapter 3, each "thing" you're asked to do is probably worth a point.

What follows is a sample free-response section. Take this as a realistic rehearsal: Take 100 minutes, plan, and write responses. If you don't have time for that, practice with individual elements: 30 minutes for a "Short-Answer Concepts" section; 30 minutes for a "Conceptual Analysis" item; and 20 minutes each for the "Country Context" questions. Assess your answers by reviewing the FRQ commentary that begins on Page 202.

Caveat: These sample questions come from one person's imagination, understanding, knowledge, and academic biases. The questions don't represent the breadth of the expertise, imagination, and experience of the AP test development committee. I do think they are realistic questions that are useful for your practice. Not everyone will agree with me. (Ah, not ambiguity in the test, too?)

Practice more than once so you get a real feel for how much time you have to do these tasks.

A Practice Version of the Free-Response Section

Short-Answer Concepts (allow 30 minutes for these five items):

For each of the following items, define or describe the concepts as instructed in the item.

1. Since comparative political science is an empirical discipline, describe a principal method used to take into account the political power of a non-empirical factor such as religious beliefs?

2. Define parliamentary sovereignty and describe one way in which a regime that includes parliamentary sovereignty differs from a regime that includes separation of powers.

3. Define, in a political context, the concept of patron-client relationship. Describe one political benefit patrons receive and one political benefit clients receive from such a relationship.

4. What is meant by political accountability? What is one procedure or one institution in Iran that is intended to provide for accountability? How is that feature intended to provide for accountability?

5. What is a primary political rationale for using proportional elections rather than plurality elections? What is one characteristic of a political culture that would discourage the use of a proportional electoral system?

Conceptual Analysis (allow 30 minutes for this item):

---

6. (a) Define the concept of "legitimate government."

   (b) Describe one public policy in the United Kingdom that promotes legitimacy and explain how it promotes legitimacy.

   (c) Describe one public policy in the Peoples Republic of China that promotes legitimacy and explain how it promotes legitimacy.

Country Context (allow 40 minutes for these two items):

---

7. Social class has not been a major factor in Nigerian politics.

   (a) Identify two causes of the absence of class-based politics in Nigeria.

   (b) Explain why each of those two factors did not prevent the development of class-based politics in the United Kingdom.

8. Continuity and change coexist in all political systems.

   (a) Describe one factor supporting continuity and one factor promoting change in the Russian political system.

   (b) Describe one factor supporting continuity and one factor promoting change in the political system of Mexico.

   (c) Using a specific example from Russia and a specific example from Mexico, compare the strength of factors supporting continuity or those promoting change in the two countries.

Answer Key for the Practice Multiple-Choice Section

ANSWERS TO THE QUESTIONS ON PAGES 168-178

1.	(D)	12.	(A)	23.	(D)	34.	(A)	45.	(A)
2.	(B)	13.	(E)	24.	(D)	35.	(D)	46.	(D)
3.	(D)	14.	(E)	25.	(C)	36.	(C)	47.	(E)
4.	(B)	15.	(E)	26.	(E)	37.	(C)	48.	(D)
5.	(D)	16.	(A)	27.	(B)	38.	(A)	49.	(A)
6.	(E)	17.	(C)	28.	(E)	39.	(C)	50.	(E)
7.	(C)	18.	(B)	29.	(D)	40.	(D)	51.	(B)
8.	(B)	19.	(A)	30.	(B)	41.	(B)	52.	(C)
9.	(B)	20.	(D)	31.	(E)	42.	(E)	53.	(B)
10.	(B)	21.	(D)	32.	(A)	43.	(D)	54.	(B)
11.	(D)	22.	(E)	33.	(C)	44.	(C)	55.	(A)

There's no way to know whether this set of questions is equivalent to the questions on an exam recently released by the College Board, but

- Nearly 95% of people with multiple-choice scores of at least 75% (41+) of the possible points earned 4s and 5s on that exam.

- Over 71% of people with multiple-choice scores of two-thirds or more (37+) of the possible points earned 4s and 5s.

- Over 86% of people with multiple-choice scores equaling 46% (25+) or more of the possible points earned 3s, 4s, and 5s.

Annotations for the Practice Multiple-Choice Section

1. In Iran, one basic political conflict arises from
    (A) Westernized groups seeking national glory and traditional groups advocating greater engagement with the global economy
    (B) the cleavages separating Azeri and Aryan ethnic groups
    (C) the need of the Islamic elite to accommodate religious minorities to stay in power
    (D) competing democratic and religious ideals
    (E) competition between *bazaaris* and the charitable Islamic foundations (*bonyads*)

    The basic conflict described in (D) is written into Iran's constitution: an elected legislature whose candidates are approved by an unelected body of religious leaders. (A) is incorrect. The ethnic cleavage described in (B) is denied by the fact that Supreme Leader Khatami is an Azeri. Choice (C) doesn't make sense. The bazaaris oppose competition from the *bonyads* (E), but make common cause with them against structural adjustment.

2. Colonial influences on the political culture of Mexico include all the following EXCEPT
    (A) the large scale state involvement in the economy
    (B) the loss of half its territory to the USA
    (C) the executive domination of the other parts of the regime
    (D) the system of unequal alliances between patrons and clients
    (E) the relative absence of Indians among the political elite

    This is an EXCEPT question. The territorial loss to the USA described in (B) happened after independence. All the other choices describe ways the Mexican political culture followed patterns established by the Spanish colonial regime.

3. Which of the following factors help explain the ongoing conflict in the Caucasus (SW Russia)?
    I.   Large numbers of people are Muslims.
    II.   Most people there are Russians.
    III. The area has rich oil and gas resources.
    IV.   Industrial development there has led to high standards of living.
    V.   Rival ethnic groups compete for political power.

    (A) I and II only
    (B) II, III, and IV only
    (C) All five factors, I, II, III, IV, and V help explain the conflict
    (D) I, III, and V only
    (E) III, IV, and V only

    While some republics in the south of Russia have significant Russian populations, most of the people in the Caucasus are Muslim and non-Russian (descriptors I and II). There are conflicts (sometimes violent) between local groups as well as

between locals and Russians (descriptor V). There's considerable oil but little industry (descriptors III and IV). Thus choice D is the best answer.

These questions are like two stage true-false exams. Sometimes there are only three descriptors. Other times there are four or five. You need to go through the descriptors and decide which ones are accurate and which ones are not. I think you ought to draw lines though the incorrect ones or circle the correct ones.

Then you need to look at the lettered choices and select the one that includes the accurate descriptors.

4. Participation in the European Union is a political controversy in the UK in large part because
    (A)   the efficiencies promoted by the Common Agricultural Policy threaten British farming techniques
    (B)   the sovereignty of the British Parliament is threatened by EU treaties and courts
    (C)   trade with Japan, China, and the USA is more important to the British economy than trade with the EU
    (D)   the EU's common defense policies conflict with the UK's membership in NATO
    (E)   the British political elite see the United Nations (and the UK's Security Council veto power) as more important to British interests than the EU

Polish agriculture might be threatened by EU policies, but not Britain's thoroughly modern system (choice A). The EU is Britain's biggest trading partner (choice C). The EU's common defense policies (choice D) might someday come into conflict with NATO, but there's no hint of conflict yet. Choice E compares the UN (global politics) with the EU and its emphasis on European and economic issues. Qualified majorities and a directly elected European parliament offer protections similar to the UN veto power.

Some Brits are as defensive of their common law system as the US is of its sovereignty. Thus the prospect of the UK being subject to international courts (choice B) is as unattractive as the prospect is to many Americans.

5. Experience with public policy making in the USSR and the Russian Federation has probably taught Russians
    (A)   the value of individual responsibility
    (B)   the value of publicly advocating policy positions
    (C)   that political leaders cultivate close relationships with grassroots organizations
    (D)   that the state, rather than being made up of the people, holds power over people
    (E)   the importance of involvement in civic groups

Key words? "Experience," "USSR," and "older Russians." Most older Russians probably learned the value of going along and relying on the state rather than taking initiative themselves (choice A). In the USSR people who advocated policy positions often suffered for their advocacy (choice B). Leaders in the USSR maintained a commanding distance from the common folk who were to follow orders (choice C). Civic groups served the state, not the members (choice E).

6. Which of the following organizations is the most powerful seat of political power in the Peoples Republic of China?
    (A) National Peoples Congress
    (B) National Party Congress
    (C) State Council Standing Committee
    (D) Politburo of the Central Committee of the National Party Congress
    (E) Politburo Standing Committee of the National Party Congress

    Knowing that political power in China is held by the Communist Party should allow you to recognize that choices A and C are incorrect. Knowing that democratic centralism concentrates power in the very top of the political hierarchy should lead you up that hierarchy to choose the Politburo Standing Committee as the peak of political power (choice E).

7. A development in the functioning of the National Peoples Congress of the PRC during the last decade is
    (A) the growing proportion of peasants among the delegates
    (B) a reduction in the percentage of Communist Party members among the delegates
    (C) the growing power of the standing committee determined to shape government policy
    (D) an increase in demands by delegates for more detailed reports from government officials
    (E) the extension of meeting times to accommodate the extensive debates over economic liberalization reforms

    If you read and talked about the NPC, you should recognize choices A, B. D, and E as incorrect. In fact, you should recognize choices D and E as nearly absurd. However, as issues have become more complex, especially in economics and technology, the power of the standing committee has grown (choice C) as the source of policy proposals.

8. The Soviet *nomenklatura* system will continue to be an obstacle for reform in the Russian state for some time to come because
    (A) private industries discriminate freely against the beneficiaries of the old system
    (B) people who rose up through the *nomenklatura* ranks are still in positions of authority
    (C) the skills and knowledge required for success in the *nomenklatura* system are irrelevant to today's market economy and republican government
    (D) foreign investors rarely have the knowledge to enable them to understand the "insider" politics involved in doing business in Russia
    (E) representative government requires a degree of transparency impossible without the record keeping of the *nomenklatura* system

    You do remember what the nomenklatura was, don't you? Discrimination against former Soviet officials wouldn't seem to be a continuing problem (choice A) since so many former officials are in charge of private industries. The officials' skills are not irrelevant in any large, bureaucratic organization (choice C). Insider politics is difficult for outsiders to understand whether nomenklatura is involved or not (choice D). The nomenklatura record-keeping system was about as far from transparent as we can imagine (choice E). However, people who rose through a centralized, authoritarian system are now in positions of power in a regime and economy that is ostensibly democratic and transparent. That would make choice B the best answer.

9. Political conflict in the Peoples Republic of China has historically been confined to the Chinese Communist Party
    (A) because of the decentralized organization of the party
    (B) because disagreement from outside the party has been harshly suppressed
    (C) through the nearly continuous use of mass campaigns to recruit new members
    (D) because competitive elections were held only within the party
    (E) by allowing open debate on policy positions at all levels of the Communist Party Congresses

    Choices A is simply inaccurate. Mass campaigns have been rare since Mao's death in '76, and except for the Cultural Revolution, they weren't aimed at recruiting new Party members (choice C). The few competitive elections held within the Party have not promoted harmony or debate on policy matters (choice D). Party Congresses have been places where leaders read long speeches to delegates, not forums for debate (choice E). However, the Party does use many resources to prevent the appearance of dissent from the official line (choice B).

10. In the United Kingdom, the monarch serves primarily as
    (A) a mediator between competing political forces
    (B) a symbol of national unity and political legitimacy
    (C) the final authority on matters of public policy
    (D) an administrator of government programs
    (E) a reminder of Great Britain's former power and wealth

    Choices A, C, and D are simply incorrect. Choice E is a reasonably accurate statement, but is it the role which the "monarch serves primarily?" The reason the Royals are featured in the popular press is not their representation of past glory, it's their representation of the country.

11. It is not unusual for outside observers to be skeptical about the constitutional nature of Nigeria's regime because
    (A) the current basic law was written so recently
    (B) the legislature in the fourth republic has never passed a national budget
    (C) so few people vote in national elections
    (D) in spite of federalism described in the constitution, powers of state governments are only vaguely defined
    (E) pragmatic compromises on major issues usually emerge before the legislature begins consideration of them

    The age of the constitution is not a reason to doubt the constitutional nature of the regime (choice A). The failures of the legislature don't include complete fiscal irresponsibility (choice B). Voting rates have varied greatly since the 1993 elections (choice C). Choice E makes no sense. However, the improvised way in which state and local governments operate (choice D) should give any observer pause.

12. Unitary states, like the UK and Iran,
    (A)   **function more successfully in countries with less ethnic or cultural diversity than in those countries with greater diversity**
    (B)   are based on sovereignty of individual units of sub-national government
    (C)   rely on written constitutions to protect of individual liberties
    (D)   are more common in Europe than in Asia
    (E)   are unusual among the world's regimes

    Choices (B), (D), and (E) are incorrect statements. Choice (C) is inaccurate when applied to the UK. Choice (A) may not seem totally acceptable, but it is the best choice among the five offered. The unity imposed on multi-ethnic countries by unitary, authoritarian regimes, as in the former Yugoslavia, is likely to be a temporary condition dependent upon the use of force.

13. A major reason for the uncertain progress Russia has made in establishing a new regime since 1991 is
    (A)   frequent turnover in the office of president
    (B)   a long tradition of decentralized political authority
    (C)   the success of economic liberalization in raising living standards
    (D)   intense competition between monarchist and democratic political parties
    (E)   **democratic centralism practiced for more than 70 years by the Communist Party in the USSR**

    Choices A, B, C, and D are inaccurate.

14. Presidential power in Mexico is limited by
    (A)   an elite group of permanent expert bureaucrats in important ministries
    (B)   a tradition of powerful legislative leadership
    (C)   limits on presidential appointment powers
    (D)   the growing influence of parastatal corporations
    (E)   **the expectation that presidents will retire from politics at the end of their terms in office**

    Choices A, B, C, and D are all incorrect statements. Parastatals, with some notable exceptions, are being privatized. While legislative leaders have become more important since the election of Vicente Fox, there is no tradition of powerful leadership in the legislature. Presidential appointment powers remain vast, and while technocrats are becoming more important, government ministries are under tight political control.

15. Since nearly all Mexicans are Roman Catholic
    (A)   the government is relieved of the task of operating schools
    (B)   the clerical elite play a large role in policy making
    (C)   moral and ethical issues rarely become public policy issues
    (D)   the impact on government of social class and ethnic cleavages is greatly reduced
    (E)   **observers are often surprised that the role of the church is a political issue in Mexico**

    Secularism or anti-clericalism has long been a key element of revolutionary politics in Mexico. Secular public schools and the exclusion of clergy from politics were applications of that idea. Ethical issues are still sometimes political and clerical power didn't just disappear. In fact, social class may be emphasized by the issue, with most supporters of the church's position coming from upper class politicians and support for religious schools coming mostly from the upper and middle classes.

16. The principle of non-reelection in Mexico
    (A)   makes legislators dependent upon civil servants for expertise
    (B)   gives a president greater power in the last years of a *sexenio*
    (C)   inspires elected officials to fulfill campaign promises quickly
    (D)   limits the influence of any single camarilla
    (E)   motivates politicians to run for office in geographically dispersed districts in successive elections

    There are no logical arguments to support choices (B), (C), and (D). Choice E might be possible in the U.S. context, but the power of camarillas and parties in Mexico rules that out. If legislators serve only single terms, they have little hope of mastering the complexities of law or technology to match the knowledge and expertise of the bureaucrats.

17. One of the keys to successful parliamentary government is
    (A)   democratic centralism
    (B)   deferential shadow cabinets
    (C)   collective responsibility
    (D)   non-assertive prime ministers
    (E)   legislative independence

    Understanding the functioning of a parliamentary system is a major part of being able to do political and governmental comparisons. Collective responsibility (choice C) should stand out from this list. You might be tempted by "legislative independence" (choice E), but think for a moment about how vague that phrase is. It could mean a number of things. Choice A should appear inappropriate. Choices B and D aren't related to the success of a parliamentary government. In fact, both might be detrimental to the success of a Westminster-style regime.

18. A major difficulty in establishing a regime in Nigeria has been the
    (A)   competition between advocates of federalism and advocates of a unitary system
    (B)   diversity of pre-colonial and colonial political experiences in the nations that make up Nigeria
    (C)   volatility of voter preferences over the past 50 years
    (D)   domination of minorities by the Hausa-Fulani majority
    (E)   unwillingness of citizens to publicly debate political issues

    Choices (A), (C), (D), and (E) are incorrect. There have been minor arguments about federalism (A), but it hasn't been a major issue. Voter preferences have been pretty consistent, there is no Hausa-Fulani majority, and people are enthusiastic debaters (when they're allowed to express themselves). The experiences of the large number of people and cultures within what is now Nigeria is highly diverse (B) and helps explain some of the largest cleavages in the country.

19. The political consensus in the United Kingdom during the 1950s and 1960s meant that government activity included
    (A)   operating airlines and railroads
    (B)   dictating wage settlements to labor unions
    (C)   setting strict limits on eligibility for welfare and unemployment payments
    (D)   creating institutions of higher education for training public administrators
    (E)   taxation policies that encouraged businesses to hire more workers

    The political consensus referred to is often called the "collectivist consensus." Choice A indicates that the government played a major role in the economy. How-

ever, it did not dictate wage settlements (choice B) because of the power of unions and the Labour Party. Choice C is inaccurate. New universities were created in the UK during the period described (choice D), but they were mostly technical schools. Taxation policies to support government programs (choice E) often discouraged hiring because of the cost of government-required benefits.

20. Which of the following is the most important source of legitimacy for Nigeria's fourth republic (beginning in 1999)?
    (A) honesty in government
    (B) a history of stable government
    (C) the promotion of a sense of national unity
    (D) maintenance of an acceptable level of law and order
    (E) the success of government-sponsored economic development

All five of these choices are, in theory, sources of legitimacy for a regime. However, in Nigeria since 1999, only (D) plays a major role, and violence in Plateau state and the Niger Delta is the biggest threat to government and regime legitimacy. Obasanjo and Yar'Adua campaigned for transparency and honesty (A), but few results are visible. Historically, Nigerian government has not been stable (B). Most politicians and citizens publicly support national unity (C), but the cleavages are still difficult to bridge. Economic development (E) has been slow and inconsistent.

21. Which Iranian institution below is correctly paired with its authority?
    (A) Expediency Council   approves candidates for elective office
    (B) Supreme Leader   appoints local officials
    (C) President   can veto Majlis legislation
    (D) Supreme Leader   appoints the Minister of Justice
    (E) Majlis   elects the Supreme Leader

Under the Guardianship of the Jurist, the Supreme Leader takes primary responsibility for the legal system and thus appoints the Justice Minister (choice D). The Guardian Council approves candidates (choice A) and can veto legislation (choice C), the president appoints local officials (choice B), The Assembly of Religious Experts chooses the Supreme Leader (choice E).

22. Nation-states must adjust to all the following trends of globalization EXCEPT
    (A) international markets for investment funds
    (B) the increasing wealth and power of corporations not exclusively associated with a country
    (C) the potential of global warming caused by human activity
    (D) the growing acceptance of the concept of "crimes against humanity"
    (E) the narrowing of the economic gap between rich and poor nations

Check out the "EXCEPT." It might be a good idea to start the test by going through all 55 questions circling the word "EXCEPT" every time you see it.

If the test writers follow precedents, the word will appear in all capital letters, usually at the end of the question or incomplete statement. Choices A, B, C, and D are all accurate descriptions of global trends. Choice E would be a global trend, but it is not true.

23. Before 2000, the political route to the presidency in Mexico centered on
    (A)   inherited wealth
    (B)   a reputation for honesty and fairness
    (C)   individual recruitment of grassroots support
    (D)   loyalty to the PRI organization and the President
    (E)   repeated electoral victory by wide margins in a legislative constituency

    **Choice (D) should stand out as the best answer. Inherited wealth (A) is less impor-
    tant than political connections. A "reputation for honesty" (B) might help, it has
    been less important than organizational loyalty. Individuals rarely win elections (C)
    and repeated victories (E) aren't possible under the non-reelection principle.**

24. A hopeful sign for the development of a republican regime in Russia is the
    (A)   electoral failures of the party that was formed from the remnants of the USSR's
          Communist Party
    (B)   the popularity of United Russia's youth group, NASHI
    (C)   popular rejection of the concept of a government-directed economy
    (D)   liberal political values held by young, urban, and well-educated Russians
    (E)   growing concentration of power in the office of president

    **Choices A and C are incorrect when applied to contemporary Russia. The suc-
    cessor to the Communist Party has been quite successful (choice A) in large part
    because so many people expect the government to be the leading economic actor
    (choice C). NASHI is a popular organization, but it acts less like a democratic party
    than like a group set on forcing acceptance of Putin's United Russia (choice B).
    The growth in power of the presidency has come primarily at the expense of other
    elected officials   (choice E).**

25. The Four Modernizations campaign in China was a response to
    (A)   declining rates of industrial production
    (B)   rapid development of new communications technology
    (C)   the emphasis on political and social goals of Mao's leadership
    (D)   increasing disparities between rich and poor in China
    (E)   failures of social service programs like education and health care

    **Choices A, D, and E are basically incorrect. By the late 1970s and early '80s indus-
    trial production was rising, standards of living were still quite egalitarian, and the
    education and health care systems had made substantial recoveries since the end
    of the Cultural Revolution. New communications technology (choice B) had not
    really begun to affect China. However, the new leadership did see the political and
    social aspects of Mao Zedong Thought (choice C) as hindrances to faster econom-
    ic and technological change.**

26. Which of the following countries is NOT correctly paired with a major unresolved issue
    in its political environment?
    (A)   China   balancing urban and rural economic development
    (B)   Iran   large scale unemployment
    (C)   Nigeria   maintaining a stable political party alignment
    (D)   Russia   mitigating conflicts caused by identity politics
    (E)   United Kingdom   eliminating political corruption

    **It's almost an "EXCEPT" question. You might not have noticed this one if you went
    through circling "EXCEPT." In any case, you should have recognized that most of**

these are obviously accurate. Remember, what you're looking for is the one item out of five that is different. In this case, which one is NOT accurate. Political corruption in the UK has been a remarkably minor problem (choice E) even considering the "Expenses" scandal of 2010.

27. Among the measures taken by Putin's government in Russia to resolve outstanding issues of federalism was the
   (A) withdrawal of Russian troops from Chechnya
   (B) legislation allowing the president to appoint regional governors
   (C) abolition of sub-national units of government below the level of republic
   (D) claim that the United States threatened Russian sovereignty through the expansion of NATO
   (E) invitation to UN mediators who were to help resolve conflicts surrounding the desires of many republics to secede

   Once again, you should be looking for the best answer. Choices A, C, and E are incorrect. Choice D is partially based on political rhetoric, but it doesn't qualify as one of the "measures taken" by the government.

28. Interest groups in the Peoples Republic of China differ from interest groups in industrialized democracies in that
   (A) the groups in China are headed by members of the political elite
   (B) interest groups in China often result from grassroots organizing
   (C) interest groups in China lobby Communist Party, not government officials
   (D) the Chinese groups aim to influence policy making, not resolve administrative and bureaucratic problems
   (E) Chinese interest groups represent the interests of the Communist Party to the affinity groups (e.g., industrial workers, peasants, and women)

   If you keep in mind that the Chinese regime is a centralized, authoritarian regime, the best answer (choice E) ought to be easy to find even if you've never heard interest groups described that way. Choices A and D describe nearly all interest groups no matter how regimes operate. Choices B and C describe things that make no sense in the Chinese context.

29. Observers have raised questions about the democratic nature of Iranian elections because of the participation of
   (A) political parties
   (B) non-Muslims
   (C) women
   (D) the Revolutionary Guard
   (E) Iranians in exile

   There are several possible answers to this question, however, only one of them appears among these choices. You should recognize immediately that the Revolutionary Guard (D) is a non-democratic element in an electoral process, and it is responsible for providing "security" for elections. That supervision often extends to deciding who can cast ballots and "guarding" ballot boxes.

30. Some people in Nigeria have advocated re-writing the Fourth Republic's constitution because that 1999 document
    (A)   gave control of elections to an independent, non-partisan commission
    (B)   was imposed on the country by a non-democratic, military government
    (C)   created too many states
    (D)   gave governors too much control over government spending for public services
    (E)   did not recognize the Muslim majority of Nigeria's population

    You should recognize the uncertain origin of the constitution in 1999 (choice B) and the argument that a constitution should be approved by the people or their representatives. The electoral commission (choice A) was created by statute, not the constitution. There is still political pressure to create more states, not eliminate some (chjoice C). The constitution is notably vague on the powers of the governors (choice D), and there is not a Muslim majority in the country (choice E).

    Refer to the following chart in answering Questions 31 and 32:

    Percentage of Elected Women in Legislatures
    (Sizes of legislatures have changed over time.)
    (Source: The Inter-Parliamentary Union)

	1997	2000	2005
Iran	4.0	3.4	4.1
Mexico	13.9	15.9	23.7
Nigeria	na	3.3	5.8
Russia	7.5	5.7	8.8
Peoples Republic of China	21.0	21.8	20.2
United Kingdom	7.8	17.0	18.7
World Average	11.7	13.8	15.9

31. From these statistics, we can infer that
    (A)   more women were elected to legislatures in 2005 than in 1997
    (B)   it is not possible to identify trends in the election of women legislators over the time period described
    (C)   nations usually described as Third World countries elected fewer women than other countries
    (D)   all the nations for which data is displayed elected more and more women over the time span described
    (E)   over the time period described, women came to play a larger role in electoral politics

    Choices A, C, and D refer to numbers of women, not percentages. Since the sizes of some of the legislative bodies changed over the time span described, there is no way to determine numbers. Choice B is only possible if you demand that every example be part of a trend. Trends or generalizations regularly include exceptions. The percentages of women elected over the years described tended to increase. Thus (E) is the best response.

32. These statistics most support the investigation of which of the following hypotheses?
    (A)   A common norm of political culture accounts for the small percentage of women elected in Iran and Nigeria.
    (B)   Ideologically driven electoral rules are important for electing larger percentages of women legislators.

(C) The higher the levels of educational achievement, the larger the percentage of women legislators elected.

(D) Long national experience with elections leads to the success of greater percentages of women candidates.

(E) Lower income countries are less likely to elect women legislators than higher income countries.

There's no evidence here about the role of ideology (B), and the range of beliefs in the political cultures of the countries described is great. It should be apparent that choices (C), (D), and (E) are inaccurate.

33. In the Iranian regime, executive power is exercised by the
(A) Supreme Leader
(B) President
(C) Supreme Leader and the President
(D) Supreme Leader, the President, and the Majlis
(E) President, the Majlis, and the Assembly of Religious Experts

Choices D and E are incorrect because of the inclusion of the legislature. The Supreme Leader AND the President are given executive powers by the constitution.

34. The universal health care system provided by the UK's National Health Service
(A) provides an example of political and social unity to citizens
(B) helps maintain the political cleavage between upper and lower classes in the UK
(C) is a controversial program which politicians regularly propose to eliminate
(D) was initiated by PM Tony Blair's government in the 1990s
(E) is not a source of political controversy

In this case, choices B, C, D, and E are inaccurate. There is controversy (choice E), but it's about costs not about eliminating NHS (choice C). NHS was created in the late 1940s (choice D) and reduces the cleavage between social classes (choice B) by narrowing the differences in health care.

35. Which of the following were goals of increasing the number of states in Nigeria in the years after independence?
I.   devolving political power to local authorities
II.   dividing the largest ethnic groups into competing political entities
III. giving more nations political bases
IV.   encouraging cooperation and alliance-making

(A) I and II only
(B) I, II, and III only
(C) II and III only
(D) II, III, and IV only
(E) I, II, III, and IV

It's another of the two stage questions. You need to go through the descriptors and decide which ones are accurate and which ones are not. I think you ought to draw lines though the incorrect ones or circle the correct ones.

Then you need to look at the choices and select the one that includes the accurate descriptors.

Remember: best answer. Most politicians and people see federalism with a strong central government as the preferred regime. There is really no discussion of devolution of political power. Dividing the dominant groups into competing sub-groups

and giving political bases to smaller groups both encourage give and take politics (choice D).

36. In the Iranian regime, which of the following is NOT able to be a check on the power of another national-level actor in the regime?
    (A)   Guardian Council
    (B)   Supreme Leader
    (C)   President
    (D)   Expediency Council
    (E)   Majlis

The Guardian Council (choice A) can veto legislation and disqualify electoral candidates. The Supreme Leader (choice B) can dismiss the president, military officers, and judges. The Expediency Council (choice D) resolves conflicts by forcing compromises. The Majlis (choice E) approves of, disapproves of, and can remove cabinet members appointed by the president. The president (choice C) is an administrator with wide appointment powers for lesser officials, but has no power to over rule other national government officials.

37. The legitimacy of Mexico's constitution is based partly on articles that
    (A)   give outgoing presidents the power to name their successors
    (B)   give official recognition to the power of members of the clergy
    (C)   prohibit foreign ownership of natural resources
    (D)   create a limited numbers of political parties
    (E)   preserve property rights of all landowners

You need to know that the power of outgoing presidents to influence the choice of their successors is not constitutional (choice A), the constitution is adamantly secular (choice B), that there is no constitutional limitation of the creation of political parties (choice D), and that the government can break up haciendas (choice E). You should easily recognize the nationalism behind the prohibition on foreign ownership of Mexican resources (choice C).

38. The concept of democratic centralism as practiced in the Peoples Republic of China is best illustrated by the
    (A)   duty of party cadres to create "correct ideas" out of the "scattered and unsystematic ideas" of the masses
    (B)   rank of the Chinese Communist Party as the largest political party in the world
    (C)   opening membership in the Communist Party to entrepreneurs
    (D)   factionalism that is the focus of intra-party competition
    (E)   recognition of eight non-communist parties in the constitutionally described "system of multiparty cooperation and political consultation"

This question is about how democratic centralism functions. If you keep that model clearly in mind as you consider the choices for this question, you should do well. Choice (B) is an accurate statement, but it is hardly relevant to the functioning of democratic centralism. The percentage of the population enrolled in the party might be. Simply opening Communist Party membership to a previously excluded group (choice C) is not by itself an illustration of democratic centralism. Factionalism within the party (choice D) might be an example of an obstacle to the functioning of democratic centralism. However, expecting party activists to articulate the ideas of the rest of the population (choice A) puts responsibility for public expression at the top of the political hierarchy. Choice E is not relevant to the operation of democratic centralism.

39. Local governments in Mexico have had limited powers because
    (A) mayors and governors in wealthier areas had access to more tax revenues than local officials in the poorer parts of the country
    (B) parties other than the PRI have long been successful in asserting power in local governments
    (C) traditionally, PRI presidents selected successful candidates
    (D) there is competition between local officials in adjacent states
    (E) recall petitions can remove governors and mayors from office

    The fact that local government, outside of Mexico City is so little discussed is a clue that local power is minimal. Why? Because of the PRI domination of local government and the PRI presidents' power to choose loyal followers as candidates (choice C). While local officials in wealthier areas might have access to more resources, that doesn't explain why their powers are limited (choice A). Only recently in the north has PAN elected governors (choice B). With loyal PRI governors in most states, there is little competition among them (choice D). Recall petitions (choice E) are unknown.

Refer to the following excerpts in answering Question 40:

Building quango spends £1.4m without laying a brick

A controversial quango set up to help build schools and hospitals have spent £1.4million — without a brick being laid.

The Scottish Futures Trust (SFT), a not-for-profit organisation launched two years ago to fund major building plans, have spent £1million on wages and £400,000 on consultants...

Aitken, Mark, " Building quango spends £1.4m without laying a brick Sunday Mail, 25 April 2010. *www.dailyrecord.co.uk/news/scottish-news/2010/04/25/building-quango-spands-1-4-m-without-laying-a-brick-86908-22210736/* (5 May 2010)

Lib Dems reject Tory plans for NHS board

The Liberal Democrats would not support Conservative plans to create an independent board to run the National Health Service, Norman Lamb, the party's health spokesman, said on Thursday...

The idea of an independent board was "crazy" and "a nonsense", Mr Lamb said... "To have an independent, non-elected quango responsible for £100bn of public money is simply incredible..."

Timmins, Nicholas, "Lib Dems reject Tory plans for NHS board." Financial Times, 29 April 2010. *www.ft.com/cms/s/o/6a44b34c-53bd-11df-abao-00144feab49a.htm* (30 April 2010)

40. Judging from these two news reports, quangos are controversial in the UK because
    (A) they are efficient vehicles for implementing public policy
    (B) they are supported by Conservative Party leaders and opposed by the leaders of the other major parties
    (C) public opinion favors a reduction of the role of government in the economy
    (D) there is too little public accountability for quangos
    (E) citizens believe that government agencies waste money

    Reports of large-scale spending by a building quango without building anything and finding it "incredible" that an "independent board" would have authority to spend

billions of pounds of public money are signs that lack of public accountability is
an issue (choice D). There's nothing in either report to suggest efficiency (choice
A) nor is there anything about favorable public opinion (choice C). The only party
mentioned is the Liberal Democrats and it was opposed to the NHS board (choice
B). There's an implication that the public believes that some quangos waste money
(choice E), but there's no evidence of a general belief.

41. Which of the following are constitutional elements of Nigeria's fourth republic?
    I.   a powerful presidency
    II.   a House of Representatives elected from single member districts
    III. a prime minister responsible to the House of Representatives
    IV.   parallel secular and sharia appellate courts
    V.   presidential veto power over bills passed by the National Assembly

    (A)   I and II only
    (B)   I, II, and IV only
    (C)   II, III, and IV only
    (D)   II, III, and V only
    (E)   IV and V only

    **This is another question that takes careful thought. There is obviously a power-
    ful presidency (descriptor I) and a lower house elected by plurality (descriptor II).
    It should also be obvious that there is no prime minister (descriptor III). Did you
    know that appellate courts can be secular or sharia (descriptor IV) and that the
    president does not have a veto power (descriptor V). The corrector answer then is
    B (descriptors I, II, and IV only).**

Refer to the following passage in answering Questions 42 through 44:

In what experts say is nothing short of a revolution [because of 2008 constitutional amendments]
Mexico is gradually abandoning its centuries-old Napoleonic system of closed-door, written
inquisitions — largely a legacy of Spanish colonial rule — that had long been criticized as rife with
corruption, opaque decisions, abuse of defendants and red tape that bogged down cases for years.

Instead, for the first time, defendants will be presumed innocent until proved guilty, instead of
the other way around, as they are now. The police will use more forensics and meticulous fact-
gathering. Plea bargains, mediation and probation, never tried before in Mexico, will become
standard [by 2016].

And, in what many consider one of the biggest leaps, courtroom doors will be thrown open to the
public for oral trials before a trio of judges where victims and the accused can confront one another
and evidence will be laid out in the open...

The effort to make the Mexican system more open and transparent is intended to bolster public
confidence in criminal justice and root out the effects of organized crime, which many legal experts
and others believe manipulates the system in its favor...

"The system is in crisis," said Carlos F. Natarén, a law professor at National Autonomous University
in Mexico City. "It doesn't leave any of the parties satisfied. There is no efficiency in combating
crime, and it's an area where we systemically find violation of rights."

Archibold, Randal C., "Mexican Prosecutors Train in U.S. for Changes in Their Legal System,"
New York Times, 24 April 2009. *www.nytimes.com/2009/04/25/us/25prosecute.html* (28 April 2010)

42. The excerpt quoted above suggests all the following EXCEPT
    (A)   many Mexicans lack faith in the old criminal justice system
    (B)   presumption of guilt made it easier to convict criminals in the old system
    (C)   adversarial processes will increase the efficiencies of the criminal justice system
    (D)   public trials will be less likely to be influenced by corruption
    (E)   transparency will reduce defendants' ability to manipulate the system to their advantage

    While transparency is a goal of the reforms, the intent is to make the justice system less amenable to manipulation that can now occur behind closed doors. That indicates that Choice E is the EXCEPT among these choices.

43. A basic concept of comparative politics discussed in this news article is that
    (A)   revolutionary changes take a long time to become effective
    (B)   legal systems serve the interests of power elites more than others
    (C)   inquisitorial justice systems are inherently unfair
    (D)   citizens' faith in their legal system is a major factor in establishing a regime's legitimacy
    (E)   scientific standards of evidence gathering are crucial requirements in inquisitorial justice systems

    "Revolutionary" changes happen, by definition, rather rapidly (choice A). Legal systems may well serve the interests of power elites better than they serve the interests of everyday citizens (choice B), but that's not a basic concept of comparative politics. Inherent unfairness of inquisitorial systems is not addressed (choice C), but the opportunity for corruption is. The excerpt explicitly states that evidence gathering and presentation will be more important in the adversarial system being established (choice E), but that is not a basic concept either. The excerpt does say that "The effort to make the Mexican system more open and transparent is intended to bolster public confidence in criminal justice…" and that is a crucial part of legitimacy.

44. Which of the following best explains a similarity between Mexico's Napoleonic system and the system in the country named below?
    (A)   Nigeria's system is similar because of colonial influences
    (B)   The UK's system is similar because of European influences on its criminal code
    (C)   China's system is similar because of the authoritarian traditions of pre- and post-revolutionary regimes
    (D)   Russia's system is similar because of that political cultures' long-standing respect for individual rights
    (E)   Iran's system is similar because open trials are required by *sharia*

    China's legal system is an inquisitorial one and that is directly connected to the authoritarian traditions of its monarchical and Leninist regimes (choice C). Colonial influences in Nigeria (choice A) would suggest its system is a common law, adversarial system, like the UK's (choice B). Individual rights in the Russian political culture (choice D) is still a novel idea. *Sharia* law does not require open trials (choice E).

45. One of the more important assets the Russian regime has in the effort to establish a rule of law is the
    - **(A) apparent acceptance of the ideas of judicial independence and due process since Gorbachev's first proposals**
    - (B) reputation of the Soviet procuracy for adhering to legal rules and transparent procedures
    - (C) high numbers of lawyers among the political elite
    - (D) high esteem in which judges have traditionally been held
    - (E) the willingness of the executive and legislative branches to abide by the decisions of the Constitutional Court since 1991

    In the Soviet procuracy, judges were low-level bureaucrats, not high level appointees (choice D). Choices B, C, and E are inaccurate statements. There are relatively few lawyers in Russia, the Constitutional Court has been ignored, and the Soviet procuracy was seen as an agent of those in political power, not as an administrator of justice. Opinion polls consistently reflect an acceptance of the ideal of judicial independence and due process (choice A) since the 1990s.

46. The legitimacy of the Iranian regime is based, in part, on all of the following EXCEPT
    - (A) nationalism
    - (B) parliamentary elections
    - (C) general acceptance of Islamic law
    - **(D) open competition among a wide range of political ideas**
    - (E) government facilitation of private social welfare systems

    This is another of those EXCEPT questions. You didn't miss that, did you?. Choices A, B, and C should be obvious bases for legitimacy. Choice E refers to the *bonyads*, which offer welfare and jobs and are free of taxes and government oversight. Open competition among ideas could be a basis for legitimacy (choice D), but it doesn't exist in Iran.

47. Hu Jintao described the goal of China's 11ᵗʰ 5-Year Plan as "building a harmonious society." Which of the following elements of that task was NOT part of earlier party plans?
    - (A) narrowing income gaps between people
    - (B) promoting honest, friendly relationships among all people
    - (C) great improvements in morals and education
    - (D) gradual improvement of the legal system
    - **(E) ordered market competition**

    This is a rather sneaky "EXCEPT" type question. You need to be alert and remember that you're looking for the choice that's "not like the others." Choices A, B, C, and D have been part of the Party line, to one degree or another since the 1930s. What is new is the idea of market competition (choice E).

48. One of the primary difficulties in studying comparative politics is that
    - (A) cultural and physical environments limit the choices that political leaders make
    - (B) competition between short-term and long-term goals frequently obscures the political decision-making processes in non-industrial countries
    - (C) governments determine the outcomes of policy decisions
    - **(D) people in various cultures value different things and prioritize their values in different ways**
    - (E) public policy is formulated in representative institutions

Choice A is a basic assumption of comparative politics. Choice B is a hypothesis that could be tested for accuracy in any country. Choice C is a basic definition used by political scientists. Choice E is only appropriate for republican regimes. Choice D suggests that cultural and political values vary from place to place and that those variations make comparisons more complex and therefore more difficult.

49. The Westminster model of representative government differs from the presidential model primarily in its
    (A)   legislative sovereignty
    (B)   federal structure
    (C)   publicly funded election campaigns
    (D)   use of proportional election procedures
    (E)   expectation that the head of government will initiate public policy proposals

    Choices B, C, D, and E could apply to either Westminster or presidential regimes. The real difference between the two types of regimes is the separation of powers in presidential regimes and the fusion of powers in parliamentary regimes (choice A).

50. Among the political beliefs held by most Nigerians is the idea that
    (A)   all people are created equal
    (B)   everyone should be politically aware and active
    (C)   traditional and elected leaders deserve citizens' loyalty
    (D)   individual action is the key to political success
    (E)   democracy is normally preferable to other kinds of government

    Polling in Nigeria has shown that most people believe that people are basically unequal (choice A), but that leaders have to earn loyalty (choice C). Choices B and D might seem like desirable bits of political culture in a functioning democracy, but neither is commonly held in Nigeria, especially in the majority of the population who live outside of urban areas. However, most people are convinced that a representative government is better than others in nearly all cases (choice E).

51. Which of the following complicated the assumption of office by Nigerian President Goodluck Jonathan in 2010?
    I.   the location of the home states of Jonathan and Yar'Adua
    II.   Jonathan's residence in New York City prior to his becoming president
    III. the isolation of Yar'Adua in hospitals in Saudi Arabia and Nigeria
    IV.   the fact that Yar'Adua and Jonathan represented different parties

    (A)   I only
    (B)   I and III only
    (C)   II, III, and IV only
    (D)   II and III only
    (E)   II and IV only

    The fact that Jonathan came from the south and Yar'Adua from the north (descriptor I) was a complicating factor as was the fact that Yar'Adua was in hospital and not seen in public for several months (descriptor III). Jonathan did not live in New York City (descriptor II) and the two men were candidates of the same party (descriptor IV). Thus Choice B is the correct answer.

52. Which of the following most adequately expresses a defensible thesis about political change in the United Kingdom?
    (A)   Membership in the European Union has created the environment favorable to constitutional change in the UK.
    (B)   Centuries of conflict with European powers (especially France) encouraged experimentation with a variety of forms of political institutions.
    (C)   Voters have regularly supported pragmatic policy changes and rejected ideologically motivated policy changes.
    (D)   economic growth like that in the 1990s, has often motivated large expansions of social welfare programs.
    (E)   Economic changes in the UK, especially outside the greater London area, have resulted in public demands for more centralized economic development policies.

    Membership in the EU (choice A) may have helped make the debate about the desirability of constitutional change more explicit, but the debate is serious and the divisions are deep. Isolation, rather than conflict (choice B) probably helped make Britain a laboratory for political experimentation. Economic growth in the '90s was not accompanied by an expansion of social welfare programs (choice D). Political demands in the UK have been for more devolution, not more centralization (choice E). For well over 100 years, voters have elected pragmatic leaders rather than ideological ones (choice C).

53. China's military organization, the Peoples Liberation Army (PLA), is linked to the Communist Party in all the following ways EXCEPT
    (A)   the assignment of political officers to all military units
    (B)   the election of the chair of the Central Military Commission, the PLA's commander-in-chief, by the National Peoples Congress
    (C)   membership of PLA representatives on the Party Central Committee
    (D)   Party General Secretary Hu Jintao's continuing role as chair of the Military Affairs Commission
    (E)   by PLA generals serving on the Party Politburo

    Here's "EXCEPT" again. Choice B should be the obvious answer since it involves the National Peoples Congress, not the Party Congress. Even if you're unsure of the other choices, that distinction should be clear.

54. Among the international challenges facing President Medvedev when he took office was
    (A)   Russia's declining economic growth rate
    (B)   Russian oil pipelines running through nationalistic former Soviet republics
    (C)   the presence of so many former KGB and FSB officers in top government positions
    (D)   the obsolescence of much of Russian industry
    (E)   the rising costs of social welfare programs

    There's really only one clearly "international challenge" among these choices. Like the previous question, if you look for the "international challenge," rather than a domestic challenge, you should be able to answer this one correctly.

55. China's Communist Party exercises direct control over which of the following means of political socialization?
    (A)   contents of the mass line
    (B)   Party and non-party newspapers
    (C)   curriculum in technical universities
    (D)   news reports on radio, television, and the Internet
    (E)   advertising by joint venture companies

    Key words? "Direct control" and "political socialization." Non-party newspapers and advertising agencies (choices B and E) are closely watched and practice self-censorship, but content is not directly controlled by the CPC. Commercial advertising is only tangentially political (choice E). Technical universities (choice C) are fairly free to determine the technical content of their curricula and avoid political content. Domestic radio and television content is tightly controlled, but satellite television and Internet content is not directly controlled by the party (choice D). The mass line (choice A) is the creation of the Party.

Commentary on the Questions in the Practice Free-Response Section

Look these terms up in Chapter 4's glossary if you're unsure of exact meanings.

To repeat a hint for answering these questions or evaluating your responses, "Read the verbs!" (See Chapter 3 on the definition of the verbs.)

To repeat another hint, "Be sure to label the various sections of your responses." Rephrasing the questions being asked is a simple way to do that.

Short-Answer Concepts (allow 30 minutes for these five items):

For each of the following items, define or describe the concepts as instructed in the item.

1. Since comparative political science is an empirical discipline, describe a principal method used to take into account the political power of a non-empirical factor such as religious beliefs?

Verbs: "describe." This simple verb asks for more than a quick sentence. Your answer should refer to identifiable correlations between stated beliefs and behaviors and political actions and/or policies. You could refer to identified public tenets of faith, facts about group unity or cleavages based on publicly-known beliefs, the religious status of political leaders, or religious practices and how those factors are historically or logically related to political behavior. The key is to explain the connection between the empirical actions and empirical facts about beliefs and behaviors. You could also describe the use of demographics to account for the proportions of populations known to adhere to one faith, sect, or denomination.

2. Define parliamentary sovereignty and describe one way in which a regime that includes parliamentary sovereignty differs from a regime that includes separation of powers.

Verbs: "define" and "describe." Here's a place for a textbook definition. (See your textbook or see "parliamentary government" and "sovereignty" in Chapter 4's glossary.) Then describe how the fusion of powers in a regime with a sovereign parliament is different from a regime in which political power is distributed among divisions that can check each other's powers.

3. Define, in a political context, the concept of patron-client relationship. Describe one political benefit patrons receive and one political benefit clients receive from such a relationship.

Verbs: "define" and "describe." This is a basic concept, See your textbook or the glossary in Chapter 4. You can use examples from Iran, Mexico, Nigeria, China, or Russia for the description here. Examples from the UK would be harder to identify.

4. Define political accountability. Identify one procedure or one institution in Iran that is intended to provide for accountability? Describe how that feature is intended to provide for accountability?

Verbs: "define," "identify," and "describe." Once again, a basic definition from your textbook or Chapter 4's glossary is needed. Then you need to name something in the Iranian regime that makes political power holders accountable for their decisions and actions (elections? the Expediency Council's mediation activities? the Supreme Leader's power to dismiss the president?) Finally you need to describe how that feature you identified works to provide for accountability.

5. What is a primary political rationale for using proportional elections rather than plurality elections? Identify one characteristic of a political culture that would discourage the use of a proportional electoral system?

Verbs: is" and "identify." It seems there are only two things to do, but you need to explain differences in outcome for these two electoral systems in order to describe the rationale. Rephrasing of the question can be an important introduction to your response. Of course, you can create your own introduction that explains what point you're trying to make. Then you need to identify a characteristic that would discourage proportional voting (small majority wishing to maintain power; insistence on ideological uniformity; long tradition of plurality voting, etc.).

Conceptual Analysis (allow 30 minutes for this item):
---

6. (a) Define the concept of "legitimate government."

(b) Describe one public policy in the United Kingdom that promotes legitimacy and explain how it promotes legitimacy.

(c) Describe one public policy in the Peoples Republic of China that promotes legitimacy and explain how it promotes legitimacy.

Verbs: "define," "describe," (twice) and "explain" (twice). In a multiple-section question like this, it's especially important to state specifically which parts you are answering with each part of your response. Your introductory definition should be as complete as you can make it. This part of the question would probably be worth 2 or 3 points and you want to include as many aspects of legitimacy as possible. The example you identify for the United Kingdom will probably relate to rule of law, elections, social welfare, national defense, or respect for precedent

and tradition. The example you choose for China will probably relate to economic growth, rising standards of living, maintaining law and order, promises of greater equality, or fighting corruption. Your explanations must include "cause and effect" relationships between the policies and the acceptance of the government's or the regime's legitimacy.

Country Context (allow 40 minutes for these two items):

---

7. Social class has not been a major factor in Nigerian politics.
    (a)   Identify two causes of the absence of class-based politics in Nigeria.
    (b)   Explain why each of those two factors did not prevent the development of class-based politics in the United Kingdom.

Verbs: "identify" (two things) and "explain." (two things). Here you want to identify things that overwhelmed class differences as political cleavages in Nigeria. Obvious choices would be religion and ethnic cleavages, although you could make a case for geographic cleavages or the fact that most people are agriculturalists. This is one of those cases when you really must introduce your identifications with a sentence restating what you are identifying. When explaining the UK system, you want to make the point (with examples) that social class cleavages are more divisive than others or that industrialization impinged on the unity that might be found in an agricultural economy.

8.   Continuity and change coexist in all political systems.
    (a)   Describe one factor supporting continuity and one factor promoting change in the Russian political system.
    (b)   Describe one factor supporting continuity and one factor promoting change in the political system of Mexico.
    (c)   Using a specific example from Russia and a specific example from Mexico, compare the strength of factors supporting continuity or those promoting change in the two countries..

Verbs: "describe" (four things) and "compare." This is probably a 6-point question. The factors could be domestic or global and they could be political, cultural, economic, geographic, or historical. Make sure that your "description" makes clear which factors promote change and which ones promote continuity. Part of that description should probably be an explanation of how the factor has the power it does. The comparison asks you to evaluate the strength of forces for change and the strength of forces against change. Given the countries you're asked to write about, the examples would probably include democratization, the economics and politics of oil production, global trade, and structural adjustment (among others).

Check for corrections and updates
at this book's supporting web site:

http://apcomparativegov.com/tools

At this site you will also find links to

- **Internet Links Cited in the Book**
- **Online Sources for Review**
- **Web Sites for Major Textbooks**
- ***What You Need to Know* Facebook Group
(for discussions and questions)**
- ***Studying Comparative*, the Blog Quiz**
- ***Teaching Comparative*, a Blog for Teachers**

Answer Sheet for Practice Multiple-Choice Section

USE TO ANSWER THE PRACTICE MULTIPLE-CHOICE QUESTIONS ON PAGES 168-178.

Name _____

Grade _____   Date _____

Fill in the oval corresponding to the answer you have selected.

1. Ⓐ Ⓑ Ⓒ Ⓓ Ⓔ	20. Ⓐ Ⓑ Ⓒ Ⓓ Ⓔ	39. Ⓐ Ⓑ Ⓒ Ⓓ Ⓔ
2. Ⓐ Ⓑ Ⓒ Ⓓ Ⓔ	21. Ⓐ Ⓑ Ⓒ Ⓓ Ⓔ	40. Ⓐ Ⓑ Ⓒ Ⓓ Ⓔ
3. Ⓐ Ⓑ Ⓒ Ⓓ Ⓔ	22. Ⓐ Ⓑ Ⓒ Ⓓ Ⓔ	41. Ⓐ Ⓑ Ⓒ Ⓓ Ⓔ
4. Ⓐ Ⓑ Ⓒ Ⓓ Ⓔ	23. Ⓐ Ⓑ Ⓒ Ⓓ Ⓔ	42. Ⓐ Ⓑ Ⓒ Ⓓ Ⓔ
5. Ⓐ Ⓑ Ⓒ Ⓓ Ⓔ	24. Ⓐ Ⓑ Ⓒ Ⓓ Ⓔ	43. Ⓐ Ⓑ Ⓒ Ⓓ Ⓔ
6. Ⓐ Ⓑ Ⓒ Ⓓ Ⓔ	25. Ⓐ Ⓑ Ⓒ Ⓓ Ⓔ	44. Ⓐ Ⓑ Ⓒ Ⓓ Ⓔ
7. Ⓐ Ⓑ Ⓒ Ⓓ Ⓔ	26. Ⓐ Ⓑ Ⓒ Ⓓ Ⓔ	45. Ⓐ Ⓑ Ⓒ Ⓓ Ⓔ
8. Ⓐ Ⓑ Ⓒ Ⓓ Ⓔ	27. Ⓐ Ⓑ Ⓒ Ⓓ Ⓔ	46. Ⓐ Ⓑ Ⓒ Ⓓ Ⓔ
9. Ⓐ Ⓑ Ⓒ Ⓓ Ⓔ	28. Ⓐ Ⓑ Ⓒ Ⓓ Ⓔ	47. Ⓐ Ⓑ Ⓒ Ⓓ Ⓔ
10. Ⓐ Ⓑ Ⓒ Ⓓ Ⓔ	29. Ⓐ Ⓑ Ⓒ Ⓓ Ⓔ	48. Ⓐ Ⓑ Ⓒ Ⓓ Ⓔ
11. Ⓐ Ⓑ Ⓒ Ⓓ Ⓔ	30. Ⓐ Ⓑ Ⓒ Ⓓ Ⓔ	49. Ⓐ Ⓑ Ⓒ Ⓓ Ⓔ
12. Ⓐ Ⓑ Ⓒ Ⓓ Ⓔ	31. Ⓐ Ⓑ Ⓒ Ⓓ Ⓔ	50. Ⓐ Ⓑ Ⓒ Ⓓ Ⓔ
13. Ⓐ Ⓑ Ⓒ Ⓓ Ⓔ	32. Ⓐ Ⓑ Ⓒ Ⓓ Ⓔ	51. Ⓐ Ⓑ Ⓒ Ⓓ Ⓔ
14. Ⓐ Ⓑ Ⓒ Ⓓ Ⓔ	33. Ⓐ Ⓑ Ⓒ Ⓓ Ⓔ	52. Ⓐ Ⓑ Ⓒ Ⓓ Ⓔ
15. Ⓐ Ⓑ Ⓒ Ⓓ Ⓔ	34. Ⓐ Ⓑ Ⓒ Ⓓ Ⓔ	53. Ⓐ Ⓑ Ⓒ Ⓓ Ⓔ
16. Ⓐ Ⓑ Ⓒ Ⓓ Ⓔ	35. Ⓐ Ⓑ Ⓒ Ⓓ Ⓔ	54. Ⓐ Ⓑ Ⓒ Ⓓ Ⓔ
17. Ⓐ Ⓑ Ⓒ Ⓓ Ⓔ	36. Ⓐ Ⓑ Ⓒ Ⓓ Ⓔ	55. Ⓐ Ⓑ Ⓒ Ⓓ Ⓔ
18. Ⓐ Ⓑ Ⓒ Ⓓ Ⓔ	37. Ⓐ Ⓑ Ⓒ Ⓓ Ⓔ	
19. Ⓐ Ⓑ Ⓒ Ⓓ Ⓔ	38. Ⓐ Ⓑ Ⓒ Ⓓ Ⓔ	